Distributed Computing by Oblivious Mobile Robots

Synthesis Lectures on Distributed Computing Theory

Editor
Nancy Lynch, *Massachusetts Institute of Technology*

Synthesis Lectures on Distributed Computing Theory is edited by Nancy Lynch of the Massachusetts Institute of Technology. The series will publish 50- to 150-page publications on topics pertaining to distributed computing theory. The scope will largely follow the purview of premier information and computer science conferences, such as ACM PODC, DISC, SPAA, OPODIS, CONCUR, DialM-POMC, ICDCS, SODA, Sirocco, SSS, and related conferences. Potential topics include, but not are limited to: distributed algorithms and lower bounds, algorithm design methods, formal modeling and verification of distributed algorithms, and concurrent data structures.

Distributed Computing by Oblivious Mobile Robots
Paola Flocchini, Giuseppe Prencipe, and Nicola Santoro
2012

Quorum Systems: With Applications to Storage and Consensus
Marko Vukolic
2012

Link Reversal Algorithms
Jennifer L. Welch and Jennifer E. Walter
2011

Cooperative Task-Oriented Computing: Algorithms and Complexity
Chryssis Georgiou and Alexander A. Shvartsman
2011

New Models for Population Protocols
Othon Michail, Ioannis Chatzigiannakis, and Paul G. Spirakis
2011

The Theory of Timed I/O Automata, Second Edition
Dilsun K. Kaynar, Nancy Lynch, Roberto Segala, and Frits Vaandrager
2010

Distributed Computing by Oblivious Mobile Robots
Paola Flocchini, Giuseppe Prencipe, and Nicola Santoro

ISBN: 978-3-031-00880-1   paperback
ISBN: 978-3-031-02008-7   ebook

DOI 10.1007/978-3-031-02008-7

A Publication in the Springer series
SYNTHESIS LECTURES ON DISTRIBUTED COMPUTING THEORY

Lecture #10
Series Editor: Nancy Lynch, *Massachusetts Institute of Technology*
Series ISSN
Synthesis Lectures on Distributed Computing Theory
Print 2155-1626   Electronic 2155-1634

Distributed Computing by Oblivious Mobile Robots

Paola Flocchini
University of Ottawa

Giuseppe Prencipe
University of Pisa

Nicola Santoro
Carleton University

SYNTHESIS LECTURES ON DISTRIBUTED COMPUTING THEORY #10

ABSTRACT

The study of what can be computed by a team of autonomous mobile robots, originally started in robotics and AI, has become increasingly popular in theoretical computer science (especially in distributed computing), where it is now an integral part of the investigations on computability by mobile entities.

The robots are identical computational entities located and able to move in a spatial universe; they operate without explicit communication and are usually unable to remember the past; they are extremely simple, with limited resources, and individually quite weak. However, collectively the robots are capable of performing complex tasks, and form a system with desirable fault-tolerant and self-stabilizing properties.

The research has been concerned with the computational aspects of such systems. In particular, the focus has been on the minimal capabilities that the robots should have in order to solve a problem.

This book focuses on the recent *algorithmic* results in the field of distributed computing by *oblivious* mobile robots (unable to remember the past). After introducing the computational model with its nuances, we focus on basic coordination problems: pattern formation, gathering, scattering, leader election, as well as on dynamic tasks such as flocking. For each of these problems, we provide a snapshot of the state of the art, reviewing the existing algorithmic results. In doing so, we outline solution techniques, and we analyze the impact of the different assumptions on the robots' computability power.

KEYWORDS

autonomous mobile robots, distributed computing, distributed algorithms, computability, obliviousness, asynchrony, coordination tasks, gathering, pattern formation, scattering, flocking

The advantage of an oblivious memory is that one enjoys several times the same good things as for the first time.

Friedrich Nietzsche

There is nothing new except what has been forgotten.

Marie Antoinette

Contents

Acknowledgments

We would like to sincerely thank our colleagues Taisuke Izumi, Franck Petit, Sebastien Tixeuil, Koichi Wada, and Masafumi Yamashita for their feedback on the manuscript and for the invaluable comments provided.

Special thanks go to Masafumi (Mark) Yamashita and to Peter Widmayer: to Mark for having introduced us to the fascinating world of mobile robots; to Peter for having shared with us the excitement of exploring this computational universe.

This work has been supported in part by NSERC Discovery Grants, by Dr. Flocchini's University Research Chair, and by MIUR of Italy under project *MadWeb*.

Paola Flocchini, Giuseppe Prencipe, and Nicola Santoro
August 2012

CHAPTER 1

Introduction

1.1 DISTRIBUTED COMPUTING AND MOBILITY

Distributed computing is the study of the computational and complexity issues arising in systems of autonomous computational entities interacting with each other (e.g., to solve a problem, to perform a task). This setting is rather different from (and in a sense more general than) that of other research areas related to concurrency, such as parallel computing and high-performance computing, because here the focus is on the *autonomy* of the entities (i.e., absence of control(lers) external to the system) and *decentralization* (i.e., absence of pre-defined controllers within the system). As such, it describes in an immediate and natural way environments such as communication networks, the web, wireless ad-hoc networks, distributed systems, peer-to-peer networks, etc.; that is, highly decentralized systems where the interaction between the entities takes place through communication.

Traditionally the entities have been assumed to be stationary and the communication to take place through explicit media (wired or wireless). However, there is a large and varied class of distributed environments where the interacting entities, autonomous and decentralized, are also *mobile*, and in some cases communication might not be explicit. They comprise very different systems, including for example: software *mobile agents* in communication networks (e.g., [37, 70]); *mobile sensors* networks (e.g., [27, 91]); *swarms* (e.g., [2, 61, 79]); *robotic networks* (e.g., [16, 102, 104, 107]); etc. In some of these settings, mobility is sometimes an additional capability given to the entities; this is for example the case with sensor networks, traditionally composed of static sensors. In most cases, however, mobility is inherent in the system; this is in particular the case with vehicular networks and robotic swarms.

Starting from the obvious fact that mobility, to take place, needs a place, we can distinguish two basic settings for the spatial universe $\mathcal{U}$ in which the autonomous mobile entities operate and move. The first setting, sometimes called *graph world* or *discrete universe*, is when the universe $\mathcal{U}$ is a simple graph, which describes, e.g., the case of mobile agents in communication networks (e.g., [37, 70]). The second setting, called sometimes *continuous universe*, is when $\mathcal{U}$ is a connected region of $\mathbb{R}^2$ (or $\mathbb{R}^3$), which describes, e.g., the case of robots moving on a terrain or in space (e.g., [2, 4, 6, 16, 71, 101]).

On the continuous setting, which is the focus of this book, there has been a large and extensive research effort, carried out within quite distinct communities of investigators; these efforts have generated the established and mature research field of *autonomous mobile robots* (which includes swarm robotics, robotic networks, and mobile sensor networks). This field has been investigated mainly by researchers in robotics (e.g., [4, 6, 71, 125]), control (e.g., [16, 102, 104, 107]), artificial intelligence (e.g., [81, 82, 101]), engineering (e.g., [91, 126]), and more recently by researchers in distributed computing.

1.2   MOBILE ROBOTS AND OBLIVIOUSNESS

Within distributed computing, an increasing number of investigations are being carried out on systems of autonomous mobile robots. The underlying research goal is to understand what kind of basic capabilities the set of robots must have in order to accomplish a given task in a distributed fashion. By assuming the "weakest" robots, it is possible to analyze in greater detail the strengths and weaknesses of distributed control; furthermore, this approach allows us to highlight the set of robots' capabilities that are necessary to accomplish a certain task.

The investigations consider rather weak robots: identical, without any central control, executing the same protocol, and without any explicit communication mechanism. The life of such a robot is an endless sequence of *Look-Compute-Move-Sleep cycles*. In each cycle, a robot observes the universe (*Look*), obtaining a snapshot of the positions of the other robots within its visibility range. Based on these positions, expressed in its local coordinate system, the robot executes the protocol (*Compute*) to compute a destination point. It then moves toward such a point (*Move*); a move may stop before the robot reaches its destination, e.g., because of energy limits. A robot then might be inactive (*Sleep*), e.g., to recharge before starting the next cycle.

Within these general guidelines, the goal has been to discover the limits of what is computable. Since the robots have no means of direct communication, any communication occurs in a totally implicit manner, by observing the other robots' positions and moving appropriately. In other words, it is the position of the robots in space at a given time, the robots *configuration*, which is meaningful, conveying information and fueling the computation. Not surprisingly, almost all the fundamental problems, already extensively investigated from an experimental and heuristic point of view in the fields of robotics, control, and AI, require in some way or another the formation of *patterns*, that is, configurations with specific properties.

For instance, the principal control problem is that of *gathering*, or *point formation*, which requires all robots to move to the same location, not known in advance; other important specific patterns are the *circle* and the *line*; another central computation, the so-called *arbitrary pattern formation* problem, requires the robots to be able to form *any* pattern specified in input; *flocking* is the problem of forming a pattern and maintaining it while moving along some trajectory; the problems of *scattering*, *filling*, and *covering* asks for the robots to distribute themselves in a bounded region of space to form a configuration where the region is uniformly covered.

The research focus has been on how cooperation, control, and interaction can occur to solve these fundamental classes of problems. Clearly, there is a large variety of parameters that can be considered and assumptions that can be made in these investigations, ranging from the (lack of) consistency between the local coordinate systems, to the level of synchronization among the robots, from the visibility range to the (lack of) ability to detect if more than one robot is at the same location. For each of these parameters and assumptions, it is important to determine whether it has an impact on the solvability of a problem under consideration, or on the complexity of its solution.

There is an element whose importance is quite clear, the (lack of) memory of the past. The *Look* operation provides the robot with the current configuration. Since communication of information is through the formation of specific patterns, the ability to remember configurations from previous cycles is clearly helpful. The main research question has been: can the robots operate based only on the current configuration? Note that this means that the robots have *no* memory of past actions and computations, and the computation is based solely on what determined in the current cycle. In other words: for the robots, every configuration occurs as if for the first time.

This feature, called *obliviousness*, has been the common concern of the distributed computing research on autonomous mobile robots (e.g. [21, 28, 30, 43, 68, 69, 94]). Indeed, the research on the impact and limitations imposed by obliviousness has been investigated also when the spatial universe $\mathcal{U}$ is discrete (e.g., in [20, 46, 64, 97, 100]). The importance of obliviousness comes from its link to *self-stabilization* [55, 57] and *fault-tolerance*; in addition to robustness, its practical advantage comes from the fact that it does not require any persistent memory (except for the protocol); its theoretical relevance derives from the fact that its presence renders the robots computationally weak and the solution to problems even more challenging.

Obliviousness is the focus of this book, which asks the following main questions: What can oblivious robots do? How?

An oblivious solution to a problem is clearly preferable to a non-oblivious one, but in some cases oblivious solutions are not known or do not exist. For this reason, there is research interest in the situation where robots have some persistent memory but that is limited to a constant number of bits; that is, the robots are just finite-state machines (e.g., [8, 40, 83]). This book also considers this case.

1.3   STRUCTURE OF BOOK

This book is organized as follows. In Chapter 2, *Computational Models*, we describe the computational model of the robots. We first define their behavior, in terms of their *Look, Compute, Move* cycles, and their activation schedule, in terms of the timing of the operations within their cycles; in particular, the FSYNC, SSYNC, and ASYNC models are defined. We then introduce the *power* of the robots, in terms of memory, sensing power, moving abilities, and local compass. Also, we introduce the fault-model that will be used to analyze fault-tolerant protocols. The chapter concludes introducing the formalism and terminology used throughout the book.

In Chapter 3, *Gathering and Convergence*, we treat fundamental problems for autonomous robots. For *Gathering* the robots are required to meet at the same physical location, unknown to the robots at the beginning; for *Convergence* they need to get arbitrarily close to such a gathering point. After presenting some basic results, we first treat the special case of gathering of two robots (also called *rendezvous*), and then the general case of gathering and convergence of more robots both in the unlimited and in the limited visibility setting. Various solutions are described depending on different assumptions and conditions mostly related to the level of synchronicity of the scheduler and the level of agreement of the robots on the local compasses. A closely related problem is then presented and solutions described, the *near-gathering*, where the robots are required to *only get close enough* to each other, without any collisions. The chapter continues by tackling *Gathering* and *Convergence* when the robots might produce inaccurate measurements during their sensing activities, and it concludes by presenting impossibility and possibility results in presence of faulty robots.

Chapter 4, *Pattern Formation*, presents another fundamental class of problems, probably the most studied in the literature. In the *arbitrary pattern formation* problem the robots must arrange themselves in the space to form any pattern given in input. Conditions for its solvability are given depending on the level of agreement the robots have on their coordinate systems. Necessary and sufficient conditions for formability of a given pattern from a specific initial configuration of the robots are also discussed, under various scenarios. Then, the specific cases of *circle formation*, where the robots have to arrange themselves in a circle, and *uniform circle formation* where they have to do so placing at regular intervals on the boundary, are discussed and solutions are described in different settings. The chapter concludes analyzing the problem of having the robots forming a *series of distinct patterns*, given in a particular order, and by characterizing the series that can be formed.

In Chapter 5 the problems of *Scatterings and Coverings* are presented: The goal is to have the robots occupy the space each in a distinct position, satisfying certain criteria, starting from arbitrary configurations possibly containing dense points (that is, positions occupied by more than one robot). First, we present solutions for the simplest problem of this class, where the robots are simply required to break the *multiplicities*, that is, to terminate in a configuration that does not contain any dense point. Next, we consider the uniform covering of very special spaces, the *line* and the *ring* on which the robots are initially located at arbitrary distinct points. The chapter concludes by presenting the *filling* problem, where, the robots are required to cover a region; the difference with the other covering problems is that at the beginning the robots are not in the region; instead, they enter the space from a point called *door*.

Chapter 6, *Flocking*, discusses the problem of the robots forming a given pattern and maintaining it while moving. There are two versions of the flocking problem, both analyzed in this book, depending on whether or not there is a special entity that decides the direction of the movement of the group. In *guided flocking*, the trajectory is given by a mobile external source, called the *leader*; the rest of the robots, the *flock*, must follow the leader maintaining the pattern without knowledge of the trajectory. A special case of guided flocking is the *intruder* problem, where the team of robots must continuously keep encircled a distinguished mobile entity, called *intruder*, regardless of its movements (unknown to the robots). In the other version of the problem, called *homogeneous flocking*, there is no external source and every robot knows the trajectory. The chapter concludes by presenting the case of homogeneous flocking in the presence of obstacles in the environment.

In Chapter 7, *Other Directions*, we present evolutions of the basic model emerged from questions on robots' memory and on the spatial universe in which the robots move. The first aspect that is presented is related to equipping the robots with a constant amount of memory that is *visible* to the other robots. In particular, the relationship between ASYNC with visible memory and both FSYNC and SSYNC is presented. The next extension presented is related to the dimension of the robots: in the basic model the robots are modeled as points, that is, they are dimensionless. Here, we consider the case of *solid robots*, where the entities occupy a physical space of some size; that is, the entities have a solid dimension. Recently, the oblivious robots model has been employed also in discrete spaces; the chapter concludes by studying computations by oblivious robots when the spatial universe is a *graph*.

We would like to stress that the book is not written as a historical survey but as a snapshot of the state of the art; hence, in most cases only the most recent/advanced result is reported (rather than the research history).

CHAPTER 2

Computational Models

2.1 GENERAL CAPABILITIES

The system is composed of a set $\mathcal{R} = \{r_1, \ldots, r_n\}$ of n mobile entities, called *robots*, each modelled as a computational unit provided with its own local memory and capable of performing local computations.

The robots are externally *identical*, that is, *a priori* indistinguishable by their appearance. They may or may not have distinct identities; if they are without identifiers that can be used during the computation they are said to be *anonymous*. The robots may or may not have a finite but *persistent* memory, that is, memory whose content is preserved during inactivity.

The robots are located and operate in a connected spatial universe $\mathcal{U} \subseteq \mathbb{R}^2$, and they are viewed as points in $\mathbb{R}^2$. Let $r(t)$ denote the position of robot r at time t; when no ambiguity arises, we shall omit the temporal indication. The global coordinate system may not be known to the robots. Each robot has its own local coordinate system: a unit of length, an origin, and a Cartesian coordinate system defined by the *directions* of two coordinate axes, identified as the X and Y axis, together with their *orientations*, identified as the positive and negative sides of the axes. However, the local coordinate systems of the robots might not be consistent with each other and there might not be any agreement on the unit of length.

A robot is capable of observing the universe, obtaining a *snapshot* of the positions of all other robots within its visibility range; since robots are viewed as points, their positions in the snapshot taken by a robot are just their coordinates in the plane with respect to its local coordinate system. How the snapshot is obtained (e.g., by activating internal sensors, from an external source such as a satellite, etc.) is not of interest here. The visibility range of the robots (i.e., the portion of the universe contained in the snapshot) might be limited.

Each robot is endowed with motorial capabilities; it can turn and move in any direction. A move may stop before the robot reaches its destination, e.g., because of energy limits.

The robots are *silent*: they have no means of direct communication of information to other robots. Thus, any communication occurs in a totally implicit manner, by observing the other robots' positions and moving appropriately.

The robots may or may not have the same notion of *time*: Each robot has a local clock, but such clocks might not sign the same value, nor run at the same rate, nor be otherwise synchronized. Robots measurements and computations are assumed to be accurate; in particular robots are capable of infinite precision real arithmetic.

2.2   BEHAVIOR

The robots are *autonomous*, that is they operate without a central control or external intervention. They all have and follow the same protocol, or algorithm.

At any point in time, a robot is either *active* or *inactive*. When *active*, a robot r executes the following three operations, each in a different state:

(i) *Look*: The robot observes the spatial environment $\mathcal{U}$; the result of this operation is a snapshot of the positions of all robots within its radius of visibility with respect to its own coordinate system. Since robots are viewed as points, their positions in the plane are just the set of their coordinates in the coordinate system of r, where the position of r is assumed to be the origin $(0, 0)$.

(ii) *Compute*: The robot executes the algorithm (the same for all robots), using the snapshot of the *Look* operation as input. The result of the computation is a destination point.

(iii) *Move*: The robot moves toward the computed destination; if the destination is the current location, the robot stays still, performing a *null movement*.

When *inactive* a robot does not perform any operation, and is said to be in state *Sleep* (or *Wait*).

The sequence *Look-Compute-Move* forms a *cycle* of the robot. The *Look* operation is assumed to be instantaneous; this is without loss of generality, since the time spent to obtain the snapshot (e.g., to activate its sensors before the snapshot is taken) and to process the information retrieved with the snapshot, can be charged to *Sleep* and to *Compute*, respectively.

2.3   ACTIVATION AND OPERATION SCHEDULE

With respect to the *activation* schedule of the robots and of the timing of the *operations* within their cycles, there are two main models, asynchronous and semi-synchronous.

In the *asynchronous* (ASYNC) model, each robot is activated asynchronously and independently from the other robots. Furthermore, the duration of each *Compute*, *Move*, and *Sleep*, as well as the time that passes between successive activities in the same cycle are finite but otherwise unpredictable. As a result, computations can be made based on totally obsolete observations, taken arbitrarily far in the past. Another consequence is that robots can be seen while moving, creating further inconsistencies in the robots' understanding of the universe. Consider for example the situation shown in Figure 2.1: Robot s in transit toward its destination, is seen by r; however, s is not aware of r's existence and, if it starts the next cycle before r starts moving, s will continue to be unaware of r. The ASYNC model, sometimes called CORDA, has been introduced by Flocchini *et al.* in [67].

In the *semi-synchronous* (SSYNC) model, the activations of the robots are logically divided into global rounds; in each round, one or more robots are activated and obtain the same snapshot; based on that snapshot, they compute and perform their move. As a consequence, no robot will ever be observed while moving, and the understanding of the universe by the active robots is always consistent. Note that such a system is computationally equivalent to a synchronous system in which the chosen robots are activated simultaneously and all operations are instantaneous. Indeed, the unpredictability is restricted to which robots are activated in each round. The SSYNC model, sometimes called SYM or ATOM, was introduced by Suzuki and Yamashita in [122]. An extreme case of SSYNC is the so-called *fully synchronous* (FSYNC) model, where in each round, *all* the robots are activated [122].

In terms of the restrictions imposed by the three models, trivially

$$\text{ASYNC} < \text{SSYNC} < \text{FSYNC} .$$

Variants of these three basic models can be defined. A particular variant which is in between ASYNC and SSYNC has been considered in [103]. In this limited form of asynchrony, called *partial* ASYNC, the time spent by a robot in the *Sleep*, *Look*, and *Compute* states is bounded by a globally predefined amount, while the time spent in the *Move* state is bounded by a locally predefined quantity (not necessarily the same for each robot).

Other restrictions can be imposed on the activation scheduler, also called *daemon*. Among those studied in the literature, the most common is the *fair scheduler*: For every robot r and time t, there exists a time $t' \geq t$ at which r is activated. The majority of the research work assumes the scheduler to be fair, as we do in this book. Note that, in the fully synchronous model the scheduler is fair by definition.

Between two successive activations of any robot r, the number of activations of the other robots is possibly unbounded. A daemon is *k-bounded* if for every $r \in \mathcal{R}$, between two successive activations of r, every other robot has been activated at most k times [42]; the bound k may not be known to the robots, in which case the daemon is called just *bounded*. Note that a k-bounded scheduler is not necessarily fair. A stronger requirement is that offered by a *k-fair* scheduler, i.e., a daemon which is both *fair* and *k-bounded*.

Note that, in the fully synchronous model, the scheduler is 1-fair by definition.

A particular daemon is the so-called *centralized* or *single activation* scheduler, where at any time at most a single robot is active [42]; notice that the centralized scheduler is not necessarily fair.

An example of 2-bounded centralized scheduler is the *slicing* scheduler: starting from time $t = 0$, after n successive activations (a *slice*), all the robots in the system have been activated exactly once [38, 42]. A particular slicing daemon is the classical *round-robin* scheduler: In each slice, the robots are activated always in the same order.

In terms of restrictions, we trivially have the diagram shown in Figure 2.2 [58].

2.4   VISIBILITY

The result of the *Look* operation is a snapshot of the spatial universe visible to the robot performing the operation. Depending on the visibility range of the robots, there are two main models, traditionally called limited visibility and unlimited visibility.

In the *unlimited visibility range* model, the range of the snapshot obtained by the robots includes the entire spatial universe; that is, a snapshot at time t contains the positions of all the

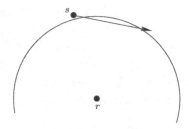

Figure 2.1: When s starts moving (the left end of the arrow), r and s do not see each other. While s is moving, r enters state *Look* and sees s; however, s is still unaware of r. After s passes the visibility circle of r, it is still unaware of r.

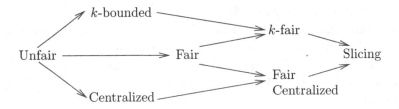

Figure 2.2: Relationship between schedulers.

robots at that time (expressed within the coordinate system of the observer). Unlimited visibility is the most commonly used model in the distributed computing investigations.

In the *limited visibility range* model, the range of the snapshot obtained by a robot $r \in \mathcal{R}$ in a *Look* at time t is the circle $C_t(r, V(r)) \subseteq \mathcal{U}$ of radius $V(r)$ and centered in $r(t)$. It is generally assumed that $V(r) = V$ for all r (unit-disc model); in this case, the parameter $\delta(r)$ is omitted. This more realistic model is employed mostly in investigations on mobile robotic sensors [66].

Regardless of whether the visibility range is limited or unlimited, there are other important visibility parameters.

In processing a snapshot, a robot can distinguish whether or not a point is empty (i.e., not occupied by any robot). However, since robots are viewed as points, the question arises of how robots occupying the same position at the same time will be perceived in a snapshot. The answer to this question is formulated in terms of the capacity of the robots to detect multiplicity of robots in a point. The robots are said to be capable of *multiplicity detection* if they can distinguish if a point is occupied by one or more than one robot. The multiplicity detection is said to be *strong* if it allows to detect the exact number of robots on the same point. Notice that, if the robots are not able to detect multiplicity, they might not be aware of the real number of robots that populate their area of visibility at the time of the *Look*; in fact, a position can be occupied by more than one robot, but the observing robot will see all these robots as just one.

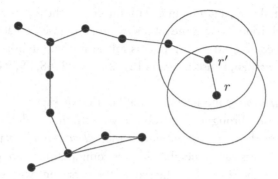

Figure 2.3: Visibility graph.

It is generally assumed that a snapshot contains the set of the positions of all the robots within the visibility range. This assumption is consistent with the fact that, since robots are viewed as points, they are *dimensionless* and thus their visibility is *unobstructed*; i.e., if three robots r, s, and z are collinear with s in the middle, s does not prevent r from viewing z. This assumption is also consistent with other scenarios, such as when the snapshot is provided from an outside source (e.g., a satellite).

One can however consider an environment where the line of sight of a robot is *obstructed* by the closest robot on that line. This is typically assumed in (and is the main motivation for) the study of robots that are *solid* (i.e., with a physical dimension) [31, 33]. Solidity does not however imply obstructed visibility; it is conceivably possible that the snapshot contains the positions of all the robots even if they are solid (e.g., in case the snapshot is provided by a satellite); the case of solid but *transparent* robots has been examined in [22].

An important concept is that of the *visibility graph* (or *distance graph*) at time t (refer also to the example depicted in Figure 2.3): The *visibility graph* $G(t) = (N, E(t))$ of the robots at time t is the graph whose node set N is the set of the robots and, $\forall r, s \in N$, $(r, s) \in E(t)$ iff r and s are at a distance no more than the visibility radius V at time t.

2.5   MEMORY

In addition to the algorithm, each robot has a local working memory, or *workspace*, used for computations and to store different amounts of information (e.g., regarding the location of other robots) obtained during the cycles. Two submodels have been identified, depending on whether this workspace is persistent or volatile.

In the *oblivious* model, all the information contained in the workspace is *cleared* at the end of each cycle. In other words, the robots have *no* memory of past actions and computations, and the computation is based solely on what was determined in the current cycle. Obliviousness is important in relation to *self-stabilization* [56, 57]. A deterministic system is said to be self-stabilizing if, regardless of its initial state, it is guaranteed to converge to the intended behavior in a finite number of steps. Since in an oblivious system the robots' memory is erased at each step, a correct solution that works for any initial configuration of robots is inherently self-stabilizing. This model, sometimes improperly called *memoryless*, is used, e.g., in [21, 28, 30, 43, 68, 69, 94], and is the one considered in this book.

In the *persistent memory* model, part (or all) of the workspace is *legacy*: unless explicitly erased by the robot, it will persist throughout the robot's cycles. In this model, an important parameter is the *size* of the persistent workspace. One extreme is the *unbounded memory* case, where no information is ever erased; hence robots can remember all past computations and actions (e.g., see [121, 123]). On the opposite side is the case when the size of the persistent workspace is *constant*; in this case, the entities are just Finite-State Machines (e.g., [8, 40, 83]), and are called *finite-state* robots. This book also considers this model.

2.6   MOVEMENTS AND COLLISIONS

Each robot is endowed with motorial capabilities, and is able to move freely in the plane. It can move only when executing *Move* and only toward the destination determined in *Compute*.

The robots move in a straight line toward the destination. It is sometimes assumed that the robots have a *guided trajectory* capability: a robot can specify a particular trajectory to the destination, and then move along that trajectory (e.g., [17, 43, 65]).

A move may end before the robot reaches its destination, e.g., because of limits to its motion energy. The assumptions about the distance a robot travels before stopping give rise to different settings.

In the more general setting, the distance traveled in a move is neither infinite nor infinitesimally small. More precisely, there exists an (arbitrarily small) constant $\delta > 0$ such that, if the destination point is closer than δ, the robot will reach it; otherwise, it will move toward it at least δ. Note that, without this assumption, an adversary would make it impossible for any robot to ever reach its destination, following a classical Zenonian argument. The quantity δ might not be known to the robots.

A stronger assumption is that of *fixed* mobility: There exists a constant $\hat{\delta} > 0$ such that every robot performing *Move* will *exactly* move $Min\{dest, \hat{\delta}\}$, where $dest$ is the destination point. The quantity $\hat{\delta}$ might not be known *a priori* to the robots. Fixed mobility is usually assumed when working in the SSYNC model.

The strongest assumption is that of *unlimited mobility*, when all robots always reach their destinations when performing *Move* (i.e., $\hat{\delta} = \infty$); this type of mobility is also called *undisturbed-motion* [28].

A moving robot might collide with other robots, moving or stationary; this happens when, while moving, it occupies the same point at the same time as another robot. More precisely, a robot r is said to *collide* with robot s at time t if $r(t) = s(t)$ and at time t, r is performing *Move*; r's collision is *accidental* if its destination is not $r(t)$.

Since robots are seen as points, it is sometimes assumed that accidental collisions are *immaterial*: A moving robot, upon causing an accidental collision, proceeds in its movement without changes, in a "hit-and-run" fashion (e.g., [123]). Another model is that of *fail-stop collision*: A moving robot stops moving when it accidentally collides with another robot (e.g., [33]). While valid from a mathematical point of view, these assumptions are pragmatically less valid. Indeed, accidental collisions are to be considered undesirable events (with possibly negative consequences), and thus to be avoided.

In this context, recall that the only time robots are aware of other robots is during *Look*. In particular, the robots have no way to detect the position of other robots while moving. This means that collision avoidance must be done algorithmically. An execution of a protocol is (accidental) *collision free* if no (accidental) collisions occur during the execution; a protocol is said to be (accidental) *collision free* if every feasible execution is (accidental) collision free. It is the responsibility of the protocol designer to engineer collision free protocols.

2.7   GEOMETRIC AGREEMENT AND ACCURACY

Each robot *r* has its own unit of length, and a *local compass* defining a local Cartesian coordinate system defined by the *directions* of two coordinate axes, identified as the *X* and *Y* axis, together with their *orientations*, identified as the positive and negative sides of the axes. This local coordinate system is self-centric, i.e., the origin is the position of the observing robot.

Depending on the level of consistency among the robots on the direction and orientation of the axes of their local compasses, different classes of *global* geometric agreement can be identified; in particular: `ConsistentCompass`, when all robots agree on both the direction and the orientation of both axes; `OneAxis` when all robots agree on the direction and orientation of only one axis; `Chirality` or *Orientation*, when the robots agree on the orientation of the axes (i.e., clockwise); and `Disorientation`, where no consistency among the local coordinate systems is known to exist.

Some of these concepts can be re-expressed in terms of accuracy of the local compasses. Let us first define the levels of inaccuracy of the compasses. We say that the compasses are *tilted* with deviation at most ϕ if each robot *r* has a local coordinate system that is tilted (with respect to the global coordinate system) by a degree $\phi(r)$ where $|\phi(r)| \leq \phi$; these inaccurate compasses, also called *dynamic*, were introduced in [93].

Another important parameter is whether the tilt of the compasses is fixed or variable. The tilted compasses are said to be *fully variable* if the actual tilt of each compass may vary at any time (but always with no more than ϕ from the global coordinate system); they are *semi-variable* if the tilt of each compass may vary (but no more than ϕ) between successive cycles, but it does not change during a cycle; they are *fixed* if the tilt of each compass never varies. Notice that, since in SSYNC the cycle is considered to be atomic, fully variable compasses are really semi-variable in SSYNC.

The type (i.e., full, semi, fixed) of inconsistency may be permanent or temporary. An example of the latter are fully variable tilted compasses that eventually become fixed; that is, after some point in time, in every compass the tilt will no longer change, but some inaccuracy may remain; we shall refer to such situation as *eventually fixed* (EF) compasses. Note that the time after which no more changes occur is *a priori* unknown to the robots. Another important situation is if/when all the inconsistencies eventually stop (e.g., because the magnetic source of instability has gone). We shall refer to such situation as *eventually consistent* (EC) compasses. Also in this case, the time after which all inconsistencies have disappeared is *a priori* unknown to the robots.

Notice that, regardless of the level of global consistency on direction and orientation of the axes, and on the level of accuracy of the compasses, there might be no agreement among the robots on the unit of length. However, observe that, in the unit-disc model of limited visibility (i.e., when all robots have the same visibility radius), the robots have a *de facto* agreement on the unit of length.

2.8   RELIABILITY AND FAULT TOLERANCE

Robots are typically assumed to be *correct*, that is to operate without faults. More realistically, failures may occur.

The robots' faults that have been investigated fall in two categories: *crash* faults (i.e., a faulty robot stops executing its cycle forever) and *Byzantine* faults (i.e., a faulty robot may exhibit arbitrary behavior and movement). Of course, the Byzantine fault model encompasses the crash fault model, and is thus harder to address.

An (n, f)-fault system is the system of n robots, of which at most f might fail at any execution. An (n, f)-crash system (resp., (n, f)-Byzantine system), is an (n, f)-fault system where the faults considered are according to the crash (resp., Byzantine) model. A *fault tolerant* algorithm for a given task in an (n, f)-fault system is required to ensure that as long as at most f robots have failed, the task is achieved by all non-faulty robots, regardless of the actions taken by the faulty ones. The actions taken by faulty robots can be seen as chosen by an adversary. The first work on fault-tolerant computing by mobile robots in the crash model is [133], and in the Byzantine model is [1].

The possible types of failures that can be considered include much more than these two classes (crash and Byzantine faults). Indeed, any deviation from an expected outcome can be seen as a fault, defining a type of failures. These include, for example, *calculation* errors during *Compute*; *moving* faults, where a robot might deviate from its path during *Move*; *vision* inaccuracy, where the robots' positions returned in *Look* might not be precise or the measurements not accurate, etc. Furthermore, any type of failure can be *transient* or *permanent*, *occasional* or *recurrent*, *local* or *global*, *detectable* or *undetectable*, etc.

2.9   GEOMETRIC DEFINITIONS AND TERMINOLOGY

In the following, robots will be denoted by letters r, s, and z, and points in the plane will be denoted by letters p, q, u, v. Also, the position of robot r at time t will be denoted by $r(t)$. Capital calligraphic letters (e.g., $\mathcal{Z}$) indicate regions; given a region $\mathcal{Z}$, we denote by $|\mathcal{Z}|_t$ the number of robots in that region at time t. In particular, $\mathcal{C}$ denotes a circle. Double lined letters (e.g., $\mathbb{E}$) indicates sets of points, sets of robots' positions in the plane, and set of robots. A *configuration* of the robots at a given time

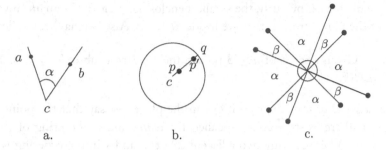

Figure 2.4: (a) Convex angle $\alpha = \sphericalangle(a, c, b)$. (b) Two points, p and p', on the same radius. (c) A biangular configuration.

instant t is the set of positions in the plane occupied by the robots at time t. A point in the plane is called *dense* if it is occupied by more than one robot; we call *plain* configuration a configuration with no dense point. When no ambiguity arises, the time reference will be omitted.

Given a set $\mathbb{E}$ of n distinct points in the plane, and a point $c \notin \mathbb{E}$ called the *center*, we will denote by $RadSet(\mathbb{E}, c) = \bigcup_i \overrightarrow{cp_i}$ the set of the half-lines, called *radiuses*, starting from c, each containing a point in $\mathbb{E}$.

Given a circle C with center c and radius Rad, and a robot $r(t)$, we will say that $r(t)$ *is on* C if $dist(r(t), c) = Rad$, where $dist(a, b)$ denotes the Euclidean distance between points a and b (i.e., r is on the circumference of C); if $dist(r, c) < Rad$, we will say that r *is inside* C. Given two distinct points p and p', with p inside C, let q be the intersection between the circumference of C and $\overrightarrow{cp}$. We say that p and p' are on the same radius if $p' \in \overline{cq}$ (see also Figure 2.4(b)). Moreover, we denote by $Rad(p)$ the radius $\overline{cq}$ where p lies; in the following we refer to $Rad(p)$ also as the *radius of* p.

Given two distinct points a and b in the plane, $\overrightarrow{ab}$ denotes the half-line that starts in a and passes through b, and $\overline{ab}$ denotes the line segment between a and b. Given two half-lines $\overrightarrow{ca}$ and $\overrightarrow{cb}$, we denote by $\sphericalangle(a, c, b)$ the convex angle (i.e., the angle which is at most 180°) centered in c and with sides $\overrightarrow{ca}$ and $\overrightarrow{cb}$ (see Figure 2.4(a)).

Given points p, p', and p'', the triangle with these three points as vertexes is denoted by $\triangle(p, p', p'')$. We use $q \in \triangle(p, p', p'')$ to indicate that q is inside the triangle or on its border.

Given a set of $n \geq 2$ distinct points $\mathbb{E}$ in the plane, we denote by $SEC(\mathbb{E})$ (or SEC if set $\mathbb{E}$ is unambiguous from the context) the *smallest enclosing circle* of the points; that is, $SEC(\mathbb{E})$ is the circle with minimum radius such that all points from $\mathbb{E}$ are inside or on the circle. An example of SEC of a set of eight points is depicted in Figure 3.6(b). The smallest enclosing circle of a set of n points is unique and can be computed in polynomial time [129]. It is well known that SEC is defined by at least three points (on its circumference), or by two opposite points (i.e., that lie on the end points of one of its diameter.). Obviously, the smallest enclosing circle of $\mathbb{E}$ remains invariant if we remove all or some of the points from $\mathbb{E}$ that are inside $SEC(\mathbb{E})$. Also, we have the following:

Property 2.1   Given a set $\mathbb{E}$ of $n \geq 3$ points, there exists a subset $\mathbb{T} \subseteq \mathbb{E}$ such that $|\mathbb{T}| \leq 3$ and $SEC(\mathbb{T}) = SEC(\mathbb{E})$.

Given a set $\mathbb{E}$ of n distinct positions in the plane, we say that the points are in a *biangular* configuration if there exists a point b, called the *center* and an ordering of the robots such that the angle $\sphericalangle(r, b, s)$ between any two adjacent robots r and s in the ordering is either α or β, and the angles alternate (see Figure 2.4(c)). If $\alpha = \beta$, we say that the configuration of the robots is *equiangular*. Note that a biangular configuration is defined only for an even number of points.

An important concept is that of *Voronoi diagram*. The Voronoi diagram of a set of points $P = \{p_1, p_2, \ldots, p_n\}$ is a subdivision of the plane into n cells, one for each point in P. The cells have the property that a point q belongs to the *Voronoi cell* of point p_i iff for any other point $p_j \in P, dist(q, p_i) < dist(q, p_j)$. In particular, the strict inequality means that points located on this boundary of the Voronoi diagram do not belong to any Voronoi cell.

IMPORTANT NOTE.   Throughout this book, unless otherwise specified, the robots considered are *anonymous*, *silent*, and *oblivious*. Note that, because of anonymity of the robots, two robots in the same location could be forced by an adversary to perform exactly the same actions for the entire duration of any algorithm, thus becoming indistinguishable.

CHAPTER 3

Gathering and Convergence

In systems of mobile entities, one of the most basic coordination and synchronization tasks is that of GATHERING: the entities, initially placed in arbitrary positions in $\mathcal{U}$, must congregate at a single location (the choice of the location is not predetermined) within finite time. This fundamental problem is also called *rendezvous* (typically for the case of two robots), or *homing*. Since the entities are seen as points, the gathering problem is sometimes called *point formation*. Note that, because of the anonymity of the robots, two robots in the same location could be forced by an adversary to perform exactly the same actions for the entire duration of any algorithm, thus becoming indistinguishable. It is thus assumed that the initial configuration contains only robots in distinct locations, unless otherwise specified.

A problem closely related to GATHERING is that of CONVERGENCE, where the robots need to be arbitrarily close to a common location, without the requirement of ever reaching it. These problems have been investigated extensively both in SSYNC and in ASYNC under a variety of assumptions about the robots' capabilities. This chapter focuses precisely on these problems.

3.1 BASIC RESULTS

We first consider some basic facts about GATHERING: It is possible in FSYNC, impossible without additional assumptions in SSYNC, and trivially achievable even in ASYNC with `ConsistentCompass`.

3.1.1 GATHERING IN FSYNC

In FSYNC, robots can gather following a very simple and rather intuitive strategy:

> *Move toward the center of gravity* $c(t) = \frac{1}{n}\Sigma_j r_j(t)$.

This protocol, called CoG and discussed in detail later (Section 3.3.1), requires simple calculations, and can be generalized to higher dimensions. More importantly, it actually achieves GATHERING in FSYNC [28]:

Theorem 3.1 [28] GATHERING *is solvable in* FSYNC *without any additional assumption.*

3.1.2   LIMITS TO GATHERING IN SSYNC: $n = 2$

A perhaps surprising result is that in SSYNC two oblivious robots cannot gather in the absence of additional assumptions; in particular, GATHERING is impossible if there is Disorientation, i.e., there is no consistency among the local coordinate systems of the two robots.

Theorem 3.2 [123]   *Without any agreement on the local coordinate systems, in* SSYNC, GATHERING *of $n = 2$ robots is* impossible, *even with strong multiplicity detection.*

To see why this is the case, consider two robots r and s that agree on one axis but not on the orientation of the other. Clearly, their view is specular. Assume by contradiction that $\mathcal{A}$ is a solution protocol. Consider an execution Act$\mathcal{S}$ of $\mathcal{A}$ where, in the last round, only one robot, say r, is activated and moves (achieving rendezvous for the first time) while the other robot does not move in that round (such an execution can be shown to exist). Consider now the execution up to (and excluding) the last round; at this point, proceed by activating not just one (as in Act$\mathcal{S}$), but both robots. When this happens, r will perform the same move as in Act$\mathcal{S}$, whose destination is the observed position of s. Since the view of s is specular, once activated, r will choose the observed position of s, as its destination. The result will be just a switch of the positions of the robots. Because they are oblivious, in the same conditions they will repeat the same actions; this means that, if they are both activated in every turn from now on, they will continue to switch without ever gathering.

This fact has motivated the study of gathering of $n = 2$ robots with chirality and tilted compasses [88], and with consistent compasses, as discussed later.

3.1.3   LIMITS TO GATHERING IN SSYNC: $n > 2$

In the case of $n > 2$, if the robots have no agreement on the coordinate system *and* are not able to detect multiplicity, the GATHERING problem is not solvable in SSYNC (and thus in ASYNC) [114]. To see why this is the case, assume that the n robots in the system have no agreement on the coordinate system and cannot detect multiplicity; given the result of Theorem 3.2, also assume that $n \geq 3$. By contradiction, let $\mathcal{A}_g$ be a deterministic algorithm that correctly solves the GATHERING problem in SSYNC.

Before showing in more detail the ideas of the impossibility proof, we observe two straightforward properties of the SSYNC setting.

Observation 3.3   If all the robots make the decision to move toward a point p at the same time instant t, then, even if a subset of them is not activated at t, all the others will still move toward p. Also, let $\mathbb{H}$ be a set of robots that at time t lie all on the same point p, and let us assume that these robots are all executing the same deterministic algorithm $\mathcal{A}$, and that they all have the same orientation of the local coordinate axes. Then at time $t + 1$ all the robots in $\mathbb{H}$ will again lie on the same position (possibly different from p).

The general idea of the impossibility proof is as follows. First, we define a scenario that we will use to defeat any possible $\mathcal{A}_g$. In particular, in this scenario

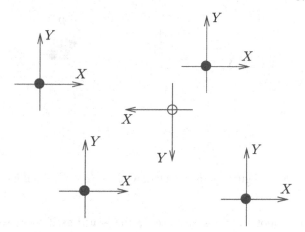

Figure 3.1: Orientation of the axes of the black robots and of the white robot, in Assum3.

Assum1. all the robots have the same unit distance;

Assum2. $\delta = \delta_1 = \ldots = \delta_n$ (with δ_i as defined in Section 2.6);

Assum3. robots $r_1, \ldots, r_{n-1}$, from now on called the *black* robots, have the same orientation and direction of the local coordinate system, while r_n, from now on called the *white* robot, has a local coordinate system where both axes have the same direction but opposite orientation with respect to the coordinate system of the black robots (see Figure 3.1).

The black and white coloring is used only for the sake of presentation, and this information is not used by the robots during the computation; also, Assum1–Assum3 are not known to the robots, hence they cannot use this information in their computations. The impossibility proof focuses on the missing multiplicity detection ability, in a setting defined by Assum1–Assum3 above: if there exists $\mathcal{A}_g$, then it must work also in a scenario described by Assum1–Assum3. Otherwise, $\mathcal{A}_g$ is not an algorithm that correctly solves the GATHERING problem. It is indeed shown that there exists no $\mathcal{A}_g$ that can be executed in such a scenario according to SSYNC and that allows the robots to gather in a point in finite time, when they cannot detect multiplicity.

By definition, if the robots execute $\mathcal{A}_g$, they will gather on the same point, say $\mathfrak{p}$, in finite time, say at time t_g. Let ActS be any execution (defined in terms of the activation of the robots) of $\mathcal{A}_g$ in SSYNC. Now, we design an alternative activation schedule of the robots, ActS', that behaves exactly as ActS until time $t_g - 1$. Then:

1. If r_n is not on $\mathfrak{p}$ at time $t_g - 1$, then in ActS', at time $t_g - 1$, r_n is inactive, and all the other robots are as in ActS. By above Observation 3.3, at time t_g the robots reach a configuration where all the black robots occupy the same position p_b, while the white robot does not: call it $\mathbb{E}_1$ (see Figure 3.2(a)).

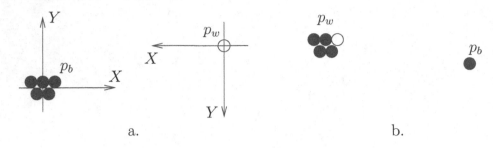

Figure 3.2: In (a) a $\mathbb{E}_1$-configuration is depicted, while in (b) a $\mathbb{E}_2$-configuration.

At time t_g the robots in the system sense the world as if there were only two robots (they cannot detect multiplicity), and these two robots have the same view of the world. Hence, by Observation 3.3 above, and by following the ideas of the impossibility proof of Theorem 3.2 for $n = 2$, we can conclude that $\mathcal{A}_g$ does not correctly solve the GATHERING problem.

2. Otherwise, in $\text{Act}\mathcal{S}'$, at time $t_g - 1$, r_{n-1} is inactive, and all the others are as in $\text{Act}\mathcal{S}$. Also in this case, at time t_g the robots reach a configuration where $n - 2$ of the black robots and the white robot occupy the same position p_w, while the last black robot does not: we will denote such a configuration as $\mathbb{E}_2$ (see Figure 3.2(b)).

In this case, the scenario is more delicate. As before, only two points on the plane are occupied by robots: on one, p_b, there is r_{n-1} (a black robot), and on the other one, p_w, there are $r_1, \ldots, r_{n-2}$ (black robots) and r_n (white robot). However, the robots on p_w do not all have the same view of the world, hence the argument of the previous case cannot be used.

We build a new activation schedule $\text{Act}\mathcal{S}''$ as follows. $\text{Act}\mathcal{S}''$ is the same as $\text{Act}\mathcal{S}'$ until time t_g. After time t_g, $\text{Act}\mathcal{S}''$ activates all the robots $r_1, \ldots, r_{n-2}$ always together (i.e., as if they were one robot); r_{n-1} and r_n are arbitrarily and fairly activated by $\text{Act}\mathcal{S}''$. Since by hypothesis $\mathcal{A}_g$ solves the problem, in a finite number of cycles, say at time $\tilde{t}$, the robots gather at $\mathfrak{p}$.

Note that at time $\tilde{t} - 1$ it is not possible that both r_n and r_{n-1} are already at $\mathfrak{p}$. In fact, this would imply that r_n (and r_{n-1}) would not move between time $\tilde{t} - 1$ and $\tilde{t}$, and that only the robots $r_1, \ldots, r_{n-2}$ would move. However, the view of the world of r_n and of $r_1, \ldots, r_{n-2}$ at time $\tilde{t} - 1$ is the same; hence, since $\mathcal{A}_g$ is assumed to be deterministic, $r_1, \ldots, r_{n-2}$ should take the same decision taken by r_n, that is to *not* move, not having the gathering at time $\tilde{t}$. A similar argument can be applied to show that

It is impossible that, at time $\tilde{t} - 1$, $r_1, \ldots, r_{n-1}$ are already at $\mathfrak{p}$, while r_n is not;

It is impossible that, at time $\tilde{t} - 1$, r_n and r_{n-1} are already at $\mathfrak{p}$, while $r_1, \ldots, r_{n-2}$ are not.

At this point, we build a further activation schedule $\text{Act}\mathcal{S}'''$ that is the same as $\text{Act}\mathcal{S}''$ until time $\tilde{t} - 1$. Then,

(a) If at time $\tilde{t} - 1$ no robot is at $\mathfrak{p}$, then in $\text{Act}\mathcal{S}'''$ robots $r_1, \ldots, r_{n-1}$ are active, while r_n is not. Hence, by Observation 3.3, at time $\tilde{t}$ the robots are in a $\mathbb{E}_1$-configuration.

(b) If at time $\tilde{t} - 1$ only r_{n-1} is at $\mathfrak{p}$, then in $\text{Act}\mathcal{S}'''$ robot $r_1, \ldots, r_{n-2}$ are active, while r_n is not. Hence, by Observation 3.3, at time $\tilde{t}$ the robots are in a $\mathbb{E}_1$-configuration.

(c) If at time $\tilde{t} - 1$ only robots $r_1, \ldots, r_{n-2}$ are at $\mathfrak{p}$, then in $\text{Act}\mathcal{S}'''$ robot r_{n-1} is active, while r_n is not. Hence, by Observation 3.3, at time $\tilde{t}$ the robots are in a $\mathbb{E}_1$-configuration.

(d) If at time $\tilde{t} - 1$ only r_n is at $\mathfrak{p}$, then in $\text{Act}\mathcal{S}'''$ robots $r_1, \ldots, r_{n-2}$ are active, while r_{n-1} is not. Hence, by Observation 3.3, at time $\tilde{t}$ the robots are once again in a $\mathbb{E}_2$-configuration.

In (a)–(c), a contradiction is reached by following the previous case. In (d), by iterating the above argument, we have that either the robots keep forming $\mathbb{E}_2$-configuration, or they form an $\mathbb{E}_1$-configuration; in both cases, it is shown that $\mathcal{A}_g$ cannot correctly solve the GATHERING problem.

Theorem 3.4 [114] *In absence of multiplicity detection and of any agreement on the coordinate systems,* GATHERING *is deterministically unsolvable in* SSYNC.

This impossibility holds even if the adversary is very restricted in the choice of the scheduler. Indeed, it holds if the scheduler is not only fair and centralized but also *slicing* (i.e., only one robot is activated in each round, and starting from time $t = 0$, after n successive rounds, all the robots in the system have been activated exactly once) [42].

3.1.4   GATHERING WITH CONSISTENT COMPASSES

By Theorem 3.4, either multiplicity detection or some form of agreement on the coordinate system is necessary for GATHERING to be solvable in SSYNC. Indeed, if there is agreement on the coordinate system, the GATHERING problem has a trivial solution that works even in ASYNC:

> *If I am not the rightmost and topmost robot, move toward it.*

which yields

Theorem 3.5   GATHERING *is possible in* ASYNC *with* ConsistentCompass *for any n.*

The question then becomes whether forms of agreement more restricted than ConsistentCompass, such as chirality and tilted compasses in ASYNC [88] and chirality and eventually consistent compasses in SSYNC [118], suffice for the problem to be solvable. The other question is whether multiplicity detection alone suffices in ASYNC [24, 25]. Both these questions are addressed later in this chapter.

3.2 RENDEZVOUS

When $n = 2$, i.e., the system contains only *two* robots, the GATHERING problem is very special, and it is often called RENDEZVOUS.

3.2.1 BASIC RESULTS

We have seen (Theorem 3.5) that, with a common coordinate system, there is an easy solution to GATHERING, and hence to RENDEZVOUS, even in ASYNC. In absence of a common coordinate system, by Theorem 3.2, the problem is not solvable even in SSYNC. Hence, the focus is on gathering in FSYNC, and on the CONVERGENCE problem. Notice that RENDEZVOUS has a trivial solution in the FSYNC model:

> *Moves to the halfway point to the other robot.*

This *move-to-half* strategy, in fact, achieves rendezvous regardless of the level of agreement among the robots' local coordinate systems; note that rendezvous would be achieved in a single round if there is *unlimited mobility* (i.e., the robots never stop before reaching their destination).

The situation is more complex in SSYNC and ASYNC. In fact, if the robots do not have a common coordinate system, in both SSYNC [123] and ASYNC [28], this *move-to-half* strategy guarantees only *convergence*; that is, the robots might not rendezvous within finite time, but only move arbitrarily close to each other.

Summarizing: the RENDEZVOUS problem of two oblivious robots without a common coordinate system is unsolvable in SSYNC (and thus ASYNC), and solvable in FSYNC. The CONVERGENCE problem of two oblivious robots without a common coordinate system is solvable even in ASYNC.

3.2.2 RENDEZVOUS WITH TILTED COMPASSES

The existing gap between trivial possibility of rendezvous in presence of `ConsistentCompass` (i.e., when the robots share a common coordinate system) and impossibility in presence of `Disorientation` (i.e., when there is no *a priori* consensus on the local coordinate systems) leads immediately to the problem of determining for which level of consistency of the coordinate systems of the two robots (i.e., accuracy of their compasses) rendezvous is still possible. In this section we consider compasses with `Chirality` (i.e., with the same notion of clockwise), where however the axes are tilted up to a certain degree. Let ϕ be the absolute value of the angle of the tilt. Clearly, if the tilt is such that $\phi \geq \frac{\pi}{2}$, the two compasses do not provide any useful information; hence rendezvous with tilted compasses might be possible only for $\phi < \frac{\pi}{2}$. In the following, for brevity, we will say that a compass has tilt ϕ to mean that the compass has a tilt whose angle has absolute value ϕ. The level of inaccuracy (i.e., the amount of tilt) tolerable will clearly depend on whether the tilt is permanent or may change from round to round.

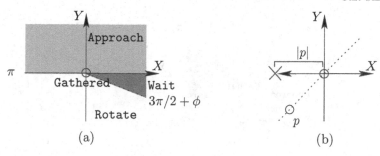

Figure 3.3: (a) An illustration of Protocol RV-A-STATIC. (b) The move of a robot state `Rotate` who looks at the other robot at p in its local coordinate system.

Fixed tilted compasses.   Let us consider the case when the two robots have fixed tilted compasses. Surprisingly, rendezvous is possible for any $\phi < \frac{\pi}{2}$ (the maximum tilt possible), even if the model is ASYNC provided there is `Chirality` [88].

The remarkably simple algorithm is as follows. Let p be the observed position of the other robot, expressed in the observer's coordinate system. The destination is determined according to the following computations, where angles are calculated modulo 2π (refer to Figure 3.3(a)):

Protocol RV-A-STATIC

Assumptions: chirality, compasses with fixed tilt $\phi < \frac{\pi}{2}$.

1. `Done`: If $p = (0, 0)$, then do not move (rendezvous is completed).

2. `Approach`: If $0 < arg(p) \leq \pi$ then move to p.

3. `Rotate`: If $\pi < arg(p) \leq \frac{3}{2}\pi + \phi$, then move to $(-|p|, 0)$.

4. `Wait`: If $\frac{3}{2}\pi + \phi < arg(p) \leq 2\pi$ then do not move.

---

where, for any point $p = (x, y) \in \mathbb{R}^2$, $arg(p) = \omega$ denotes the *argument* (or *phase*) of p, i.e., $0 \leq \omega < 2\pi$ and $(x, y) = |p|(\cos\omega, \sin\omega)$.

While the actions in state `Approach`, `Wait`, and `Done` are rather intuitive, the move of a robot in state `Rotate` is less so (refer to Figure 3.3(b)); this operation is indeed the crucial component of the algorithm.

Theorem 3.6 [88]   *With* chirality, *rendezvous of two asynchronous and semi-synchronous robots with static tilted compasses can be achieved if and only if* $\phi < \frac{\pi}{2}$.

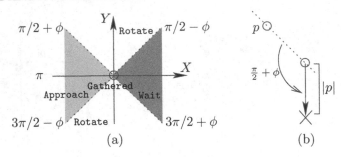

Figure 3.4: (a) An illustration of Protocol RV-S-DYNAMIC. (b) The move of a robot state `Rotate` who looks at the other robot at p in its local coordinate system.

Compasses with variable tilt in SSYNC. Let us focus now on the case of tilted compasses with chirality when the tilt is fully variable and semi-variable. Clearly, the amount of tolerable tilt in these compasses is less than that with fixed tilt. Unlike the static case, the result depends on whether the robots operate in SSYNC or ASYNC. Observe that in SSYNC there is no difference between semi-variable and fully-variable tilt.

An important observation is that the amount of tolerable tilt is strictly less than that tolerable with static compasses. In fact, if $\phi \geq \frac{\pi}{4}$ then rendezvous is *impossible* [88]. On the other hand, rendezvous is possible for any $\phi < \frac{\pi}{4}$.

The algorithm is still rather simple [88]. Let p be the observed position of the other robot, expressed in the observer's coordinate system. The destination is determined according to the following computations, where angles are calculated modulo 2π (refer to Figure 3.4(a)):

Protocol RV-S-DYNAMIC
Assumptions: SSYNC, chirality, compasses with variable tilt $\phi < \frac{\pi}{4}$.

1. `Done`: If $p = 0$ then do not move (rendezvous has been accomplished).

2. `Approach`: If $\frac{\pi}{2} + \phi < arg(p) \leq \frac{3}{2}\pi - \phi$ then move toward p.

3. `Wait`: If $-\frac{\pi}{2} + \phi < arg(p) \leq \frac{\pi}{2} - \phi$ then do not move.

4. `Rotate`: If $\frac{\pi}{2} - \phi < arg(p) \leq \frac{\pi}{2} + \phi$ or $\frac{3}{2}\pi - \phi < arg(p) \leq \frac{3}{2}\pi + \phi$ then move to $\rho_{\frac{\pi}{2}+\phi}(p)$.

---

where $\rho_\omega(p)$ denotes the point obtained by rotating p by angle ω with respect to the rotation center $(0, 0)$ (refer to Figure 3.4(b)).

Theorem 3.7 [88] *With chirality, rendezvous of two semi-synchronous robots with compasses with variable tilt can be achieved if and only if $\phi < \frac{\pi}{4}$.*

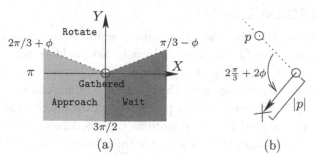

Figure 3.5: (a) An illustration of Protocol RV-A-SemiDynamic. (b) The move of a robot state Rotate who looks at the other robot at p in its local coordinate system.

***Compasses with variable tilt in* Async.**   If the two robots with compasses with variable tilt are asynchronous, the situation is not as precise as in the other cases. Observe that, unlike Ssync, in Async compasses with semi-variable and fully-variable tilt are quite different.

In the case of semi-variable tilt, a rendezvous protocol for $0 \leq \frac{\pi}{6}$ exists, following the same lines as the ones discussed before [88] (refer to Figure 3.5):

Protocol RV-A-SemiDynamic

Assumptions: chirality, compasses with semi-variable tilt $\phi < \frac{\pi}{6}$.

1. Done: If $p = 0$ then do not move (rendezvous has been accomplished).

2. Approach: If $\frac{2}{3}\pi + \phi \leq arg(p) < \frac{3}{2}\pi$ then move toward p.

3. Wait: If $-\frac{\pi}{2} \leq arg(p) \leq \frac{\pi}{3} - \phi$ then do not move.

4. Rotate: If $\frac{\pi}{3} - \phi < arg(p) < \frac{2}{3}\pi + \phi$ then move toward $\rho_{\frac{2}{3}\pi + 2\phi}(p)$.

Theorem 3.8 [88]   *With chirality, rendezvous of two asynchronous robots with compasses with semi-variable tilt can be achieved if $\phi < \frac{\pi}{6}$.*

It is not known if this is the best possible bound for semi-variable tilt in Async. Nothing is known for rendezvous with fully-variable tilt in Async.

3.3   GATHERING WITH UNLIMITED VISIBILITY

The gathering problem has been extensively investigated both experimentally and theoretically in the unlimited visibility setting, that is assuming that the entities are capable to sense ("see") the entire space (e.g., see [1, 24, 28, 42, 68, 89, 121, 123]).

3.3.1   CONVERGENCE IN ASYNC

As stated by Theorem 3.4, when no additional assumptions are made in the model, there is no deterministic solution to the GATHERING problem in SSYNC. However, CONVERGENCE is possible even in ASYNC: The robots get closer to a gathering point, but never reach it in finite time.

A very general and intuitive approach for letting n robots converge to a common location is to have each robot calculate some median position of all the observed positions (also called *target function*) and to move toward it. The algorithms described below can be generalized to higher dimensions; we however focus only on the case of the plane (i.e., $\mathcal{U} = \mathbb{R}^2$).

Convergence via Center of Gravity.   The Center of Gravity (CoG) (a.k.a. center of mass / baricenter) is probably the most natural target function. The center of gravity is not invariant to the robots' movement; in spite of that, a simple algorithm that uses it as a target function converges even in ASYNC for any number of robots [28]; it actually achieves GATHERING in FSYNC, as mentioned in Section 3.1.1. The protocol is quite simple:

Protocol CoG (for robot r_i at time t).
Assumptions: none.

1. Compute the Center of Gravity $c_i(t) = \frac{1}{n}\Sigma_j r_j(t)$;

2. Move toward $c_i(t)$.

This strategy has several advantages: in fact, it uses simple calculation, and it can be applied to any number of dimensions and to any number of robots.

The crucial property on which convergence is based is that, even if the center of gravity changes with the movements of the robots, there is still an invariant measure that allows the robots to get closer and closer. Define the destination point $\psi_i(t)$ of robot r_i to be the final point of the movement made by r_i following the last *Look* performed by r_i before or at time t. Let $H(t)$ denote the convex hull of the points $r_i(t)$ and $\psi_i(t)$. Then the convex hull $H(t)$ cannot increase in time. In other words, using protocol CoG, we have that:

Theorem 3.9   [28]   CONVERGENCE *is solvable in* ASYNC *without additional assumptions.*

The *convergence time* of the solution can be studied, based on the notion of *rounds*. Starting at time t, a round is said to terminate at the earliest point in time t' when all robots have performed at least one complete cycle (*Look–Compute–Move*) during the time between t and t'. With this definition, the convergence time is defined as the number of rounds that are required to halve the convex hull [28]. As expected, the convergence time depends on the synchronicity level of the model; it also depends on the type of mobility, that is whether the usual mobility model is assumed, where the robots move toward the destination of at least a small amount δ, or the *unlimited mobility* model is assumed, where the robots always reach their destination.

Let h be the initial diameter of the convex hull, and δ the minimum traveled distance. Then:

Theorem 3.10 [28] *In any execution of the* CoG *algorithm, the convex hull of robot locations and of the* CoGs *computed by all robots is halved: (i) Over any* $O(n^2 + \frac{nh}{\delta})$ *rounds for* ASYNC. *(ii) Over any* $\lceil \frac{8\sqrt{2}h}{\delta} \rceil$ *rounds for* FSYNC. *(iii) Over any* $O(n^2)$ *rounds for* ASYNC *under unlimited mobility. (iv) Over any* $O(n)$ *rounds for* SSYNC *under unlimited mobility. (v) Over any* $O(1)$ *round for* FSYNC *under unlimited mobility.*

In all cases, a simple lower bound of $\Omega(n)$ rounds can be shown. As mentioned in Section 3.1.1, the protocol actually achieves GATHERING in FSYNC. The results can be generalized to higher dimensions [28].

Other Target Functions.   Other target functions have been investigated with the main goal of improving the convergence time in ASYNC [32]. In particular, a property of target functions that guarantees convergence is described and, for this class of functions, convergence time bounds are given.

This property, called ϵ-*inner property* for a parameter $\epsilon \in (0, \frac{1}{2}]$, intuitively requires that when a robot computes a new target point, this point is significantly within the current "axes aligned minimal box" containing all robots. Note that this property holds also when the point is the center of gravity.

Let $f(r_1(t), \ldots, r_j(t), \ldots, r_k(t))$ be any function with the ϵ-*inner property* (also called ϵ-*inner target function*); a generalization of the CoG protocol becomes as follows.

Protocol CONVERGE (for robot r_i at time t).
Assumptions: None.

1. Compute the target point $c_i(t) = f(r_1(t), \ldots, r_j(t), \ldots, r_k(t))$;

2. Move toward $c_i(t)$.

Theorem 3.11 [32] *In* ASYNC *with* unlimited mobility, *in any execution of the convergence algorithm with a ϵ-inner target function, the diameter of the minbox around all robot positions and target points is halved after* $O(\frac{1}{\epsilon})$ *rounds.*

Since it is easy to see that the function that computes the center of gravity is a ϵ-*inner target function* with $\epsilon = \frac{1}{n}$, one obtains that a better analysis of the center of gravity algorithm gives the optimal $\Theta(n)$ convergence time under unlimited mobility. Moreover, let D_{max} be the maximum distance between any two robots positions and target points at any time, and let δ be the maximum traveled distance by a robot in one cycle. Then:

Theorem 3.12 [32] *In* ASYNC *with* unlimited mobility, *in any execution of the convergence algorithm with a ϵ-inner target function, the diameter of the minbox around all robot positions and target points is halved after* $O(\frac{1}{\epsilon} + \frac{D_{max}}{\epsilon\delta})$ *rounds.*

3.3.2   GATHERING IN ASYNC WITH MULTIPLICITY DETECTION

As seen earlier, gathering is impossible in absence of any form of agreement on the coordinate system and of multiplicity detection (see Theorem 3.4); this is true even if the robots have unlimited mobility (i.e., they always reach their destination in a single round). The question then becomes what additional consistency/power the robots need to have for gathering to be possible. The algorithm described in this section achieves GATHERING in ASYNC and uses, as an additional assumption, multiplicity detection.

Problems with Solutions Based on Invariant Target Points.   As seen earlier, the simpler CONVERGENCE problem, where the robots are required only to move "very close" to each other, without necessarily gathering at the same point, can be easily solved by having each robot compute some appropriate target point (e.g., the center of gravity) and move there. The reason moving toward the center of gravity does not work for GATHERING is because the center of gravity is not invariant with respect to robots' movements toward it, and the robots are oblivious. Once a robot makes a move toward the center of gravity, its position changes; since the robots act independently and asynchronously from each other and have no memory of the past, a robot (even the same one) observing the new configuration will compute and move toward a different point.

The obvious solution strategy for gathering would be then to choose as destination a point that, unlike the center of gravity, is *invariant* with respect to the robots' movements toward it. The only known point with such a property is the unique point in the plane that minimizes the sum of the distances between itself and all positions of the robots. In fact, this point, known as the *Weber* (or *Fermat* or *Torricelli*) *point*, does not change when moving any of the robots straight toward it [98, 128]. Unfortunately, the Weber point is not expressible as an algebraic expression involving radicals since its computation requires finding zeroes of high-order polynomials [5]. In other words, the Weber point is *not computable* even by radicals; thus it cannot be used to solve the gathering for $n \geq 5$. Interestingly, even *convergence* toward the Weber point cannot be guaranteed due to its instability with respect to changes in the point set [59]. A very different strategy, then, must to be devised.

Background and Difficulties.   If robots can detect multiplicity, a strategy starting from distinct initial positions of the robots could be to have some of them create a unique point of multiplicity and then have all the other robots move there, so to occupy the exact same point. This general idea has been employed first in the SSYNC model, with the assumption of *fixed mobility* (i.e., a robot always travels the minimum between the distance to its destination and a fixed δ, reaching its destination point) [123]: The point where multiplicity is created is the center of the smallest enclosing circle containing all the robots (special algorithm deals with the case of three robots). Such a solution is however heavily based on instantaneous movements and on synchronicity.

In the asynchronous setting the general strategy of creating a unique dense point can be employed, but in this case the overall gathering algorithm is very complex [25]. In fact, several difficulties have to be overcome because of the combination of asynchrony and obliviousness. Among

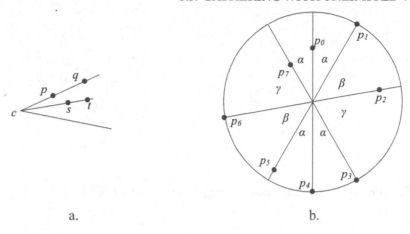

a.   b.

Figure 3.6: (a) Definition of $\texttt{succ}(p, c)$ and $\texttt{pred}(q, c)$. (b) Example of the string of angles of $P = p_0, \ldots, p_7$, computed with respect to their *SEC*, with a clockwise orientation of the circle. We have $SA^+(P, c)[1] = \langle \alpha, \beta, \gamma, \alpha, \alpha, \beta, \gamma, \alpha \rangle$; $LexMinString(P, c) = \langle \alpha, \alpha, \beta, \gamma, \alpha, \alpha, \beta, \gamma \rangle$; $StartSet^+(P, c) = \{p_3, p_7\}$; and $StartSet^-(P, c) = \emptyset$.

them is the difficulty of avoiding *collisions*: since the robots do not look while moving, and the destination is computed based on possibly outdated information about the position (and moves) of the other robots, to avoid collisions, the computation of a robot r must take into account all possible movements of all the other robots from the time t of the *Look* to the *unknown* and a priori *unbounded* time $t' > t$ when r will actually end its move. An additional difficulty due to obliviousness and related to collisions is that if two robots (accidentally or by design) terminate a cycle at the same location, then they become potentially indistinguishable, and from that moment on they might behave exactly in the same way (in fact there is at least one execution in which they will do so); in particular, it might not be possible for them to separate ever again. More generally, due to asynchrony, symmetric configurations are more difficult to break.

Important Concepts.   We now introduce some important terminology used in the algorithm. Given a set P of n distinct points in the plane, a point $c \notin P$ called the *center*, and the set $RadSet(P, c)$, we define the successor of $p \in P$ with respect to c, denoted by $\texttt{succ}(p, c)$, as the point $q \in P$ such that (refer to Figure 3.6(a)):

- either q is the closest point to p on the radius where p lies, with $dist(c, q) > dist(c, p)$, if such a point exists;

   or $\overrightarrow{cq}$ is the radius following $\overrightarrow{cp}$ in the order implied by the clockwise direction, and q is the closest point to c on $\overrightarrow{cq}$.

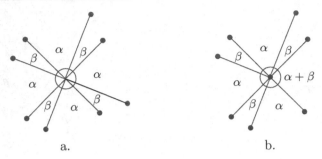

Figure 3.7: (a) A regular biangular and (b) irregular biangular set of 8 points.

Symmetrically, given a point $q \in P$, the predecessor of q with respect to c, denoted by $\text{pred}(q, c)$, is the point $p \in P$ such that $\text{succ}(p, c) = q$.

The functions $\text{succ}()$ and $\text{pred}()$ define a unique cyclic order on P, which we shall denote by $< p_0, p_1, \ldots, p_{n-1} >$, where $p_{i+1} = \text{succ}(p_i)$, and all operations on indices are modulo n. This, in turns, defines a cyclic *string of angles* $SA^+(P, c) =< \alpha_0, \alpha_1, \ldots, \alpha_{n-1} >$, where $\alpha_i = \sphericalangle(p_i, c, p_{i+1})$; p_i is called the (clockwise) *start point* of α_i. The string of angles in the opposite direction is denoted by $SA^-(P, c) =< \alpha_{n-1}, \ldots, \alpha_0 >$.

Associated to the cyclic string of angles $SA^+(P, c)$ there is the set of strings $SA^+(P, c)[i] =< \alpha_i, \alpha_{i+1}, \ldots, \alpha_{i+n-1} >$, with $0 \le i \le n - 1$ (refer to the example depicted in Figure 3.6(b), where the string of angles are computed with respect to the *SEC* of the eight points); similarly, associated to $SA^-(P, c)$ there is the set of strings $SA^-(P, c)[i] =< \alpha_{i-1}, \ldots, \alpha_i >$; here and in the following, all operations on the indices are modulo n. We define the *start point* of $SA^+(P, c)[i]$ as the start point of α_i, that is p_i. Finally, let $SA(P, c)[i] = SA^+(P, c)[i] \cup SA^-(P, c)[i]$, and $SA(P, c) = \bigcup_i SA(P, c)[i]$.

We say that $SA(P, c)$ is *simple* if $SA^+(P, c)$ does not contain any angle of zero degrees; otherwise, at least two points are on the same radius, and we say that $SA(P, c)$ is *mixed*.

We denote by $LexMinString(P, c)$ the lexicographically minimum string among all strings in $SA(P, c)$. Let $StartSet^+(P, c) = \{p_i \in P | SA^+(P, c)[i] = LexMinString(P, c)\}$ be the set of start points of $LexMinString(P, c)$ in $SA^+(P, c)$, and let $StartSet^-(P, c)$ be defined similarly. Let $StartSet(P, c) = StartSet^+(P, c) \cup StartSet^-(P, c)$.

We now refine the definition of biangular configuration introduced in Section 2.9. In particular, we say that a set of n distinct points in the plane P is *biangular* if there exists a point b such that $\forall i \ge 0 \, \alpha_i = \alpha_{i+2} > 0$ where $SA^+(P, b) =< \alpha_0, \ldots, \alpha_{n-1} >$; b is then called *center of biangularity* of P. Given a set P of $n - 1$ points on the plane we say that P is *biangular with one gap* and center b if there exists a point $x_g \notin P$, such that $P \cup \{x_g\}$ is *biangular* with center b. Analogous definition holds for a set of points *biangular with two gaps*. Finally, given a set P of n points, we say that P is *irregular biangular* if there exists a point $p \in P$, the center, such that $P \setminus \{p\}$ is *regular biangular with one gap* with center p (refer to Figure 3.7(b)). Note that it can be shown that, if P is irregular biangular, then its center is unique. Similarly, to the "gaps" introduced for a biangular set of points, we say that a set P of $n - 1$ points is *periodic with one gap* if there exists a string W, with $|W| \geq 3$, and $e \geq 2$ such that $SA^+(P, c) = W^{e-1} \circ W'$, with $W = \langle w_0, \ldots, w_{n/e-1} \rangle$ and $W' = \langle w_0, w_1, \ldots, w_{i-1}, \overline{w}, w_{i+2}, \ldots, w_{n/e-1} \rangle$, for some $0 \leq i \leq n/e - 1$, and with $\overline{w} = w_i + w_{i+1}$ (refer to Figure 3.9(b)). Note that, since $n \geq 5$ and $e \geq 2$, if P is periodic with one gap, then i is unique. Furthermore, we say that a set P of n points is *irregular periodic*, if one of the points in P is at c, and $P \setminus \{c\}$ is periodic with one gap.

ASYNCHRONOUS GATHERING ALGORITHM ± GOGATHER
Assumptions: Multiplicity detection

$\mathcal{R} :=$ Set of positions of the robots;
If One dense point p **Then** `moveIfFreeWay`(p).
Else
   If The robots are in regular (resp. irregular) biangular configuration **Then**
     $b :=$ Center of regular (resp. irregular) biangularity;
     `moveIfFreeWay`(b).
   Else
     $SEC :=$ Smallest Enclosing Circle of all robots;
     $c :=$ Center of SEC;
     If No robot is at c **Then**
       Compute the set of strings $SA(\mathcal{R})$, $LexMinString(\mathcal{R})$;
       Compute $StartSet^+(\mathcal{R})$, $StartSet^-(\mathcal{R})$;
       $s := |StartSet^+(\mathcal{R}) \cup StartSet^-(\mathcal{R})|$;
       If $SA(\mathcal{R})$ is simple **Then** Case 1. **Else** Case 3.
     Else %*One robot r is at c*%
       $\overline{\mathcal{R}} := \mathcal{R} \setminus \{c\}$;
       Compute the set of strings $SA(\overline{\mathcal{R}})$, $LexMinString(\overline{\mathcal{R}})$;
       Compute $StartSet^+(\overline{\mathcal{R}})$, $StartSet^-(\overline{\mathcal{R}})$;
       $s := |StartSet^+(\overline{\mathcal{R}}) \cup StartSet^-(\overline{\mathcal{R}})|$;
       If $SA(\overline{\mathcal{R}})$ is simple **Then** Case 2. **Else** Case 4.
     End If
   End If
End If

Strategy. The overall strategy follows this general principle: at the beginning the robots are in distinct locations (forming a *plain* configuration); within finite time, a unique *dense* point (i.e., where there is more than one robot) is created, and all other robots gather there. However, since the robots are disoriented and oblivious, and operate in a totally asynchronous manner, this strategy is not simple to enact. For example, ensuring that a unique dense point is created requires that during the execution of the algorithm no collisions occur at any point other than the final gathering one. As

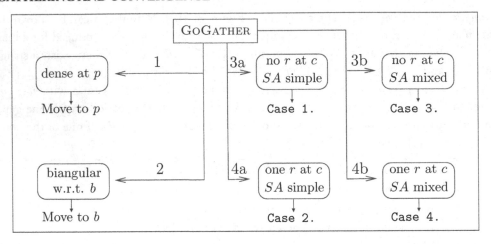

Figure 3.8: Schematic overview of the solution; the numbers on the arrows represent the ordering of the tests performed by Algorithm GoGather.

mentioned earlier, an additional difficulty is in recognizing if a symmetric configuration is being formed during the execution. For instance, if all the robots initially are the vertices of a n-gon (a configuration called *equiangular*), then the trivial strategy in this case would be that the robots move toward the center of the n-gon; however, if such a configuration is created by the movement of some robots during the execution, the still robots might observe the equiangular configuration and decide to apply the go-to-center strategy, while those already moving continue their procedure (possibly destroying the newly formed equiangularity). The algorithm ensures that, if a symmetric configuration is formed during the execution, *all* robots become aware of it (recall, however, that the robots are oblivious and do not remember previous observations), so that *all* robots follow the same strategy.

In particular, the protocol works by examining the configuration observed by a robot in the *Look* operation (see also Figure 3.8). The first test a robot does when computing is to determine whether there is a single dense point, p; if so, the robot moves toward p. In absence of a dense point, the robot checks for the presence of a *biangular* configuration.

If the check for a biangular configuration is positive, the robot will move toward the center of biangularity b. The algorithm ensures that, if this case is recognized by one robot, then *all* robots will recognize it, and will move toward b; in this case, within finite time b will become dense.

Should the first two tests fail, the robot analyzes the *string of angles* (SA) of the robots with respect to the center c of the smallest enclosing circle (see an example in Figure 3.9).

The algorithm distinguishes four cases depending on whether there is one or no robot at the center of *SEC*, and on whether the *SA* is *simple* (i.e., the string does not contain any angle of zero

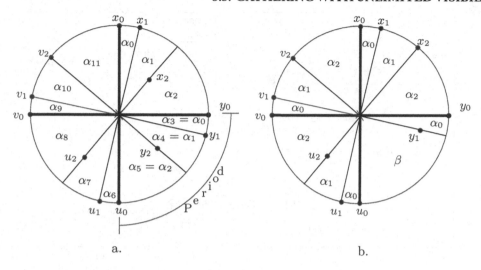

a.   b.

Figure 3.9: (a) Example with $|StartSet^+(P, c)|=4$, $LexMinString(P, c) = \langle \alpha_0, \ldots, \alpha_{11} \rangle$ with period $\langle \alpha_0, \alpha_1, \alpha_2 \rangle$. There are $\frac{n}{k} = \frac{12}{3} = 4$ periods, with $\beta = 90°$. The thick lines represent the starting points of each of the four periods. Robots x_i, y_i, u_i, and v_i, $0 \le i \le 2$, are *equivalent*. (b) If y_2 is removed from P, we obtain an example of a set of points that is periodic with one gap, with $\beta = \alpha_1 + \alpha_2$.

degrees) or *mixed* (i.e., at least one angle of zero degrees is in the string; this implies that at least two robots are on the same radius).

In all cases, the algorithm uses the string of angles of the robots to "elect" a subset of the robots. Several cases arise (see Figure 3.10 where s is the size of the elected set) and the algorithm is complicated by various technicalities. At a general level, if the elected set consists of a single robot, that robot moves until it reaches another robot, thus creating a single dense point. Otherwise, the robots of the elected set move toward c, the center of the smallest enclosing circle, ensuring that the smallest enclosing circle is not changed by their movements, and paying particular attention to *potential* biangular configuration that might be formed during their movements (all moves are done *cautiously*). In fact, it is possible that the elected robots reach, during their movements, points that render the configuration biangular; such points are called *critical*. The algorithm explicitly computes these points; in particular, if elected robot has a critical point on its way, the algorithms ensure that it reaches it; also, the algorithm ensures that the configuration is *still* (i.e., no robot is moving or about to move) when this happens. Hence, if a biangular configuration is formed during the movements of the elected robots, all other robots will observe it in their next *Look* state, and will eventually gather on the center of biangularity, as described above. Otherwise, if no biangular configuration is formed, the elected robots will create a unique dense point at c, where all other robots will gather. Correctness is proven by the following sequence of theorems.

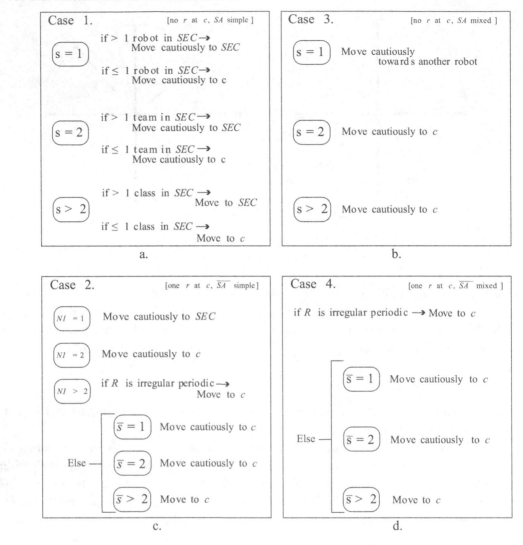

Figure 3.10: The four cases of the algorithm when there is no dense point, and the configuration is not biangular. Recall that s is the number of start points in the string of angles; $\bar{s}$ is the number of start points in the string of angles built not considering c (such string of angles is denoted by $\overline{SA}$ in the figure); and NI is the number of robots inside SEC. Note that the figure specifies only the kind of movement that is performed in each case, and not which robot (or subset of robots) is performing it.

Lemma 3.13 [25] *Let p be the only dense point at time t. If at that time all the robots are either still or safely acting on p, then there exists a time $t' > t$ when all robots gather at p.*

Lemma 3.14 [25] *Let at time t the configuration be plain, still and biangular (either regular or irregular) with center b. Then there exists a time t' > t when all robots gather at b.*

Lemma 3.15 [25] *From any initial configuration $\mathbb{E}$, within a finite number of cycles, the robots reach a configuration that is either biangular (regular or irregular) and still, or dense and still, or dense with all acting robots safely acting on the dense point.*

Finally:

Theorem 3.16 [25] *In ASYNC, with multiplicity detection, $n \geq 5$ robots can solve the GATHERING problem within finite time.*

Since the Weber point can be computed for $n < 5$, this fact as well as the availability of multiplicity detection, can be exploited to solve GATHERING in ASYNC also for $n = 3$ and $n = 4$ [26].

3.3.3 GATHERING IN SSYNC: TILTED COMPASSES

Also in SSYNC, GATHERING is impossible in absence of any form of agreement on the coordinate system and of multiplicity detection. In this section we see that Chirality and *unlimited mobility* suffice for making the problem solvable if the tilt of the local compasses is $\phi < \frac{\pi}{4}$ [86]; here, it is assumed that the tilts are variable.

We remind that $arg(p) = \omega$ denotes the *argument* (or *phase*) of p, i.e., $0 \leq \omega < 2\pi$ and $(x, y) = |p|(\cos \omega, \sin \omega)$. The algorithm consists of two sub-algorithms. The first one, called GATHERLDS, achieves gathering under the assumption that the point set of the initial configuration has a unique *longest-distance segment* (LDS), where LDS at time t is the maximum-length segment among all pairs of robots' locations at time t. If the LDS is not unique, a preprocessing algorithm, ELECTONELDS, is executed first. As a result of this preprocessing, the system reaches a configuration where either a unique LDS is elected, or gathering is achieved.

Let us consider first the case when there is a uniquely determined LDS at time t; let $a(t)$ and $b(t)$ be the coordinates of the two endpoints of the LDS, and let $L(t) = b(t) - a(t)$. Let us assume, without loss of generality, that $\frac{\pi}{2} - \epsilon < arg(L(t)) \leq \frac{3}{2}\pi - \epsilon$. Let $R(t)$ be the set of robots at the end points of LDS at time t; i.e., $R(t) = \{r_i \in \mathcal{R} : r(t) = a(t) \text{ or } r(t) = b(t)\}$. If $R(t) = \mathcal{R}$, we say that the configuration is 2-gathered.

The algorithm GATHERLDS first gathers all robots at the endpoints of the unique LDS. This is done as follows. If robot r, with $r(t) \notin R(t)$, observes and recognizes that the current configuration is not 2-gathered, it moves to either $a(t)$ or $b(t)$. All robots in $R(t)$ wait until the current configuration becomes 2-gathered.

Once the current configuration is 2-gathered, the algorithm gradually reduces the angle $arg(L(t))$ to $\frac{\pi}{2}$. The robots do so by rotating the LDS counter-clockwise (recall that the robots have chirality). This process is repeated until either the robots are gathered at one point, or $arg(L(t))$ is close to $\frac{\pi}{2}$ and all robots are gathered at two endpoints of $L(t)$; in the latter case, all robots will gather within finite time. All this is done as follows. Let r be at $a(t)$ and become active at time t; then r it executes the 2GATHEREDRULE below:

Protocol 2GATHEREDRULE

Assumptions: SSYNC, chirality, unlimited mobility, compasses with variable tilt $\phi < \frac{\pi}{4}$.

1. Approach: If $\pi \le arg(b(t)) < \frac{3}{2}\pi + \epsilon$ then move to $b(t)$.

2. Wait: If $0 \le arg(b(t)) \le \frac{2}{\pi} + \epsilon$ then do not move.

3. Rotate: Otherwise, move at angle $arg(b(t)) + \pi - 2\epsilon$ by length $b(t)$.

Similarly, if r is at $b(t)$ and becomes active at time t, it executes the same rule replacing $b(t)$ by $a(t)$.

Notice that, even if all robots are gathered at the endpoints of the LDS before the rotation, robots may end up at more than two points after the rotation; this is because two robots at a same point can behave differently because of the difference in their compasses. However, even in this case it is possible to uniquely determine an LDS with endpoints $a(t+1)$ and $b(t+1)$ satisfying $\epsilon \le arg(L(t) - L(t+1)) \le 2\epsilon$, where $L(t+1) = a(t+1) - b(t+1)$. Again all robots not already at the end points $a(t+1)$ and $b(t+1)$, go to one of them; so within finite time, all robots are 2-gathered. This entire process is repeated until either the robots are gathered at one point, or $arg(L(t))$ is close to $\frac{\pi}{2}$ and all robots are 2-gathered at the endpoints of $L(t)$. In the latter case, all robots perform in 2GATHEREDRULE either Approach or Wait, and they will gather within finite time.

Observe that, if there is a unique LDS, GATHERLDS guarantees that any following configuration has a unique LDS unless it achieves gathering.

Lemma 3.17 **[86]** *Let $\mathbb{E}(t)$ be a configuration having a unique LDS. Then, in any following configuration there is a unique LDS unless gathering is achieved.*

The only missing component of the algorithm is ELECTONELDS that reduces any configuration to one where there is a unique LDS or gathering is achieved. By Lemma 3.17, once the system reaches the configuration having a unique LDS, ELECTONELDS is never needed again. Let us see how this algorithm works. Call a configuration *contractable* if (1) its convex hull $H(t)$ is symmetric (i.e., its edges have the same length) and every robot is either at a vertex of $H(t)$ or at the center of gravity of $H(t)$, or (2) $H(t)$ is not symmetric and there are no robots inside $H(t)$.

The algorithm first of all reduces the current configuration to a contractable one, if it is not already so. This is done by having each active robot that is not at a vertex of $H(t)$ (nor at the center of gravity of $H(t)$, if $H(t)$ is symmetric) move to a vertex of $H(t)$.

Once $H(t)$ is contractable, a unique LDS is elected by decreasing the number of edges of the convex hull, until the configuration has a unique LDS (this will always happen because the convex hull eventually will become a single edge). If $H(t)$ is contractable but symmetric, any active robot moves to the center of gravity of $H(t)$. Since the robots have *unlimited moving* capabilities, each active robot reaches its destination. This means that, if all robots are activated, they all gather at the center of gravity; otherwise, the number of edges of the convex hull decreases.

If $H(t)$ is contractable but asymmetric, the number of edges is decreased by some robots moving so to contract shortest-length edges in $H(t)$. This is done as follows. Each robot r on a vertex of $H(t)$ considers the distance to the right (i.e., clockwise) and left (i.e., counter-clockwise) neighboring vertices of vertex of $H(t)$; it becomes *contracting* if the edge on the left is a shortest-length edge in $H(t)$, while the one on the right is not. Obviously there is at least one contracting robot since $H(t)$ is asymmetric. All non-contracting robots do not move. A contracting robot, when active, moves to the neighboring vertex on the left, in this way decreasing the number of edges of the convex hull. Summarizing,

Theorem 3.18 [86]   *In* SSYNC *it is possible to gather robots having* unlimited mobility, chirality, *and compasses with variable tilt* $\phi < \frac{\pi}{4}$.

3.3.4   GATHERING IN SSYNC: DENSE INITIAL CONFIGURATIONS

A capability that can be considered instead of a common coordinate system is a stronger form of multiplicity detection, where robots can detect the exact number of robots located at a given position [53]. Adding this capability, it is impossible to solve the problem for all possible initial configurations containing an even number of robots; however the robots can gather from an arbitrary configuration with n robots, when n is odd. In this case, *arbitrary* configurations include dense configurations (i.e., containing more than one robot on the same point). Since this algorithm is correct starting from all possible configurations provided n is odd (even the ones containing more than one robot), it is truly self-stabilizing.

The general idea of the algorithm is to transform an arbitrary configuration P into one where there is exactly one point $p_{max} \in P$ that contains the highest number of robots. When such a configuration is reached, all the robots which are not at p_{max} move toward it, avoiding creating another point containing the same number of robots, or more.

If there exists a unique p_{max} then all other robots move toward it. Two more cases are identified by the authors depending on whether there are two such maximal points, or more than two.

If there are two, then each robot moves toward the closest between them, avoiding creating another maximal point. Since the number of robots is odd, eventually one of the two will contain more than the other and the robots on the one containing fewer robots will move to the other.

If there are more than two, the strategy consists in creating a unique maximal point inside the smallest enclosing circle *SEC* of all the robots. Let $Max\mathcal{P}$ be the set of points containing the highest number of robots. Three situations are identified:

- 1. If there is no robot inside *SEC*, then all the robots can move toward the center of *SEC*.

- 2. If all the robots inside *SEC* are at the center of *SEC*, then only the robots in $SEC \cap MaxP$ can move toward the center of *SEC*.

- 3. If some robots inside *SEC* are not at the center of *SEC*, then only the robots inside *SEC* are allowed to move toward the center of *SEC*.

All movements have to be carefully designed so not to create undesired high multiplicity. With this algorithm it is shown that:

Theorem 3.19   [53]   *With* strong multiplicity detection, *the* GATHERING *problem is solvable in* SSYNC *starting from any (possibly dense) initial position if and only if n is odd.*

3.4   CONVERGENCE AND GATHERING WITH LIMITED VISIBILITY

In general, and more realistically, robots can sense only a surrounding within a radius of bounded size V (refer to the example depicted in Figure 2.1). This setting is understandably more difficult; for example, a robot might not even know the total number of robots nor where they are located if outside its radius of visibility. Not surprisingly, not many algorithmic results are known (e.g., [2, 3, 68, 102, 103, 118]).

In this setting, obviously neither convergence nor gathering can be performed if the initial visibility graph $G(0)$ is not connected (refer to Section 2.4). So, in all the literature, $G(0)$ is assumed to be connected.

3.4.1   CONVERGENCE IN SSYNC

In the SSYNC model, a convergence gathering solution exists even if the robots do not agree on a common coordinate system [2].

Let $\mathcal{R}(t) = \{s_1(t), \ldots, s_n(t)\}$ denote the set of the n robots' positions at time t. Also, let $\mathcal{R}_i(t)$ denote the set of robots that are within distance V from s_i at time t; that is, the set of robots that are visible from s_i (note that $s_i \in \mathcal{R}_i(t)$). $SC_i(t)$ denotes the smallest enclosing circle of the set $\{s_j(t) | s_j \in \mathcal{R}_i(t)\}$ of the positions of the robots in $\mathcal{R}_i(t)$ at t; let $c_i(t)$ be the center of $SC_i(t)$. The algorithm is described below (refer also to Figure 3.11).

LV-SS-Converge
Assumptions: Ssync.

1. If $\mathcal{R}_i(t) = \{s_i\}$, then $x = s_i(t)$.

2. $\forall s_j \in \mathcal{R}_i(t) \setminus \{s_i\}$,

    2.1. $d_j := dist(s_i(t), s_j(t))$,
    2.2. $\theta_j := c_i(t)\widehat{s_i(t)}s_j(t)$,
    2.3. $l_j := (d_j/2)\cos\theta_j + \sqrt{(v/2)^2 - ((d_j/2)\sin\theta_j)^2}$,

3. $limit := \min_{s_j \in \mathcal{R}_i(t) \setminus \{s_i\}}\{l_j\}$,

4. $goal := dist(s_i(t), c_i(t))$,

5. $amount := \min\{goal, limit\}$,

6. $p :=$ point on $\overline{s_i(t)c_i(t)}$ at distance $amount$ from $s_i(t)$.

7. Move toward p.

Every time a robot s_i becomes active, it moves toward $c_i(t)$, but only over a certain distance $amount$. Specifically, if s_i does not see any robot other than itself, then s_i does not move at all. Otherwise, the algorithm chooses as destination for s_i the point p on the segment $\overline{s_i(t)c_i(t)}$ that is closest to $c_i(t)$ and that satisfies the following condition:

For every robot $s_j \in \mathcal{R}_i(t)$, p lies in the disk $\mathcal{C}_j$ whose center is the midpoint m_j of $s_i(t)$ and $s_j(t)$, and whose radius is $V/2$.

This condition ensures that s_i and s_j will still be visible after the movement of s_i, and possibly of s_j (see Figure 3.11(a)).

The correctness proof is based on the following reasoning. First, two robots that are connected in the visibility graph at time t, will stay connected at time $t + 1$. In fact, if $s_i(t)$ and $s_j(t)$ are connected, then $s_j(t) \in \mathcal{R}_i(t)$ and $s_i(t) \in \mathcal{R}_j(t)$ and then, by definition of $limit$, both $s_i(t + 1)$ and $s_j(t + 1)$ lie inside the disc with center m_j (Figure 3.11(a)). Second, let $H(t)$ be the convex hull of the robots at time t, for any $t \geq t_0$, $H(t + 1) \subseteq H(t)$ leading to the proof that $H(t)$ converges to a point. Then we have:

Theorem 3.20 **[2]** Convergence *with limited visibility is possible in* Ssync.

The convergence time (assuming fully synchronous executions) of the algorithm above has been recently analyzed and a tight bound of $O(n^2)$ rounds has been shown [45].

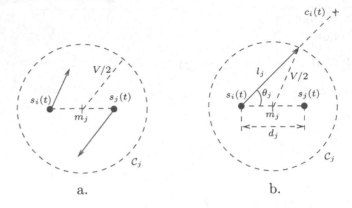

Figure 3.11: Convergence gathering in SSYNC [2].

Variants. Variants and generalizations of the LV-SS-CONVERGE algorithm have also been studied. In FSYNC the algorithm is generalized and a family of solutions for the convergence problem with limited visibility are devised [102].

3.4.2 CONVERGENCE IN FSYNC IN NON-CONVEX REGIONS

The CONVERGENCE problem has also been studied when the robots operate in a *non-convex* region $\mathcal{U} \subseteq \mathbb{R}^2$ (of which they have no map) [74].

In such a space (see Figure 3.12), two robots s and s' are said to be *mutually visible* at time t if not only their distance is at most V but also the segment connecting their positions at time t is completely contained in $\mathcal{U}$; for instance, robots s and s' in Figure 3.12 are within distance V, but they are not mutually visible. The approach used to solve the problem is that of computing a set of constraints that the robots have to follow when moving so that (a) the mutual visibility graph stays connected during the movements, and (b) the distances between robots strictly decrease at each time step.

The first set of constraints is derived from those discussed in Section 3.4.1, and guarantees that condition (a) is met; in particular, it imposes that if two robots s_i and s_j are mutually visible at time t, they stay connected at time $t + 1$: let $p_i = s_i(t)$ and $p_j = s_j(t)$ be the positions of robots s_i and s_j at time t, respectively, then s_i and s_j are allowed to moving inside the ball $\mathcal{C}$ of radius $\frac{V}{2}$ centered in the mid-point of p_i and p_j (see Figure 3.11). Clearly, since the robots operate in a non-convex environment, the robots are limited to moving inside any convex area contained in the intersection between $\mathcal{C}$ and $\mathcal{U}$. The computation of such a convex area by any pair of mutually visible robots can easily be done [74].

The overall idea of the gathering algorithm can be summarized as follows: at each time step t, every robot computes all convex areas for all its neighbors in the V-range visibility graph at t; the area where it is allowed to move in order to verify condition (a) is therefore the intersection of

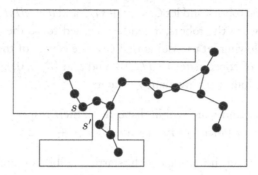

Figure 3.12: An example of non-convex environment for the gathering problem in [74]. The edges between robots represent the edges of the visibility graph.

all these areas. The robot moves now toward the circumcenter of its allowed moving zone, i.e., the center of the smallest circle enclosing this area. It can be shown that this choice satisfies condition (b) above. Hence,

Theorem 3.21   [74]   *In* FSYNC, *robots with limited visibility operating in a non-convex region can solve* CONVERGENCE.

3.4.3   CONVERGENCE IN ASYNC

***Convergence in partial* ASYNC.**   A limited form of asynchrony, here called *partial* ASYNC, has also been considered in regard to the convergence problem. In *partial* ASYNC the time spent by a robot in the *Sleep*, *Look*, and *Compute* states is bounded by a globally predefined amount, while the time spent in the *Move* state is bounded by a locally predefined quantity (not necessarily the same for each robot). This form of asynchrony lies in between the ASYNC model and the SSYNC model. A slight variation of the LV-SS-CONVERGE Algorithm, described in Section 3.4.1, can be shown to achieve convergence in such a model.

Theorem 3.22   [103]   CONVERGENCE *with limited visibility is possible in* partial ASYNC.

***Convergence in 1-fair* ASYNC.**   CONVERGENCE with limited visibility is possible in ASYNC under a *1-fair scheduler* [95]: Between two successive activations of each robot r, all other robots have been activated at most once. As a consequence, from the moment r observes the current situation to the moment it finishes its movement, no other robot performs more than one *Look*.

The proposed approach looks for restrictions on robot's movements that preserve the connectivity of the initial visibility graph, and that allow robots to converge toward a point.

Let r and s be two robots, and let $C = (r + s)/2$ and $d = dist(r, s)$; since the visibility radius V is a parameter known to the robots, it can be assumed to be the common unit distance for the robots. Also, in the following let us assume that C is the center of the coordinate systems for r and s (i.e., r is in position of coordinates $[-d/2, 0]$, and s at $[d/2, 0]$). In order to keep the visibility graph connectivity, the following invariant I is kept:

> **[I]** If two robots r and s are within distance V, their respective destinations d_r and d_s are chosen within distance $1/2$ from point $C = (r + s)/2$.

If this invariant is kept for any initial edge of the starting visibility graph, the connectivity is preserved.

In order to preserve the above invariant, two independent restrictions on the movements of the robots are introduced, called, respectively, *move toward* and *move around*. In *move toward*, robot s chooses as its destination any point inside the circle having $\overline{Cs}$ as diameter; in *move around* robot s chooses as its destination any point inside the circle with center s and having radius $l = (1 - d)/4$.

Lemma 3.23   [95]   *If any pair of robots r and s within visibility distance choose their destination point according to the above* move toward *or* move around *restrictions, then the invariant I is preserved.*

Now, each robot r first computes, for each robot r_j in its visibility range, the set of all allowed destination points, say $T_j(r)$, consisting of the union of the allowed destinations as specified by *move toward* or *move around*. Let $CH(t)$ be the convex hull of all robots at time t, and $CH_r(t)$ be the convex hull of all robots observed by r at time t, including r. In order to converge, robots inside CH should not move toward the boundary of CH; actually, the robots on the boundary of CH should move inside CH. This rule is transformed into a third restriction on the possible movement of the robots: Let $T^*(r)$ be the set of points that are not further than halfway from the boundary of CH_r. Then, the destination point of r is chosen to be inside $\overline{T} = \cap_{j=1}^{k} T_j(r) \cap T^*(r)$, with $r_1, \ldots, r_k$ the robots visible by r; in particular, robot r chooses as its destination the point in $\overline{T}$ that is further from its current position. Using these rules $CH(t)$ shrinks, converging toward a point; thus

Theorem 3.24   [95]   *Convergence with limited visibility is possible in* Async *under a* 1-*fair scheduler.*

3.4.4   GATHERING WITH CONSISTENT COMPASSES IN ASYNC

The most difficult setting for the gathering problem is clearly the *asynchronous* one, where no timing assumptions are made.

In spite of the severity of this setting, GATHERING with limited visibility can be achieved in finite time using only ConsistentCompass [68]. In particular, the algorithm does not assume that the robots have the capability of multiplicity detection.

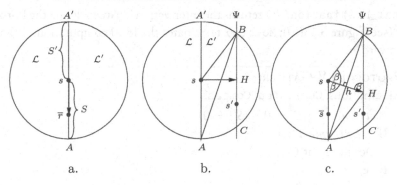

a.   b.   c.

Figure 3.13: (a) Notation used in the Gathering Algorithm. (b) Horizontal move. (c) Diagonal move.

Let *Right* be the rightmost vertical axis where some robots initially lie. The idea of the algorithm is to make the robots move toward *Right*, in such a way that, after a finite number of steps, they will reach it and gather at the bottommost position occupied by a robot at that time.

Let s perform a *Look* operation at time t; as a result, it has available its circle of visibility $C_s(t)$ with the positions of all the robots in it at time t: Different destination points will be computed depending on the positions of the robots inside this circle. Once the computation is completed, s starts moving toward its destination (but it may stop before the destination is reached). Informally,

- If s sees robots to its left or above on the vertical axis passing through its position (from now on, this axis will be referred to as *its vertical axis*), it does not move.

- If s sees robots only below on its vertical axis, it moves down toward the nearest robot.

- If s sees robots only to its right, it moves horizontally toward the vertical axis of the nearest robot (details below).

- If s sees robots both below on its vertical axis and on its right, it computes a destination point and performs a diagonal move to the right and down, as explained below.

To describe the diagonal movement in detail we need to introduce some notation (refer to Figure 3.13). Let $\overline{AA'}$ be the vertical diameter of $C_s(t)$ with A' the top and p the bottom end point; let $\mathcal{L}'_s$ denote the topologically open region (with respect to $\overline{AA'}$) inside $C_s(t)$ and to the right of s and let $S = \overline{sA}$ and $S' = \overline{sA'}$, where both S' and S are topologically open on the s side (i.e., s belongs neither to S' nor to S). Let Ψ be the vertical axis of the robot in $\mathcal{L}'_s$, if any, nearest to s with respect to its projection on the horizontal axis passing through s. The algorithm for gathering in a point, described for robot s, is detailed in the next LV-GATHERING PROTOCOL.

The algorithm makes use of the functions Nearest(), Horizontal_Destination(Ψ), and Move(p); Nearest() returns the vertical axis Ψ of the robot in $\mathcal{L}'$ nearest to s with respect to its projection on the horizontal axis passing through s (robot s' in Figure 3.13(b));

`Horizontal_Destination`(Ψ) returns the intersection between Ψ and the horizontal line passing through s (see Figure 3.13(b)); `Move`(p) terminates the local computation of the calling robot and moves it toward p.

PROTOCOL LV-GATHERING
Assumptions: `ConsistentCompass`.

$\quad$ *Extreme* := $\big(|\mathcal{L}| = 0 \wedge |S'| = 0\big)$;
$\quad$ **If** $\neg$*Extreme* **Then**
$\qquad$ `Do_nothing`();
$\quad$ **Else**
$\qquad$ **Case** $(|\mathcal{L}'|, |S|)$
$\qquad\quad \bullet(0, 0)$:
$\qquad\qquad$ `Do_nothing`();
$\qquad\quad \bullet(0, \neq 0)$: %*Vertical Move*%
$\qquad\qquad \bar{s}$:= nearest visible robot on S;
$\qquad\qquad$ `Move`($\bar{s}$).
$\qquad\quad \bullet(\neq 0, 0)$: %*Horizontal Move*%
$\qquad\qquad \Psi$:= `Nearest`();
$\qquad\qquad H$:= `Horizontal_Destination`(Ψ);
$\qquad\qquad$ `Move`(H).
$\qquad\quad \bullet(\neq 0, \neq 0)$: %*Diagonal Move*%
$\qquad\qquad \Psi$:= `Nearest`();
$\qquad\qquad$ `Diagonal_Movement`(Ψ).
$\quad$ **End If**

In the last case of the algorithm, s sees some robots below it and some to its right (robots $\bar{s}$ and s' in Figure 3.13(c)); to avoid losing some robots, s moves diagonally, according to the following routine:

`Diagonal_Movement`(Ψ)
$\quad B$:= upper intersection between $\mathcal{C}_s(t)$ and Ψ;
$\quad C$:= lower intersection between $\mathcal{C}_s(t)$ and Ψ;
$\quad A$:= point on S at distance v from s;
$\quad 2\beta = A\widehat{s}B$;
$\quad$ **If** $\beta < 60°$ **Then**
$\qquad (B, \Psi)$:= `Rotate`(s, B);
$\quad$ **End If**
$\quad H$:= `Diagonal_Destination`(Ψ, A, B);
$\quad$ `Move`(H).

---

where `Rotate`() and `Diagonal_Destination`() are as follows:

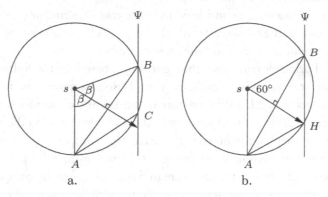

Figure 3.14: Routine Rotate(): in (a), $\beta < 60°$; in (b) the scenario after Rotate() has been executed.

- Rotate(s, B) rotates the segment $\overline{s\,B}$ in such a way that $\beta = 60°$ and returns the new position of B and Ψ. This choice of angle ensures that the destination point is not outside the circle. (see Figure 3.14).

- Diagonal_Destination(Ψ, A, B) computes the destination of s in the following way: the direction of s's movement is given by the perpendicular to the segment $\overline{AB}$; the destination of s is the point H on the intersection of the direction of its movement and of the axis Ψ.

The correctness of the algorithm is proven by first showing that the robots which are initially visible will stay visible until the end of the computation, and then that the robots' movement leads to non-infinitesimally-small progress toward gathering, thus concluding that all robots will gather in a point on *Right* in finite time.

Theorem 3.25 [68] *In* ASYNC, *robots with limited visibility can solve the* GATHERING *problem with* ConsistentCompass.

3.4.5   GATHERING WITH UNSTABLE COMPASSES IN SSYNC

As we have seen in the previous Section 3.4.4, the presence of ConsistentCompass allows the robots to gather in finite time even in the ASYNC model (and thus also in the SSYNC model).

Consider now the problem of gathering when compasses are unstable for some arbitrary long periods. Provided that the compasses have Chirality and that they eventually stabilize, the robots can gather in finite time in the SSYNC model with fixed mobility [118]. In this solution, which we describe now, the robots do not use multiplicity detection; knowledge of the number of robots is however necessary.

Recall that compasses are considered to be *eventually consistent* (see Section 2.7) if there is a time GST (unknown to the robots) after which compasses become consistent; before that time, they are arbitrarily different, but they share the same chirality.

The general principles on which the algorithm is based are the following: (1) Robots that are visible at time t must remain visible at time $t + 1$; (2) Robots move close to each other until they all become visible to each other; (3) When robots are sufficiently close, robots that perceive themselves located on the leftmost side at time t move toward the visible robots on their right side at time $t + 1$.

These three principles, combined with the fact that compasses are eventually consistent, guarantee that, when robots become close enough, they will eventually move to the position of the rightmost-bottommost robot, gathering there in finite time after the compasses become consistent.

Let $s \in \mathcal{R}_r(t)$, with $\mathcal{R}_r$ the set of robots in the visibility range of r at time t, and let $\mathcal{C}(r, s)$ be the circle with center $\frac{(r+s)}{2}$, and with radius $\frac{V}{2}$. For any robot r, if the intersection $\cap_{s \in \mathcal{R}_r} \mathcal{C}(r, s)$ contains all robots in $\mathcal{R}_r$, then robot r considers that the system has sufficiently converged.

Let Ψ_r be the vertical axis passing through robot r according to its compass at time t. We denote by $Left_r(t)$ and $Right_r(t)$, the regions, respectively, to the left and to the right of Ψ_r, excluding Ψ_r. Let also Φ_r be the perpendicular axis to Ψ_r passing by r. Then, we denote by $Top_r(t)$ and $Bottom_r(t)$ as the regions above and below Φ_r, respectively, excluding Φ_r. Finally, Ψ_r^{above} and Ψ_r^{below} denote the intersections of $Top_r(t)$ and Ψ_r, and of $Bottom_r(t)$ and Ψ_r, respectively. When no ambiguity arises, temporal indications are omitted.

The idea of the algorithm is the following: when a robot r becomes active, it considers all the robots in its visibility region $\mathcal{R}_r(t)$ and it decides its movement depending on whether the system has been sufficiently converged or not. If r sees that the system has not converged sufficiently, it calculates its destination as follows:

- If robot r is collinear with all robots in $\mathcal{R}_r(t)$, and r is not in between two robots, then r moves linearly to the nearest robot.

- If there are robots neither on $Left_r$ nor in Ψ_r^{above}, and there are some robots on $Right_r$ or in Ψ_r^{below}, then r computes the positions of the two outermost robots r_a and r_b. Afterward, r computes the height of the triangle that it forms with the two outermost robots, r_a and r_b, whose base is the segment $\overline{r_a r_b}$. Let H be the foot of the perpendicular to this segment starting at r. Then, r moves to H if H is inside the triangle $\triangle(r, r_a, r_b)$ (see Figure 3.15(a)). Otherwise, if H is outside $\triangle(r, r_a, r_b)$, then r moves to the robot, between r_a and r_b, which is closest to it (e.g., robot r_b in Figure 3.15(b)).

If instead r sees that the system has converged sufficiently, it calculates its destination as follows:

- If r sees robots to its left or above on its vertical axis, it does not move.

- If there are robots neither on $Left_r$ nor in Ψ_r^{above}, and r is collinear with all robots in $\mathcal{R}_r(t)$, then r moves linearly to the nearest robot (e.g., robot r_2 in Figure 3.15(c)). Observe that in this case, r must be the topmost or leftmost robot in the line.

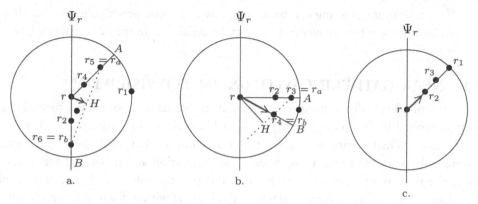

Figure 3.15: (a) r determines the position of the two outermost robots r_a and r_b. H is inside $\triangle(r, r_a, r_b)$, hence r moves to H. (b) r determines the position of the two outermost robots r_a and r_b. Since H is inside $\triangle(r, r_a, r_b)$, then r moves to r_b instead of H. (c) r is collinear with all robots in $\mathcal{R}_r$ and is the leftmost robot; in this case, r moves to r_2.

- If there are robots neither on $Left_r$ nor in Ψ_r^{above}, and there are some robots on the $Right_r$ or in Ψ_r^{below}, then r moves to the position of the closest robot to Ψ_r^{below}, if any, otherwise it moves to the position of the closest robot to it on $Right_r$.

Correctness of the algorithm is proven in two steps. In the first, it is shown that connectivity of the visibility graph is preserved before and after the time when the compasses become consistent. That is, the robots that are initially visible remain always visible during the entire execution of the algorithm. In the second step, it is shown that all the robots will gather at one point in a finite number of steps.

Theorem 3.26 [118]   *In* Ssync, *robots with* Chirality *and* eventually consistent compasses, *can gather in finite time.*

An adaptation of the above algorithm can be shown to work also in Async, but only for the case of $n = 4$ robots [116].

3.5   NEAR-GATHERING

A problem that is very close to the convergence problem is Near-Gathering, where robots are required to get close enough to each other, without any collisions. In the Near-Gathering problem, at the beginning a set of n robots is arbitrarily placed in the plane on distinct positions (the *initial configuration*, denoted by $\mathbb{I}$). In finite time, the robots are required to move within distance ε from each other for some predefined ε (the *final configuration* $\mathbb{F}$).

Note that near-gathering can be achieved by any convergence solution that does not allow collisions during the robots' movements. In fact, by definition, in the near-gathering two robots can never lie on the same point.

3.5.1   NEAR-GATHERING WITH UNLIMITED VISIBILITY

In the unlimited visibility setting, the algorithm where each robot moves toward the center of gravity described in Section 3.3.1 [28] would achieve NEAR-GATHERING in ASYNC with slight modifications. When moving toward the target function, a robot would have to determine if there are other robots on the straight line toward the destination and it would have to move without passing the next robot on that line (if any). In this way the solution still converges, collisions are avoided, and near-gathering is reached when all robots are within distance ε to each other. Thus, we have:

Theorem 3.27   [28]   *The* NEAR-GATHERING *problem is solvable in* ASYNC *with unlimited visibility.*

3.5.2   NEAR-GATHERING WITH LIMITED VISIBILITY

In the limited visibility setting we assume that the robots know how many they are, so to be able to achieve explicit termination. In this setting, solving the near-gathering is particularly important as a solution to a NEAR-GATHERING problem would possibly overcome the limitations of having robots with limited visibility. In fact, NEAR-GATHERING could be a "pre-processing" module to have all the robots within visibility radius; at this point one might exploit the majority of studies done in the unlimited visibility setting. To be able to use a NEAR-GATHERING algorithm as a first step to solve another problem with unlimited visibility, one would still have to coordinate it with the subsequent activity, a task that might not be straightforward, especially in ASYNC.

Precisely this idea is employed in the gathering algorithm presented in the Section 3.4.5 where, in SSYNC with limited visibility, chirality, and eventually consistent compasses, near-gathering is achieved as a first step toward gathering.

Even more general is the convergence algorithm of [2] for SSYNC described in Section 3.4.1, which could be slightly modified so to solve near-gathering in SSYNC without compasses.

Theorem 3.28   *The* NEAR-GATHERING *problem can be solved in* SSYNC *with limited visibility.*

3.5.3   NEAR-GATHERING WITH LIMITED VISIBILITY IN ASYNC

We describe below a recent near-gathering algorithm that works in the ASYNC setting [112] with `ConsistentCompass`. This algorithm assumes that all distances are induced by the *infinity norm*: $\|p\|_\infty = \max\{p.x, p.y\}$, where $p.x$ and $p.y$ denote the coordinates x and y of point p. The result can be then generalized to other norms (and in particular to the classical Euclidean distance considered

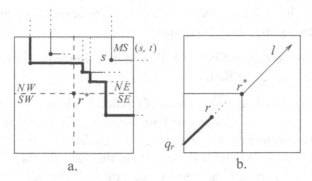

Figure 3.16: (a) The area above and to the right of s defines the *Move Space* of s. The fat line is the *Contour* of r^*. (b) Computation of the length of movement in the algorithm.

everywhere else in this book), with the requirement that the initial distance graph $G(0)$ is however connected with respect to the infinity norm.

Let $G(t) = (N, E(t))$ be the *distance graph* at time $t \geq 0$, where N is the set of the input robots and, for any two distinct robots r and s, $(r, s) \in E(t)$ iff $0 \leq \|r(t) - s(t)\|_\infty \leq V$. Let r be a robot, and let us divide its visible area into four quadrants, denoted by $\mathcal{NW}(r), \mathcal{NE}(r), \mathcal{SE}(r)$, and $\mathcal{SW}(r)$ (see the example depicted in Figure 3.16(b)). For technical reasons, the vertical and the horizontal segment of length V starting from r and going South and West, respectively, (including the location of r itself), are part of $\mathcal{SW}(r)$; the vertical (resp. horizontal) segment of length V passing through r and going North (resp. East) is part of $\mathcal{NW}(r)$ (resp. $\mathcal{SE}(r)$). When not necessary, the reference to r will be dropped. Similarly, a reference to time may be added. Next, we define the *Move Space* of a robot r at time t, denoted by $\mathcal{MS}(r, t)$, as the set $\left\{ (x', y') \in \mathbb{R}^2 \mid x' \geq r(t).x \wedge y' \geq r(t).y \right\}$ (refer to the example depicted in Figure 3.16(a)).

Based on the previous definition, we define the *Contour* of a robot r at time t, denoted by $\mathcal{CT}(r, t)$, as the boundary of the set $\bigcup_s \mathcal{MS}(s, t)$, where s ranges through all the robots in $\mathcal{NW}(r, t) \cup \mathcal{NE}(r, t) \cup \mathcal{SE}(r, t)$ (refer again to Figure 3.16(a)). We will call a *peak* of the contour any convex corner of $\mathcal{CT}(r)$; the concave corners will be called *valleys*. An easy property of $\mathcal{CT}(r, t)$ is stated in the following

Observation 3.29   If there are robots in both $\mathcal{NW}(r)$ and in $\mathcal{SE}(r)$, and no robot in $\mathcal{NE}(r)$, then $\mathcal{CT}(r)$ has exactly one valley in $\mathcal{NE}(r)$.

Informally, let r^* be any robot. At each cycle, r^* first computes the direction of movement according to the following rules:

- If r^* can see robots only in $\mathcal{SW}$, then it will not move; that is, in this case the destination point is the point of coordinates $(0, 0)$.

- If r^* can see robots only in $\mathcal{NW} \cup \mathcal{SW}$, then its direction of movement is given by the half-line l starting in r^* and going North.

- If r^* can see robots only in $\mathcal{SW} \cup \mathcal{SE}$, then its direction of movement is given by the half-line l starting in r^* and going East.

- Otherwise, the direction of movements of r is decided based on the shape of the Contour of r^*. In particular, if in $\mathcal{NE}$ there is at least one robot, the direction of movement is given by the half-line l starting from r^* and passing through the robot in $\mathcal{NE}$ closest to r^*. Otherwise, there must be robots in both $\mathcal{NW}$ and $\mathcal{SE}$; in this case, the direction of movement is given by the half-line l starting from r^* and passing through the only valley in $\mathcal{CT}(r^*)$.

In order to establish the length of the movements along l, r^* checks two main factors: First, it must not enter the Move Space of any robot it can see (this contributes to guaranteeing collision avoidance); second, the new position must be within distance $V/2$ from any of the robots it is currently seeing (this contributes to guaranteeing both collision avoidance and the connectedness of the initial distance graph). In order to ensure these two factors, first, for each $r \in \mathcal{NW} \cup \mathcal{NE} \cup \mathcal{SE}$, it computes the intersection p_r between l and $\mathcal{MS}(r)$ (notice that robots move only upward and rightward). Second, for each visible robot r, the intersection q_r between the visible area of r^* and the line parallel to l and passing through r is computed. The distance d_r between r and q_r is the maximum distance robot r^* is allowed to move in order to not lose visibility with r (assuming r does not move). Thus, if p is the point closest to r^* among the points in $\{p_r\} \cup \{d_r\}$, the destination point of r^* is the median point dp on the segment between r^* and p. A consequence of the computation of dp as just described is that the distance graph never gets disconnected; also, collisions are avoided.

A robot terminates its execution as soon as it sees n robots at a distance less than a given tolerance ε. Let us call *Right* the vertical axis passing through the rightmost robot(s) in $\mathbb{I}$, and *Top* the horizontal axis passing through the topmost robot(s) in $\mathbb{I}$; also, let f be the intersection point between *Right* and *Top*.

Lemma 3.30   [112]   *The following properties hold:*

1. *The connectedness of $G(0)$ according to the infinity norm is preserved during the execution of the algorithm.*

2. *All robots converge toward point f without ever colliding.*

Based on these properties it can be shown that:

Theorem 3.31   [112]   *After finite time, all robots terminate their execution, being at distance ε from each other.*

The algorithm also solves the NEAR-GATHERING problem in a model that uses other norms, including the usual Euclidean distance: each robot r just "ignores" any point p such that $\|r - p\|_\infty >$

V, thus pretending to be in the infinity norm model. Of course, this is guaranteed to terminate correctly only if $G(0)$, computed with the infinity norm, is connected. In other words:

Theorem 3.32   [112]   *In* ASYNC *with limited visibility, a set of anonymous oblivious robots with* ConsistentCompass *can solve the* NEAR-GATHERING *problem when the initial distance graph is connected with respect to the* infinity norm.

3.6   GATHERING WITH INACCURATE MEASUREMENTS

In our discussion so far, we have assumed that measurements are accurate. In particular, the snapshot obtained in *Look* is a perfect map of the locations of the other robots relative to itself. However, the measurements may suffer from non-negligible inaccuracies in both distance and angle estimations. In this section we examine the GATHERING and the CONVERGENCE problems where the inputs are obtained by inaccurate visual sensors [29, 78, 79, 105]. The goal is to understand how much inaccuracy (if any) is tolerable, i.e., still allows the robots to gather or converge.

For every two robots r_i and r_j denote by $\vec{r}_{i,j}[t]$ the vector from $r_i[t]$ to $r_j[t]$, and by $\vec{v}_{i,j}[t]$ the vector from r_i to the location of robot r_j as measured by r_i at time t, translated to the global coordinate system (unknown to the robots). We consider the case when the imprecision on the location estimation is bounded by some known accuracy parameter. This imprecision can affect both distance and angle estimations.

A *distance imprecision* ϵ means that the measurement $\vec{v}_{i,j}[t]$ will satisfy $(1 - \epsilon)r_{i,j}[t] < v_{i,j}[t] < (1 + \epsilon)r_{i,j}[t]$ (for a vector $\vec{p}$ we denote by p its scalar length $p = |\vec{p}|$). A *direction imprecision* $\theta_0 \leq \pi$ means that the angle θ between the actual distance vector $\vec{r}_{i,j}[t]$ and the measured distance vector $\vec{r}_{i,j}[t]$ satisfies $\theta \leq \theta_0$.

If the robots may have inaccuracies in distance estimation but not in directions then r_i will measure $\vec{r}_{i,j}[t]$ as $\vec{v}_{i,j}[t] = (1 + \epsilon_{i,j})\vec{r}_{i,j}[t]$, where $-\epsilon < \epsilon_{i,j}[t] < \epsilon$ is the local error factor at robot r_i in estimating the position of r_j at time t. For robots with inaccuracy in angle measurement as well, r_i will measure the true distance $r_{i,j}[t]$ as $v_{i,j}[t] = (1 + \epsilon_{i,j})r_{i,j}[t]$ and the angle θ between $\vec{r}_{i,j}[t]$ and $\vec{v}_{i,j}[t]$ satisfies $|\theta| \leq \theta_0$. In the following, the parameter t is omitted whenever clear from the context.

3.6.1   IMPOSSIBILITY OF GATHERING

We first start with some impossibility results. The proofs of these results are based on the ability of the adversary to partition the space of possible initial configurations into countably many regions each of uncountably many configurations (on the basis of the initial distance between the robots) such that within each region the outcome of the algorithm (i.e., the instructions to the robots on how far to move in each round) are the same

Theorem 3.33   [29]   GATHERING *of* $n - 2$ *robots with inexact distance measurements is impossible in* FSYNC *even with* ConsistentCompass *and* strong multiplicity detection.

Proof. Partition the real line into disjoint segments a_i, b_i such that $\frac{b_i}{a_i} < \frac{1+\epsilon}{1-\epsilon}$ for each i. Whenever the true distance is a point in the i-th segment, the adversary may always choose as outcome of the robot's measurement a single measurement result m_i in the range $(1-\epsilon)b_i < m_i < (1+\epsilon)a_i$. Consider first the *round robin* scheduler (i.e., each robot is activated at alternate rounds). At each round, the algorithm only has one input, namely the result of the measurement and the partition allows the introduction of only countably many such results. Therefore, the total distance traveled by a robot after n cycles is the sum of n outputs of the algorithm. Since this is the sum of a finite number of vectors from a countable basis, this set is still countable. Thus, gathering is never achieved from almost every starting configuration. In FSYNC, both robots are activated at each round; still the above argument can be applied to the sum of movements of both robots.   □

Note that adding *persistent memory*, allowing robots to store their previous measurements, as well as allowing the use of *randomness* will not help; therefore the robots cannot gather even with constant probability [29].

It is unclear whether the same impossibility holds for $n > 2$, at least in SSYNC, although it is so conjectured:

Conjecture 3.34 [29]   GATHERING of $n > 2$ robots with inexact distance is impossible in SSYNC even with `ConsistentCompass` and *strong multiplicity detection*.

What is certain is that if both distance *and* angle inaccuracies are present then the problem is unsolvable:

Theorem 3.35 [29]   GATHERING *of $n > 2$ robots with inaccurate distance and angle measurements is impossible in SSYNC even with* `ConsistentCompass` *and* strong multiplicity detection.

Proof. The distances $r_{i,j}$ may again be partitioned similarly to Theorem 3.33. The angles may be partitioned into $n > \frac{2\pi}{\theta_0}$ disjoint intervals. The adversary chooses a single measurement outcome for each such interval; then the set of possible measurement outcomes is again countable. Choosing a *slicing* activation schedule (i.e., where the robots are activated in non-overlapping time intervals), the adversary ensures that the robots will gather only for countably many initial configurations for any possible algorithm.   □

3.6.2   POSSIBILITY OF CONVERGENCE WITH UNLIMITED VISIBILITY

First observe that Protocol CoG (described in Section 3.3.1) solves CONVERGENCE in FSYNC with unlimited visibility, even if measurements are not guaranteed to be accurate:

Lemma 3.36 [29]   *In FSYNC, a group of n robots performing Protocol CoG with inaccurate distance and angle measurements converges, provided $\epsilon < \frac{1}{2}$.*

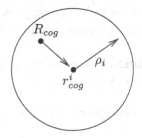

Figure 3.17: Illustration of Protocol RCoG.

The following slightly more involved algorithm Restricted CoG, or RCoG, is based on calculating the center of gravity of the group of robots and also estimating the maximum possible error in the center of gravity calculation. A robot approaches the estimated center of gravity while staying out of the circle of possible error. We fix a conservative error estimate parameter $\epsilon_0 > \epsilon$. A formal description of the algorithm is below (see also Figure 3.17):

Protocol RCoG (for robot r_i).
Assumptions: none.

1. Estimate the measured Center of Gravity $vc_i = \frac{1}{n}\Sigma_j v_j$;

2. $dm_i := \max_j\{v_{i,j}\}$;

3. $\rho_i := \frac{\epsilon_0}{1-\epsilon_0}dm_i$;

4. If $vc_i(t) > \rho_i$ then move toward $c_i := (1 - \frac{\rho_i}{vc_i})vc_i$.

With only inaccurate distance measurements, it is not difficult to prove that Protocol RCoG converges in FSYNC:

Lemma 3.37 [29] *In* FSYNC, *a group of n robots performing Protocol* RCoG *with inaccurate distance converges, provided* $\epsilon_0 < 0.2$.

It can actually be shown that CONVERGENCE can also be achieved when angle measurement inaccuracies are present, and even in SSYNC for appropriate choice of accuracy parameters:

Theorem 3.38 [29] *In* SSYNC, *a group of n robots performing Protocol* RCoG *with inaccurate distance and angle measurements converges, provided* $\epsilon_0 > \sqrt{2(1 - \epsilon)(1 - cos\theta_0) + \epsilon^2}$.

It is not known whether protocol RCoG converges also in Async, at least with just inaccurate distance measurements, although it is so conjectured:

Conjecture 3.39 [29] CONVERGENCE of n robots performing Protocol RCoG with inaccurate distance measurements is possible in Async.

It is however known that it does converge in the *unidimensional space*, i.e., when $\mathcal{U} = \mathbb{R}$.

Theorem 3.40 [29] *Let $\mathcal{U} = \mathbb{R}$. Then* CONVERGENCE *of n robots performing Protocol* RCoG *with inaccurate distance measurements is possible in* Async.

It is interesting to note that the simpler Protocol CoG does *not* converge in Async with inaccurate distance measurements [29].

3.6.3 POSSIBILITY OF CONVERGENCE WITH LIMITED VISIBILITY

The CONVERGENCE problem has also been studied in the presence of some inaccuracies both in distance and direction when the robots have limited visibility [105]. The type of inaccuracies considered are *radial errors*: A robot s in the radius of visibility of r at time t can be seen by r anywhere within distance σ from $s(t)$; i.e., within the circle or radius σ centered in $s(t)$.

Solutions exist tolerating radial errors in Fsync with ConsistentCompass, provided they are not too large with respect to the visibility radius.

Theorem 3.41 [105] CONVERGENCE *with limited visibility with radial error σ is possible in* Fsync *with* ConsistentCompass, *provided* $\sigma < \frac{V}{7}$.

The algorithms are all variants of the general idea of algorithm LV-SS-CONVERGE discussed in Section 3.4.1.

3.7 GATHERING WITH FAULTY ROBOTS

In all investigations we have discussed so far on the gathering of oblivious robots, the robots themselves function without failures. Clearly, the gathering problem becomes more difficult to resolve if the robots are prone to failures. The faults that have been investigated fall in two categories: *crash* faults (i.e., a faulty robots stops executing its cycle forever) and *Byzantine* faults (i.e., a faulty robot may exhibit arbitrary behavior and movement). Of course, Byzantine faults include crash faults as a particular case, and are thus harder to address.

In this section, we discuss the issues, limitations, and solutions for gathering when f out of the n robots may be faulty. A *fault-tolerant* (n, f)-GATHERING algorithm in the crash (resp. Byzantine) fault model ensures that as long as at most f robots have failed in the crash (resp. Byzantine) fault model, all non-faulty robots gather within finite time, regardless of the actions taken by the faulty ones; similarly, a *fault-tolerant* (n, f)-CONVERGENCE algorithm ensures that as long as at most f

robots have failed, for every $\epsilon > 0$, there is a time t such for all $t' \geq t$ all non-faulty robots are within distance at most ϵ of each other. Investigations on fault-tolerant gathering have been started in [1], and include [42].

As discussed in Section 3.1, without some additional capability or knowledge (e.g., multiplicity detection, common coordinate systems, etc.) gathering is impossible in fault-free environments, let alone in the presence of failures. As we see now, even with additional capabilities, with few exceptions, the presence of faults may render the gathering task very difficult if not impossible.

3.7.1   CRASH FAULTS

In this section we consider crash failures; that is, faulty robots can stop functioning at any time, becoming permanently inactive.

Crash Faults in ASYNC.   Let us first consider gathering in spite of robot crashes in the more general and difficult setting ASYNC. We first observe that, with consistent compasses, (n, f)-gathering can be achieved for any number $f < n$ of crashes, even if n is not known. The algorithm is remarkably simple (see Section 3.7): when active, a robot r sets as its destination the location of the north-most east-most robot in the configuration. Since the robots have consistent compasses, this location does not change as the non-faulty robots move there. The only technical problem, of easy resolution, is how to avoid collisions and deadlocks (e.g., a robot s on the path from r to its destination might be crashed and hence that path will never be cleared). In other words:

Theorem 3.42   *With* ConsistentCompass, *the* (n, f)-*gathering problem can be solved in* ASYNC *for any number* $f < n$ *of crashes,* $n \geq 1$.

Notice that the above result does not use multiplicity detection; however, consistent compasses do imply chirality.

Let us consider next what the availability of multiplicity detection and chirality (without, however, consistent compasses) allows in terms of crash-tolerant gathering in ASYNC. As it turns out, not too much: There is currently no gathering algorithm for $n \geq 4$ that tolerates a single crash failure with multiplicity detection and chirality alone; for the special case $n = 3$ it turns out that the gathering algorithm given in [26] can be shown to operate correctly also in the presence of one crashed robot.

Crash Faults in SSYNC.   The situation is better in SSYNC. Indeed, in SSYNC, with multiplicity detection alone it is possible to solve the $(n, 1)$-gathering problem in the crash model, for any $n \geq 3$ [1].

Let us start with some terminology. Given the set of robots $\mathcal{R}$ and its $SEC(\mathcal{R})$, let us denote the robots of $\mathcal{R}$ on the circumference of $SEC(\mathcal{R})$ by $C_{cir}(\mathcal{R})$ and let $C_{int}(\mathcal{R}) = \mathcal{R} \setminus C_{cir}(\mathcal{R})$. For a circle C and a set of points $P = \{p_1, \ldots, p_l\}$ on its circumference, denote the partition of the circle C into Voronoi cells according to the points in P by $Vor(C, P)$, and denote by $Cell(p_k)$ the cell

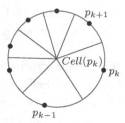

Figure 3.18: Example of a circle division according to the Voronoi cells.

defined by the point $p_k \in P$ (see Figure 3.18). Two points q and q' in $\mathcal{C}$ are said to share the cell $Cell(p_k)$ if they both lie inside the cell or on its boundary.

Consider the following Algorithm GATHERCRASH for $(n, 1)$-gathering in SSYNC, where it is assumed $n \geq 4$ (the case $n = 3$ is treated differently as explained later):

Algorithm GATHERCRASH($SEC(\mathcal{R})$)
Assumptions: SSYNC, multiplicity detection.

   If $\mathcal{C}$ contains a dense point **Then** GoToMULT($\mathcal{R}$).
   Else CREATEMULT($SEC(\mathcal{R})$).

---

where procedure GoToMULT($\mathcal{R}$) is as follows. We say that robot r_i, has a "free corridor" to point p at time t if no other robot is currently located on the straight line segment $\overline{r(t)p}$.

Procedure GoToMULT($\mathcal{R}$) (for robot r_i)
/* The configuration contains a dense point p^* */

   If r_i has a free corridor to p^* **Then** Move toward p^*.
   Else
      (a) Translate the coordinate system to be centered at p^*;
      (b) Compute for each robot r_j the angle μ_j of $\overrightarrow{p^*r_j}$ counterclockwise from the X axis;
      (c) Find the robot r_k with smallest angle $\mu_k > \mu_i$;
      (d) Set $\mu = \frac{1}{3}(\mu_k + 2\mu_i)$, and $d = dist(r_i, r_k)$;
      (e) Move toward the point p_i' at distance d and angle μ from p^*.
   End If

Procedure GoToMULT guarantees that within finite time all non-faulty robots gather at p^* while avoiding the creation of additional dense points. Every robot with a free corridor toward p^* goes toward p^* and will arrive at p^* within a finite time. If a robot r_i detects another robot on its trajectory toward p^*, it looks for a free corridor by moving orthogonally to the dense point, while making sure that it does not obstruct the free corridor of any other robot. This is ensured by moving only so as to change its angle with respect to the X axis and p^* by a third of the angle to the closest-angle neighboring robot r_j. Note that it is possible that r_j will also enter the same sector, due to the lack of a consistent coordinate system. However, even if r_j enters that clear sector, it will be in the "far" third of the sector. It is also possible for $k \geq 3$ robots to share a common corridor to p^*. In this case, the one of them closest to p^* will move toward p^*, and the others might take the same new trajectory to p^*; on this new trajectory, only $k > 1$ robots might collide, so the closest to p^* has a free corridor, and only $k - 2$ robots must shift orthogonally again. Hence, if a robot has more than one robot on its trajectory toward p^*, it may shift finitely many times until it has a free corridor toward p^*, and will eventually arrive there. Procedure CREATEMULT($SEC(\mathcal{R})$) is as follows:

Procedure CREATEMULT($SEC(\mathcal{R})$)

1. **If** $|C_{int}(\mathcal{R})| = 0$ **Then** move toward the center of $SEC(\mathcal{R})$.

2. **If** $|C_{int}(\mathcal{R})| = 1$ **Then** move toward the single robot in $C_{int}(\mathcal{R})$.

3. **If** $|C_{int}(\mathcal{R})| = 2$ **Then** the robots $r_k \in C_{cir}(\mathcal{R})$ do not move, while the two robots r_i and r_j in $C_{int}(\mathcal{R})$ do the following:

   (a) Compute the Voronoi partition $Vor(SEC(\mathcal{R}), C_{cir}(\mathcal{R}))$.

   (b) **If** r_i and r_j do not share cells **Then** r_i and r_j move toward the center of $SEC(\mathcal{R})$.

   (c) **If** r_i and r_j share a single cell, $Cell(r_k)$ **Then** r_i and r_j move toward r_k.

   (d) **If** r_i and r_j share two cells, i.e., both robots lie on the radius forming the boundary between two adjacent cells $Cell(r_k)$ and $Cell(r_{k+1})$ **Then** the robot closer to the circle, say r_i, chooses the first of r_k, r_{k+1} in its clockwise direction, say r_k, and moves toward r_k; the other robot, r_j, moves toward r_i.

4. **If** $|C_{int}(\mathcal{R})| \geq 3$ **Then** the robots in $C_{cir}(\mathcal{R})$ do not move, and each robot r_k in $C_{int}(\mathcal{R})$ recursively invokes Procedure CREATEMULT($C_{int}(\mathcal{R})$).

The case $n = 3$ is handled in a simpler special way. The observing robot acts as follows: if the configuration contains a dense point p^*, then the robots move toward p^*; if the three robots r_1, r_2, r_3 are collinear (with r_2 in the middle), then the robots move toward r_2; if the three robots form an acute triangle, then the robots move toward the intersection point of the three angle bisectors; and finally, if $\exists i \in \{1, 2, 3\}$ such that $\sphericalangle(r_j, r_i, r_k) \geq \frac{\pi}{2}$ (i.e., the three robots form a square or obtuse triangle), then the robots move toward r_i.

Theorem 3.43   [1]   *With multiplicity detection, the $(n-1)$-gathering problem can be solved in SSYNC in the crash model, with $n \geq 3$.*

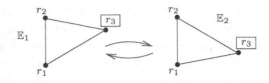

Figure 3.19: Proof of Lemma 3.45.

Recently, it has been shown that if there is `Chirality` and strong multiplicity detection, the fault-tolerance level can be extended significantly:

Theorem 3.44 [12]   *With* strong multiplicity detection *and* chirality, *the* (n, f)-*gathering problem can be solved in* SSYNC *in the crash model, for any* $f < n$.

3.7.2   BYZANTINE FAULTS: IMPOSSIBILITY IN SSYNC

In this section we consider Byzantine failures; that is, faulty robots can behave arbitrarily, moving whenever they want and to wherever they choose.

Clearly, this is the most severe type of failure, and even with additional capabilities, the presence of Byzantine faults renders the gathering task impossible in SSYNC (and clearly in ASYNC).

In fact, in SSYNC it is impossible for any algorithm to achieve even convergence (and thus gathering) of three robots in the presence of at most one Byzantine robot; that is, it is impossible to perform (3, 1)-convergence in Byzantine systems [1], even if the robots have strong multiplicity detection capabilities (i.e., to determine the exact number of robots that occupy a position) and chirality.

To see why this negative result holds, consider first the class of *hyperactive* gathering algorithms, that is, those algorithms that instruct each active robot to always make a move until gathering is achieved.

Lemma 3.45 [1]   *In* SSYNC, *any* non-*hyperactive algorithm will fail to achieve* (3, 1)-*gathering or convergence in a Byzantine system, even if the robots are endowed with strong multiplicity detection and chirality.*

Proof. Given three robots r_1, r_2, r_3, consider a non-hyperactive gathering algorithm $\mathcal{A}$; thus, there exists a fault-free execution of $\mathcal{A}$ in which, at some configuration $\mathbb{E}_1$, r_1 is active but, according to $\mathcal{A}$, it must not move. The adversary can now do the following. It designates r_3 as faulty, and in $\mathbb{E}_1$ it makes r_1 active and r_2 inactive. As a result, neither r_1 nor r_2 moves in this round. In addition, the adversary moves r_3 to create a configuration $\mathbb{E}_2$ that from r_2's point of view is equivalent to what r_1 has seen in $\mathbb{E}_1$ (refer to the example depicted in Figure 3.19). The adversary now activates r_2 but not r_1. Since r_2's state is equivalent to r_1's state in the previous configuration, the algorithm will now instruct r_2 to stay in place. The adversary can now switch from configuration $\mathbb{E}_1$ to $\mathbb{E}_2$ and back, forcing r_1 and r_2 to stay in place indefinitely. Therefore, the algorithm fails to achieve gathering or convergence of the non-faulty robots. □

A distributed algorithm is *diverging* in a $(3, 1)$-Byzantine system if there exists a configuration in which the instructions of the algorithm combined with the actions of the adversary can cause two non-faulty robots to increase the distance between them. The following can then be shown:

Lemma 3.46 [1] *In* Ssync, *any* diverging *algorithm will fail to achieve* $(3, 1)$-*gathering or convergence in a Byzantine system, even if the robots are endowed with strong multiplicity detection and chirality.*

Considering these properties together, it is then possible to prove the impossibility.

Theorem 3.47 [1] *In a* $(3, 1)$-*Byzantine system in* Ssync, *gathering and convergence are impossible even with strong multiplicity detection.*

Proof. Consider a gathering algorithm $\mathcal{A}$ and an initial setting in which the three robots r_1, r_2, and r_3 are collinear, with r_2 in the middle. If the algorithm instructs r_2 to remain stationary, then it is non-hyperactive, and by Lemma 3.45 will not achieve gathering. On the other hand, it can be shown that $\mathcal{A}$ is always diverging. Thus, by Lemma 3.46, algorithm $\mathcal{A}$ fails to achieve gathering or convergence. □

This impossibility holds even if the adversary is very restricted in the choice of the scheduler. Indeed, it holds if the scheduler is not only fair and centralized but also *slicing* (i.e., only one robot is activated in each round, and starting from time $t = 0$, after n successive rounds, all the robots in the system have been activated exactly once) [42].

It has just been claimed that indeed in Ssync it is not possible to tolerate a single Byzantine fault, generalizing all the above results; surprisingly, this impossibility holds even if the robots are not oblivious, and there is `ConsistentCompass` and mobility is unlimited:

Theorem 3.48 [84] *In a* $(n, 1)$-*Byzantine system,* Gathering *is impossible in* Ssync *even if there is* `ConsistentCompass`, *mobility is unlimited, and the robots are not oblivious.*

3.7.3   BYZANTINE FAULTS: GATHERING IN FSYNC

As we have seen, in presence of Byzantine faults, there are only negative results for gathering in SSYNC and ASYNC. The situation changes drastically in FSYNC. In fact, with multiplicity detection, in FSYNC (n, f)-gathering is possible for $f < \frac{n}{3}$ Byzantine faults [1].

The main idea of the algorithm achieving this result is to ensure that the destination point selected in each round falls in the convex hull of the non-faulty robot locations. This would ensures that the geometric span of the set of locations of the non-faulty robots decreases by at least $\frac{1}{4}\delta$, thus the robots will meet within a finite number of cycles.

The main difficulty with this approach clearly lies in the fact that a non-faulty robot r does not know which are the other non-faulty robots, and hence it does not know which is the convex hull of the non-faulty robots. It, however, knows that at most f robots are faulty. For each possible choice of f robots as the faulty ones, e.g., $s_1, s_2, \ldots, s_f$, the convex hull of the remaining robots is a possible candidate. Thus, r can locally compute all the $BIN(n, f)$ candidate convex hulls. Fortunately there is a well known property of convex sets, Helly's Theorem, that allows us to usefully employ this information:

Theorem 3.49   (Helly's Theorem)   *Let A be a finite family of at least three convex sets in $\mathbb{R}^2$. If every three members of A have a point in common, then there is a point common to all members of A.*

Since $n \geq 3f + 1$, any three candidate convex hulls have at least a point in common; hence, according to Helly's Theorem the intersection H^f of all the candidate convex hulls is non-empty. At this point the algorithm consists of r locally computing all the $BIN(n, f)$ candidate convex hulls, calculating their intersection H^f, and then moving toward the center of gravity CoG of such a region:

Procedure GATHERBYZ($\mathcal{R}$)
Assumptions: FSYNC, multiplicity detection.

1. Compute H^f.

2. Move toward $CoG(H^f)$.

The fact that the robots do not just converge but actually gather within finite time is due to the following property:

Lemma 3.50   [1]   *If a set of k robots move toward a point p in their convex hull, then their geometric span decreases by at least $c\delta$ for some constant $c \geq \frac{1}{4}$.*

Consequently, the robots will meet within a finite number of cycles. That is,

Theorem 3.51   [1]   *Algorithm GATHERBYZ solves the gathering problem in an (n, f)-Byzantine system for any $n \geq 3f + 1$ under the FSYNC model with multiplicity detection.*

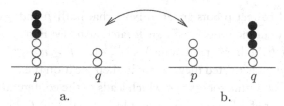

Figure 3.20: Impossibility of convergence in SSYNC with $n \leq 3f$, black robots are Byzantine. (a) Configuration $\mathbb{E}_1$. (b) Configuration $\mathbb{E}_2$.

This result still leaves out the $(3, 1)$-Byzantine system. For this special case, a simple protocol for gathering in FSYNC with multiplicity detection indeed exists [1]: If the points are collinear, the destination is the middle point; otherwise, the destination is the intersection of the three angle bisectors of the triangle formed by the points.

3.7.4 BYZANTINE FAULTS IN UNIDIMENSIONAL SPACE

The convergence problem in the presence of Byzantine faults has also been studied for the restricted spatial universe $\mathcal{U} = \mathbb{R}$, that is, when the space is a simple *line*.

In this unidimensional universe, there are some basic limitations. An important fact is that if at least $n - f$ robots are co-located in the same position, then any convergence algorithm will instruct them to stay in this position. More precisely:

Lemma 3.52 [15]   *Let $\mathcal{U} = \mathbb{R}$, and let at least $n - f$ robots be co-located in the same point p at time t. In absence of other assumptions, all destinations computed by any convergence algorithm at time t are equal to p, even with strong multiplicity detection.*

Theorem 3.53 [14, 15]   *Let $\mathcal{U} = \mathbb{R}$. Then in absence of other assumptions, it is impossible to solve:*

1. *$(n, 1)$-Byzantine convergence with weak multiplicity detection in SSYNC.*

2. *$(n, \frac{n}{5})$-Byzantine convergence with strong multiplicity detection in SSYNC.*

3. *$(n, \frac{n}{3})$-Byzantine convergence with strong multiplicity detection and a 2-bounded scheduler in SSYNC.*

4. *$(n, \frac{n}{2})$-Byzantine convergence with strong multiplicity detection in FSYNC.*

To see, for example, why (3) holds, consider n robots of which $f \geq \frac{n}{3}$ are Byzantine and at least two are non-faulty. Assume that the non-faulty robots are spread over two distinct points p and q in the line. Let $\mathbb{E}_1$ be an initial configuration in which $\lceil \frac{n-f}{2} \rceil$ correct robots are located at p and the remaining $\lfloor \frac{n-f}{2} \rfloor$ correct robots are at q. Note that both p and q contain at least one correct robot each. All the Byzantine robots in $\mathbb{E}_1$ are located at p (see Figure 3.20(a)). Therefore, the total number of robots at p (whether correct or not) is $\lfloor \frac{n-f}{2} \rfloor + f \geq n - f$. Thus, by Lemma 3.52, when the correct robots at p are activated they remain in their location (i.e., p) and do not move. Next, the adversary moves the Byzantine robots to q which leads to the configuration $\mathbb{E}_2$ (see Figure 3.20(b)). Again, the total number of robots at q in $\mathbb{E}_2$ is at least equal to n/f. Therefore, the correct robots at q do not move upon their activation. So by repeatedly alternating between the two configurations $\mathbb{E}_1$ and $\mathbb{E}_2$, the robots at p and q always remain at their initial positions and never converge.

Convergence in FSYNC **with strong multiplicity detection.**   Let us consider convergence in $\mathbb{R}$ when the robots are fully synchronous. By Theorem 3.53, we know that weak multiplicity detection is not sufficient for convergence, and that even with strong multiplicity detection FSYNC convergence is impossible for $f \geq \frac{n}{2}$. On the other hand, if $f < \frac{n}{2}$ then FSYNC convergence is possible with strong multiplicity detection.

The protocol is very simple:

1. Remove from consideration the f largest and f smallest values from the multiset of the robots, positions in the snapshot;

2. compute the point p in the middle of the range of the robots positions;

3. move toward p.

And indeed it guarantees convergence in FSYNC with strong multiplicity detection if the majority of the robots are not-faulty:

Theorem 3.54   [15]   *Let* $\mathcal{U} = \mathbb{R}$. *Then* $(n, \frac{n}{2} - 1)$-*Byzantine convergence with* strong multiplicity detection *is possible in* FSYNC.

Convergence in ASYNC **with k-fair scheduler.**   By Theorem 3.53, we know that $(n, \frac{n}{3})$-Byzantine convergence is impossible in SSYNC even with strong multiplicity detection and a 2-bounded scheduler. On the other hand, if $f < \frac{n}{3}$, Byzantine agreement is possible with strong multiplicity detection and a k-bounded scheduler even in ASYNC.

The idea of the algorithm is an interesting variation of the one for FSYNC described above: each robot computes the median point of the positions of the robots seen in its last *Look*, ignoring the f largest positions if they are larger than its own position, and the f smallest positions if they are smaller than its own position; it then moves toward there.

Algorithm GATHERBYZLINE
Assumptions: Strong multiplicity detection, k-fair scheduler, $f < \frac{n}{3}$.

1. Among the f largest positions, remove from consideration those that are greater than my position. Among the f smallest positions, remove from consideration those that are smaller than my position.

2. Compute the point p in the middle of the range of points still under consideration

3. Move toward p.

Theorem 3.55 [15] *Let $\mathcal{U} = \mathbb{R}$. Then $(n, \frac{n}{3} - 1)$-Byzantine convergence with* strong multiplicity detection *and k-fair scheduler is possible in* ASYNC.

The general idea of the proof is to show that the destination points computed by the non-faulty robots are located either around the middle of the range of their positions and/or in the neighborhood of only one end of this range. If all computed destinations are located around the center of the range of the non-faulty robots, then the diameter of this range decreases. Otherwise, if some computed destinations are located in the neighborhood of one end of the range, then there is a time at which none of the non-faulty robots will be in the neighborhood of the other end of the range; hence the range of the positions of the non-faulty robots decreases also in this case.

Convergence in ASYNC *with strong multiplicity detection*   We have just seen that the simultaneous presence of strong multiplicity detection and k-fair scheduler allows us to solve convergence on the line in ASYNC for $f < \frac{n}{3}$. The next question is what type of convergence can be achieved in ASYNC *without* the restriction on the scheduler to be bounded, i.e., relying solely on strong multiplicity detection.

By Theorem 3.53, we know that, with strong multiplicity detection alone, convergence is impossible if $f \geq \frac{n}{5}$ even in SSYNC. On the other hand, using yet another variant of the same strategy as in the other cases, if $f < \frac{n}{5}$, convergence is possible with strong multiplicity detection in ASYNC.

The variant is the following: each robot computes the median point p of the positions of the robots seen in its last *Look* ignoring the $2f$ largest positions if they are larger than its own position, and the $2f$ smallest positions if they are smaller than its own position; if its position was not among the f smallest nor among the f largest, it then moves toward p.

Theorem 3.56 [14] *Let $\mathcal{U} = \mathbb{R}$. Then $(n, \frac{n}{5} - 1)$-Byzantine convergence with* strong multiplicity detection *is possible in* ASYNC.

CHAPTER 4

Pattern Formation

The PATTERN FORMATION problem is one of the most important coordination problems for robotic systems. Initially the entities are in arbitrary positions. Within finite time they must arrange themselves in the space to form a pattern given in input. The pattern can be given as a set of points in the plane (expressed in their Cartesian coordinates), or as a geometric predicate (e.g., "form a *circle*").

The standard requirements are that, initially, no two entities are in the same position (i.e., there are no dense points), and that the number of points prescribed in the pattern and the number of robots are the same. The robots are said to *form the pattern* if, at the end of the computation, the positions of the robots coincide, in everybody's local view, with the points of the pattern (or satisfy the predicate). Depending on the application, the formed pattern may be *translated*, and/or *rotated*, and/or *scaled*, and/or *flipped* into its mirror position with respect to the initial pattern. If dense points are allowed in the robots configurations and in the pattern, the problem is called *pattern formation with multiplicity*.

The PATTERN FORMATION problem is practically relevant because, if the robots can form a given pattern, they can agree on their respective roles in a subsequent, coordinated action.

The more general and difficult version of this problem is the ARBITRARY PATTERN FORMATION problem, where the robots must be able to form *any* arbitrary pattern $\mathbb{P}$ they are given in input, starting from *any* arbitrary initial configuration where the robots occupy a distinct location. The pattern formation problem, in its general as well as in the more specific versions, has been extensively investigated (e.g., see [3, 21, 43, 44, 69, 92, 94, 121, 123, 124, 127]).

4.1 VIEWS AND SYMMETRICITY

Useful tools to study what patterns are formable by oblivious robots are based on the notion of *view* [123].

Let Z_i denote the local coordinate system of robot r_i, then the *global view* $GV_i(t)$ from robot r_i at time t is the infinite rooted tree defined as follows (refer also to Figure 4.1):

1. The root v_i of $GV_i(t)$ corresponds to r_i.

2. Node v_i has $n - 1$ children, one for each robot r_j, with $j \neq i$. The edge from node v_i to node v_j corresponding to r_j is labeled $((a, b), (c, d))$, where (a, b) is the position of r_j with respect to Z_i, and (c, d) is the position of r_i with respect to Z_j.

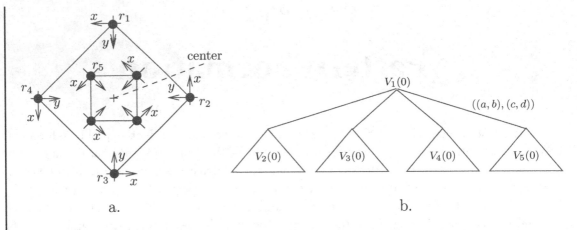

Figure 4.1: (a) A configuration of robots. (b) The global view of r_1.

3. Node v_j, with $j \neq i$ has $n-1$ children, one for each robot r_l, with $j \neq l$; the edge from v_j to v_l is labeled $((a', b'), (c', d'))$, where (a', b') is the position of r_j with respect to Z_i, and (c', d') is the position of r_i with respect to Z_j.

Since in general a robot does not know the coordinate systems of the other robots, which are an integral part of the definition of global view, the global view of a configuration is in general not available to the robots and, in most cases, impossible to derive.

Something that the robots can locally compute in absence of any other information is the *local view*. The *local view* $LV_i(t)$ *of* robot r_i at time t is the set of vectors $vec(r_i, r_j)$ for all $j \neq i$ with respect to Z_i. In other words, the local view $LV_i(t)$ corresponds to the information that r_i obtains when performing *Look* at time t. Two local views $LV_i(t)$ and $LV_j(t)$ are said to be *equivalent* $(LV_i(t) \equiv LV_j(t))$ if they are equal up to rotations, mirroring, and scaling.

An important property of the equivalence classes defined by the views (both in the case of global views, and of local views) is that they all have the same size.

Lemma 4.1 [123]   *Given a configuration $\mathbb{E}$ at time t, all the equivalence classes of robots with the same global (resp., local) view, have the same cardinality m.*

Moreover, when there is chirality, the robots can be partitioned into $\frac{n}{m}$ groups of m robots each, such that two robots have an equivalent view if and only if they belong to the same group. Note that, in the case of global view, the equivalence relationship is equality.

Lemma 4.2 [123]   *If the system has* Chirality, *given a configuration $\mathbb{E}$ at time t, the robots in the same equivalence class form a regular m-gon, and the regular m-gons formed by all the groups have a common center.*

The size m of the equivalence classes, called *symmetricity*, is denoted by $\sigma(\mathbb{E})$ in the case of global views, and by $\rho(\mathbb{E})$ in the case of local views.

For example, in the configuration of robots depicted in Figure 4.1(a) there are two classes of symmetry, each containing four robots, both when considering global and local views: In this case, $\sigma(\mathbb{E}) = \rho(\mathbb{E}) = 4$. Moreover, since in this example there is chirality, Lemma 4.2 holds and the robots can be partitioned into two groups of four robots each group forming a 4-gon with a common center.

Note that Lemma 4.2 does not hold when there is no chirality, i.e., when the axis of the coordinate systems of the robots are not rotationally symmetric. Consider, for example, the configuration depicted in Figure 4.1(b). It is clear that all robots have the same global and local views, thus belong to the same equivalence class; they however do not form a single n-gon, but rather two distinct $\frac{n}{2}$-gons.

More examples are shown in Figure 4.2 where, in all cases, the robots have the same local views; thus $\rho(\mathbb{E}_1) = \rho(\mathbb{E}_2) = \rho(\mathbb{E}_3) = n$. On the other hand, the global views are not always the same. More precisely, in Figure 4.2(a), we have that $\sigma(\mathbb{E}_1) = 1$ because all global views are different; in Figure 4.2(b), $\sigma(\mathbb{E}_2) = n$ because the global views are all identical; finally, in Figure 4.2(c), $\sigma(\mathbb{E}_3) = \frac{n}{2}$.

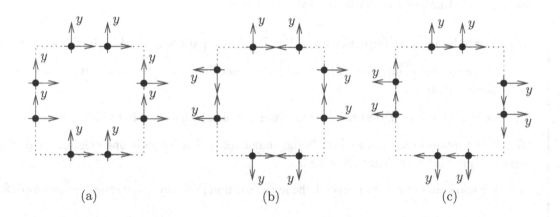

Figure 4.2: Three configurations of robots: (a) $\mathbb{E}_1$, with $\rho(\mathbb{E}_1) = n$ and $\sigma(\mathbb{E}_1) = 1$; (b) $\mathbb{E}_2$, with $\rho(\mathbb{E}_2) = \sigma(\mathbb{E}_2) = n$; and (c) $\mathbb{E}_3$, with $\rho(\mathbb{E}_3) = n$ and $\sigma(\mathbb{E}_3) = \frac{n}{2}$.

So far we have defined the symmetricity in terms of configurations; this concept can be extended also to patterns. The symmetricity of a pattern $\mathbb{P}$ can be defined analogously to the one of a configuration with respect to local views from the points of the pattern. It shall be indicated with $\rho(\mathbb{P})$.

4.2   ARBITRARY PATTERN FORMATION

In the most general version of the problem, the robots are required to form any *arbitrary* pattern $\mathbb{P}$ they are given in input, starting from any *arbitrary* plain initial configuration; that is, they are required to solve the ARBITRARY PATTERN FORMATION problem. We note that, since rotation is allowed, two robots always form the desired pattern. Therefore, we will assume to have at least three robots in the system.

4.2.1   ARBITRARY PATTER FORMATION AND LEADER ELECTION

A problem related to the ARBITRARY PATTERN FORMATION problem is the LEADER ELECTION problem: the robots in the system are said to *elect a leader* if, after a finite number of cycles, all the robots deterministically agree on (i.e., choose) the same robot l, called the leader. A deterministic algorithm that lets the robots in the system elect a leader in a finite number of cycles, given any initial configuration, is called a *leader election algorithm*.

The relationship between the arbitrary pattern formation problem and the leader election problem, is as follows:

Theorem 4.3   [69]   *If it is possible to solve the* ARBITRARY PATTERN FORMATION *problem for* $n \geq 3$ *robots, then the* LEADER ELECTION *problem is solvable too.*

Proof.   Let $\mathcal{A}$ be a pattern formation algorithm. Let $\mathbb{P}$ be a pattern defined in the following way:

1. All the robots but one are evenly placed on the same line $\mathcal{L}$; the distance between two adjacent robots is d; and

2. the last robot is on $\mathcal{L}$, but the distance from its unique adjacent robot is $2d$.

After all the robots execute $\mathcal{A}$ to form $\mathbb{P}$, the unique robot that has only one neighbor, and whose distance from it is $2d$, is identified as the leader.   □

We will now show that in general, the leader election problem is deterministically unsolvable.

Theorem 4.4   [69]   *Without any additional assumption, there exists no deterministic algorithm that solves the* LEADER ELECTION *problem, even in* FSYNC *with* Chirality.

Proof.   By contradiction, let $\mathcal{A}$ be a deterministic algorithm for solving the LEADER ELECTION problem, and let us assume that the robots have no agreement on the local compasses (i.e., Assumption Disorientation holds). Consider any pattern different from a regular n-gon or a single point, and let the initial positions be such that the robots form a regular n-gon. Let $\alpha = 360°/n$ be the characteristic angle of the n-gon, and let the local coordinate system of each robot be rotated by α with respect to its neighbor on the polygon (see Figure 4.3). In this situation, all the robots have the same (local) view of the world. Now, for any move that any one robot can make in its local

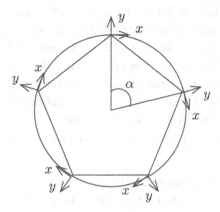

Figure 4.3: Theorem 4.4: The unbreakable symmetry of a 5-gon.

coordinate system by executing algorithm $\mathcal{A}$, we know that each robot can make the same move in its local coordinate system. If all of them move in the exact same way at the same time (i.e., they move according to a synchronous schedule), they again end up in a regular n-gon or a single point. Therefore, by letting all the robots move at the same time in the same way, we always proceed from one regular n-gon or single point to the next. Hence, no leader can be elected. The same argument applies even if Chirality holds.   □

Thus, by Theorem 4.3, we can state the following:

Corollary 4.5   *In a system with $n > 2$ anonymous robots, without any additional assumption, the* ARBITRARY PATTERN FORMATION *problem is unsolvable.*

Furthermore, even if the robots agree on the direction of one axis and direction (condition OneAxis), the LEADER ELECTION problem is still unsolvable when n is even.

Theorem 4.6 [69]   *Let the robots agree only on the direction and orientation of one axis; there exists no deterministic algorithm that solves the* LEADER ELECTION *problem, hence the* ARBITRARY PATTERN FORMATION *problem, when n is even.*

Proof. By contradiction, let $\mathcal{A}$ be a deterministic leader election algorithm. Without loss of generality, let us assume that the robots agree on the direction and orientation of the Y axis, and consider an initial placement of the robots symmetric with respect to a vertical axis; i.e., each robot r has a *specular partner* $\widehat{r}$. In addition, let the local coordinate systems be specular with respect to the symmetry axis: the directions of the X axis of r and of the X axis of $\widehat{r}$ are opposite; thus the (local) view of the world is the same for r and $\widehat{r}$. In this setting, at time $t = 0$, both r and r are in the same state; i.e., $\tau(r, 0) = \tau(\widehat{r}, 0)$. Consider now a semi-synchronous scheduler: robots are activated at discrete time instants; each robot is activated infinitely often; an active robot performs its operations instantaneously. Additionally, if a robot r is activated at time $t \geq 0$, the scheduler will activate at that time also $\widehat{r}$. As a consequence, if $\tau(r, t) = \tau(\widehat{r}, t)$, since the two robots execute the same protocol $\mathcal{A}$, their next state will still be the same: if r moves to d, $\widehat{r}$ moves to the point $\widehat{d}$ specular to d with respect to the symmetry axis. In other words, in this execution of protocol $\mathcal{A}$, $\tau(r, t) = \tau(\widehat{r}, t)$ for all $t \geq 0$. On the other hand, since $\mathcal{A}$ is an election protocol, a time $t' > 0$ must exist such that a robot, say r', becomes leader. Since the leader is unique, $\tau(r', t') \neq \tau(r, t')$ for all $r \neq r'$, contradicting the fact that $\tau(r', t') = \tau(\widehat{r'}, t')$. $\square$

Let us consider now the converse relationship between the ARBITRARY PATTERN FORMATION problem and the LEADER ELECTION problem. Assume that all robots share a common protocol LEADER($\mathbb{E}$) that, given any configuration $\mathbb{E}$, deterministically returns a unique leader in $\mathbb{E}$. We can now employ such a protocol to form an arbitrary target pattern $\mathbb{P}$, i.e., to solve the ARBITRARY PATTERN FORMATION problem, assuming that the robots agree on a common chirality. The overall idea of the algorithm consists of three main steps [54]: (1) the robots move to some appropriate positions, and build a kind of global coordinate system; (2) next, they compute the final positions to occupy in order to form the input pattern; (3) finally, the robots move toward these final positions, paying attention to maintain unchanged the global coordinate system.

In particular, given a set of points P and its $SEC(P)$, we call the *concentric enclosing circles* of $SEC(P)$ all the circles having the same center of $SEC(P)$ and passing through at least one point in P. Starting from a *leader configuration* (i.e., a configuration where a leader can be located), the robots first move to an *agreement configuration*:

Definition 4.7   Agreement Configuration   A configuration $\mathbb{T}$ is an agreement configuration if and only if both following conditions hold:

1. There exists a robot r_l in $\mathbb{T}$ such that r_l is the unique robot located on the smallest concentric enclosing circle of $SEC(\mathbb{T})$;

2. There is no robot at the center of $SEC(\mathbb{T})$.

In order to achieve an agreement configuration from a leader configuration $\mathbb{E}$, the robots act as follows. If there is a robot r that is located at the center c of $SEC(\mathbb{E})$, let s be the closest robot to c among the robots in $\mathbb{E} \setminus \{r\}$, and p the median point on the segment $\overline{rs}$. Then, by moving r toward p, an agreement configuration is achieved. Otherwise (no robot is at c), we consider the smallest concentric enclosing circle of $SEC(\mathbb{E})$, call it $\mathcal{C}$; if there is only one robot on this circle, then the robots are already in an agreement configuration. Thus, let us assume there is more than one robot on $\mathcal{C}$. Now, the availability of protocol LEADER() is exploited: let $r^* = \text{LEADER}(\mathbb{E})$, and let r be the first robot on $\mathcal{C}$, according to the clockwise orientation, with respect to the half-line $\overrightarrow{cr^*}$ (recall that Assumption `Chirality` holds). By moving r toward the median point of the segment $\overline{rc}$, an agreement configuration is obtained. Note that the previous strategy works also when all robots are on $SEC(\mathbb{E})$ (i.e., when $\mathcal{C} \equiv SEC(\mathbb{E})$): the only difference is in the way robot r is chosen. In fact, in this case, r is the first *non-critical* robot on $\mathcal{C}$, i.e., the first robot on $\mathcal{C}$ whose movement would not change $SEC(\mathbb{E})$ (in this case r might coincide with r^*).

Once the robots are in an agreement configuration $\mathbb{T}$, they can also agree on their final positions: in particular, the center c of $SEC(\mathbb{P})$ is mapped onto the center o of $SEC(\mathbb{T})$; the pattern is rotated so that $\overrightarrow{or_l}$ is mapped onto $\overrightarrow{cs}$, with s the first non-critical point located on the smallest concentric enclosing circle of $\mathbb{P}$; and $\mathbb{P}$ is scaled with respect to the radius of $SEC(\mathbb{T})$ so that all the distances are expressed according to the radius of $SEC(\mathbb{T})$ (in particular $SEC(\mathbb{T}) = SEC(\mathbb{P})$).

Then, the robots occupy these positions, starting from those situated on SEC, and then on all the circles concentric to SEC from the largest to the smallest. During this phase, the final positions are maintained unchanged, by making sure that the robots remain in an agreement configuration until the pattern is formed. In particular, the protocol makes sure that no angle above $180°$ is created on SEC (otherwise the smallest enclosing circle changes), and that the leader of the agreement configuration remains the unique closest robot from the center of SEC and does not leave the radius where it is located. In other words,

Theorem 4.8 [54] *In* Async, *assuming* Chirality, *for any $n \geq 4$ if the* Leader Election *problem is solvable, then the* Arbitrary Pattern Formation *problem is solvable.*

4.2.2 ARBITRARY PATTERN FORMATION AND COMPASSES

The solvability of the Arbitrary Pattern Formation problem, and in general which patterns can be formed regardless of the starting configuration, strictly depend on the level of agreement that the robots have about their local coordinate systems.

Following the ideas of the proof of previous Theorem 4.4, it is possible to show a *necessary* condition for the solvability of the Arbitrary Pattern Formation problem: the absence of common agreement on the coordinate system leads to the inability to form arbitrary patterns.

Theorem 4.9 [69] *Without any agreement on the local compasses,* Arbitrary Pattern Formation *is* impossible, *even in* Fsync *with chirality.*

As a consequence, some agreement is necessary.

Sense of Direction. Total agreement on the coordinate system (Assumption ConsistentCompass) is indeed *sufficient* to solve the Arbitrary Pattern Formation problem even in Async. To see how, consider the following protocol [69]:

1. Each robot establishes the (lexicographic) total order of the points of the local pattern (Figure 4.4(a)).

2. Each robot establishes the (lexicographic) total order of the robots' positions retrieved in the last *Look* (Figure 4.4(b)). As we will see, this order will be the same for all robots.

3. The first and second robots move to the positions matching the first and second pattern points. This movement can be performed in such a way that the order of the robots does not change (Figure 4.4(c) and (d)). Once this is done, the first two robots' positions will determine the translation and scaling of the pattern (Figure 4.4(e)).

4. All other robots go to the other points of the pattern. This can be done by moving the robots sequentially to the pattern's points. The sequence is chosen in such a way to guarantee that, after one robot has made even only a small move toward its destination, no other robot will move before that one has reached its destination (Figure 4.4(f)).

We note that the final positions of the robots are not rotated w.r.t. the input positions; in other words the algorithm keeps the "orientation" given by the input pattern. Moreover, in this case Theorem 4.3 holds also for $n = 2$, since the rightmost and topmost robot in the system can always be identified as the leader.

Theorem 4.10 [69]   *With* ConsistentCompass, ARBITRARY PATTERN FORMATION *is solvable in* ASYNC.

Partial Agreement: Odd Number of Robots.   Let us now consider the case when the robots have partial agreement: they agree only on the orientation of one axis, say Y; that is, there is common agreement also on the direction of the X axis, but not on its orientation (assumption OneAxis). Note that this case, if there is also chirality, would trivially coincide with the total agreement one.

As stated by Corollary 4.5, the ARBITRARY PATTERN FORMATION problem is unsolvable in general; furthermore, by Theorem 4.6, it is also unsolvable by an even number of robots when the Assumption OneAxis considered in this section holds, since symmetric initial configuration can impede the formation of arbitrary patterns. However, for breaking the symmetry, it is sufficient to know that the number n of robots is odd: in this case, in fact, either the robots are in a symmetric initial situation, in which there is a unique middle robot that will move in order to break the symmetry; or the initial situation is not symmetric, and this asymmetry can be used to identify an orientation of the X axis.

In more detail, let us define some *references* related to a set of points $\mathbb{E}$ that will be used in the following:

- The two vertical lines that are tangent to the convex hull of $\mathbb{E}$, and the vertical axis $\Phi_m^{\mathbb{E}}$ that is in the middle between them.

- These three vertical lines delimit two regions (or *sides*): one to the left of $\Phi_m^{\mathbb{E}}$ and one to its right. Let $\mathcal{M}_{\mathbb{E}}$ and $\mathcal{L}_{\mathbb{E}}$ denote the side in $\mathbb{E}$ with more and less points, respectively. If the two

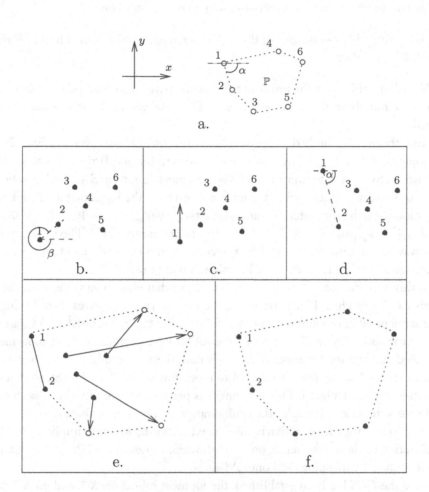

Figure 4.4: An example of the arbitrary pattern formation protocol in presence of `ConsistentCompass`. (a) The input pattern $\mathbb{P}$. The robots have complete knowledge on the local coordinate systems. The numbers represent the lexicographical ordering the robots give to the points of $\mathbb{P}$, and $\alpha = \texttt{Angle}(p_1, p_2)$. (b) The robots sort the robots' positions retrieved in the last *Look* state, and compute $\beta = \texttt{Angle}(r_1, r_2)$. (c) r_1 moves in such a way that $\texttt{Angle}(r_1, r_2) = \alpha$. (d) The relative positions of r_1 and r_2 are such that $\texttt{Angle}(r_1, r_2) = \alpha$. (e) At this point, all the robots can translate and scale the input pattern according to $\overline{r_1 r_2}$. Then, all the robots, one at a time, reach the final positions of the pattern to form. (f) The final configuration.

sides have the same number of points, then $\mathcal{M}_{\mathbb{E}}$ is the rightmost side. If $|\mathcal{M}_{\mathbb{E}}| \neq |\mathcal{L}_{\mathbb{E}}|$, then $\mathbb{E}$ is said to be *unbalanced*; otherwise, we will call it *balanced*.

- Finally, $\Phi_{\mathcal{M}}^{\mathbb{E}}$ denotes the one of the two axes tangent to the convex hull of $\mathbb{E}$ that lies in $\mathcal{M}_{\mathbb{E}}$, and $\Phi_{\mathcal{L}}^{\mathbb{E}}$ the other.

We will describe now the protocol to form any pattern with an odd number of points, where the points are not all on the same vertical line. The case, where the robots have to form a vertical line is easier.

First, the robots check that the robots are not on the same vertical line Ξ; otherwise, the second topmost robot on this line, say r, moves toward its (local) right, up to a distance equal to the distance between the topmost and the bottommost robot on Ξ (no other robot move until r reaches this distance). At this point, the references on both the input pattern $\mathbb{P}$ and on the observed configuration $\mathbb{D}$ can be computed: in particular, let $\Upsilon_m = \Phi_m^{\mathbb{P}}$, $\Upsilon^+ = \Phi_{\mathcal{M}}^{\mathbb{P}}$, $\Upsilon^- = \Phi_{\mathcal{L}}^{\mathbb{E}}$ the references in $\mathbb{P}$, and $K_m = \Phi_m^{\mathbb{D}}$, and $K^+ = \Phi_{\mathcal{M}}^{\mathbb{D}}$, $K^- = \Phi_{\mathcal{L}}^{\mathbb{E}}$ the references in $\mathbb{D}$. The final goal of the robots is to find a way of mapping these two sets of references onto each other so that the final destinations the robots have to reach to form $\mathbb{P}$ can be uniquely computed.

To this aim, the robots need to *unbalance* $\mathbb{D}$, so that also an agreement on the orientation of the x axis can be reached. If $\mathbb{D}$ is balanced, the symmetry that derives from having the two sides with the same number of robots is broken as follows. First all the robots[1] in $\mathcal{M}_{\mathbb{D}}$ are moved on K^+ and all the robots in $\mathcal{L}_{\mathbb{D}}$ on K^-. After all the robots have performed these movements, since $\mathbb{D}$ is still balanced and the total number of robots is odd, there is an odd number of robots on K_m: the topmost robot on K_m, say top^*, is selected to move toward its (local) right, so that an unbalanced configuration can be achieved. This movement is performed carefully since, as soon as top^* leaves K_m and enters the side to its right, the configuration will become unbalanced.

The fact that the configuration is unbalanced allows the robots to implicitly reach an agreement on the direction of the x axis; hence, on a *global coordinate system (GCS)*: the common orientation of the x axis is given by mapping $\mathcal{M}_{\mathbb{P}}$ onto $\mathcal{M}_{\mathbb{D}}$.

Once the *GCS* has been established, the topmost robots on K^+ and on K^- (top^+ and top^-, respectively) move vertically on K^+ and on K^-, respectively, until they reach positions corresponding to the two topmost points on Υ^+ and Υ^- in $\mathbb{P}$. Once top^+ and top^- place themselves in the correct positions, they will never move again. At this point, the set of final positions of the robots can be easily computed, by scaling the pattern according to these mappings. Note that here the pattern does not need to be rotated.

Now, all robots are ready to reach their final destinations. Note that at this point it might be possible that the unbalancing process is not completed yet; i.e., top^* is still moving toward its destination. Should this be the case, the other robots can, however, detect it, and will not start their move until top^* stops. The robots reach their final destinations sequentially:

---

[1]Note that, since at this time the robots still do not have a common agreement on the direction of the X axis, for some robots $\mathcal{M}_{\mathbb{D}}$ and $\mathcal{L}_{\mathbb{D}}$ might be different. All of them, however, agree on K_m.

- First, the robots in S^- (side of $\mathbb{D}$ where K^- lies) sequentially fill the final positions that are in S^-. If there are more robots than available final positions, the "extra" robots are sequentially moved toward K_m, starting from the topmost robots that are closest to K_m.

- Second, the robots in S^+ (side of $\mathbb{D}$ where K^- lies), except for the bottommost on K^+, sequentially fill the final positions in S^+. If there are more robots than available final positions, the "extra" robots are sequentially moved toward K_m, starting from the topmost robots that are closest to K_m.

- Third, if there are still unfilled final positions in S^+ (that is, there were not enough robots in S^+ in the second step), the robots on K_m are sequentially moved in S^+, starting from the topmost, to fill the final positions occupied by no robots.

- Fourth, if there are still unfilled final positions in S^- (that is, there were not enough robots in S^- in the first step), the robots on K_m are sequentially moved in S^-, starting from the topmost, to fill the final positions still available.

At this point, all the robots not on K_m occupy the correct positions except one: the bottommost robot on K^+, say r.

- If there is an available destination in S^+, then r goes there. At this point, all the robots but those on K_m are in correct positions. Note that now all available destinations are also on K_m: thus, the robots on K_m move sequentially (and only vertically on K_m) toward the available final destinations.

- If there are no available final positions inside S^+ and S^-, r moves toward K_m. Once it reaches the median axis, all the robots but those on K_m are in correct positions, and again the algorithm proceeds as in the previous case.

- If there is an available destination in S^-, r first moves toward K_m. Then, the topmost robot on K_m moves in S^- on the last unfilled final position. Once this position also becomes occupied, only the robots on K_m must be adjusted, as in the two previous cases.

Thus, the above plus Theorem 4.6 imply the following:

Theorem 4.11 [69] *With* OneAxis, ARBITRARY PATTERN FORMATION *is solvable only if n is odd, and this can be done in* ASYNC.

Partial Agreement: Even Number of Robots. By Theorem 4.6, an arbitrary pattern cannot be formed by an even number of robots with OneAxis. In this section, we are interested in determining which class of patterns, if any, can be formed in this case starting from any initial position. Again, we will assume that the robots in the system have common agreement on the direction and orientation of only the Y axis, and that the number n of robots in the system is even.

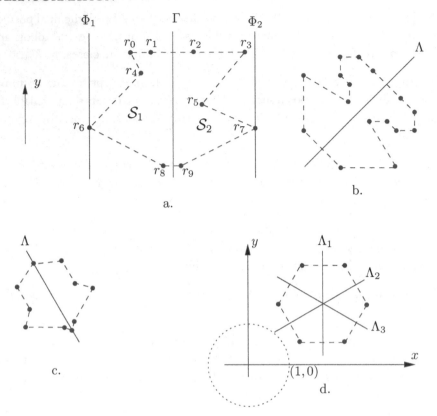

Figure 4.5: (a) An unachievable asymmetric pattern. (b) An achievable pattern with one axis of symmetry not passing through any vertex. (c) An unachievable pattern. (d) An achievable pattern that has three axes of symmetry not passing through any vertex. Note that this pattern has also axes of symmetry passing through vertexes.

We say that $\mathbb{P}$ is a *symmetric pattern* if it has at least one axis of symmetry Λ; that is, for each $p \in \mathbb{P}$ there exists exactly another point $p' \in \mathbb{P}$ such that p and p' are symmetric with respect to Λ (see Figures 4.5(b), (c), and (d)).

The proof of the unsolvability result of Theorem 4.6 is useful to better understand what kind of patterns cannot be formed, hence what kind of pattern formation algorithms cannot be designed. In fact, the ability to form a particular type of patterns would imply the ability to elect a robot in the system as the leader. Formally,

Theorem 4.12 [69] *If an algorithm $\mathcal{A}$ lets the robots form (a.) an asymmetric pattern, or (b.) a symmetric pattern that has all its axes of symmetry passing through some vertex, then $\mathcal{A}$ is a leader election algorithm.*

From Theorem 4.6 and Theorem 4.12, it follows that

Corollary 4.13 *There exists no pattern formation algorithm that lets the robots in the system form (a) an asymmetric pattern, or (b) a symmetric pattern that has all its axes of symmetry passing through some vertex.*

Let us call $\mathfrak{T}$ the class containing all the arbitrary patterns, and $\mathfrak{P} \subset \mathfrak{T}$ the class containing only patterns with at least one axis of symmetry not passing through any vertex (e.g., see Figures 4.5(b) and 4.5(d)); let us call *empty* such an axis. Corollary 4.13 states that if $\mathbb{P} \in \mathfrak{T} \setminus \mathfrak{P}$, then $\mathbb{P}$ cannot be in general formed; hence, according to Part (b), the only patterns that might be formed are symmetric ones with at least one *empty axis*.

The idea behind the algorithm that solves the ARBITRARY PATTERN FORMATION problem with partial agreement and an even number of robots is as follows. First, the robots compute locally an *empty axis* of the input pattern $\mathbb{P}$, say Λ, and then rotate $\mathbb{P}$ so that Λ is parallel to the common understanding of the orientation of y; let us denote by $\mathbb{P}_R$ the rotated pattern.

If the robots lie all on the same line, the algorithm forces them to place on at least two distinct vertical lines, Γ and Γ' (this is achieved as for the odd case). Then, the topmost robot on Γ, say *Out*, and the topmost robot on Γ', say *Out'*, move so that they place themselves in the correct position: in particular, since $\mathbb{P}_R$ is symmetric with respect to Λ, *Out* and *Out'* must place themselves to the same height. This is because, by Corollary 4.13, the input pattern cannot be a vertical line.

At this point, the set of final positions can be computed, by scaling the input pattern with respect to $\overline{\Gamma\Gamma'}$, and by translating it so that the topmost point on the rightmost vertical axis tangent to $\mathbb{P}$ is mapped onto *Out*, and the topmost point on the leftmost vertical axis tangent to $\mathbb{P}$ is mapped onto[2] *Out'*.

At this point, the robots move to reach a balanced configuration, with each side containing half of the robots. The balancing is obtained as follows. Let $\mathcal{S}$ and $\mathcal{S}'$ be the two sides determined by Γ_m, the vertical median axis between Γ and Γ'.

- In the side that has more than $n/2$ robot (if any), the robots are moved sequentially (starting from the topmost with the smallest horizontal distance from Γ_m) toward Γ_m, using a path that avoids collisions, until there are exactly $n/2$ robots in that side.

- In a side that has $\leq n/2$ robots, the robots are moved toward the final positions in that side.

- The robots that are on Γ_m wait until $|\mathcal{S}| \leq n/2$ and $|\mathcal{S}'| \leq n/2$, and all the robots in the two sides are on a final position. At this point, sequentially (from the topmost) they move toward the final positions still available in the two sides. In fact, by the way the input pattern has been rotated, no final positions can be on Γ_m.

[2]Note that, since $\mathbb{P}_R$ is symmetric, including the topmost point on the leftmost vertical axis tangent to $\mathbb{P}$ is mapped onto *Out*, and the topmost point on the rightmost vertical axis tangent to $\mathbb{P}$ is mapped onto *Out'*.

Thus, we can state the following:

Theorem 4.14   [69]   *With* OneAxis, *when n is even only patterns in* $\mathfrak{P}$ *can be formed, and this can be done in* ASYNC.

No Agreement.   In absence of any additional assumption, and in particular in absence of any agreement on the compasses, Theorem 4.4 implies that no asymmetric pattern can be formed from all arbitrary initial configurations. Furthermore, as discussed later in Section 4.3, a symmetric pattern $\mathbb{A}$ with symmetricity $\sigma(\mathbb{A})$, can be formed only with the same or lower symmetricity. This means that the only pattern that can (possibly) be formed from all initial configurations is the *uniform circle* (i.e., a circle along which the robots are placed at equal distance) or *n-gon*. Note that this fact holds regardless of the synchronicity (i.e., even in FSYNC).

The problem of forming a uniform circle is important in its own right, and is analyzed in Section 4.4. Interestingly, to date it is not known whether this problem can be solved in ASYNC without additional assumptions; in the case of SSYNC it is solvable.

4.2.3   LANDMARKS COVERING: FORMATION OF VISIBLE PATTERNS

An interesting problem related to ARBITRARY PATTERN FORMATION (APF) is the LANDMARKS COVERING problem: In the space there are *n* points, the *landmarks*, visible to all robots[3]; the problem is for the robots to reach a configuration where at each landmark there is precisely one robot. A solution protocol must enable the robots to cover the landmarks, regardless of the location of the landmarks and of the initial location of the robots.

In other words, the LANDMARKS COVERING problem is precisely the ARBITRARY PATTERN FORMATION problem when the points of the input pattern are globally visible. Clearly, any solution to APF under some conditions, will solve also LANDMARKS COVERING under those conditions. The research interest is whether LANDMARKS COVERING can be solved more efficiently than APF, or with fewer conditions than APF, or in situations where APF is not (known to be) solvable. In terms of efficiency, the main goal of any LANDMARKS COVERING solution protocol is that of minimizing the robot's movements, i.e., the total amount traveled by the robots to reach the final configurations in which all landmarks are covered.

Interestingly, unlike the ARBITRARY PATTERN FORMATION problem, the LANDMARKS COVERING problem can always be solved in ASYNC, provided there is Chirality. Furthermore, this can be done always with minimal travel costs and without collisions [73].

The solution strategy consists in the robots computing a unique perfect *matching* between robots and landmarks which minimizes the total travel costs from each robot to the landmark assigned by the matching; each robot then moves until it reaches the assigned landmark, avoiding collisions. The clear difficulty is to perform this process obliviously; to do so, the determined matching must be *invariant* to the movements of the robots toward their destination, so that each robot, every

---

[3]Equivalently, the position of the landmarks is known *a priori* to all robots.

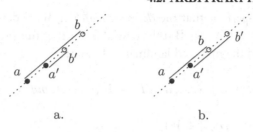

a.   b.

Figure 4.6: Examples of matchings.

time it becomes active, can determine which landmark was initially assigned it, regardless of the progress made by the other robots toward their assigned landmarks.

Consider the initial configuration of the robots $\mathbb{A}$ and let $\mathbb{B}$ denote the pattern of the landmarks. We can view a perfect matching M from $\mathbb{A}$ to $\mathbb{B}$ as a set of pairs $\{(a, b)\}$ where a is a robot location in $\mathbb{A}$ and b is a landmark in $\mathbb{B}$, and its *cost* is the sum $\sum_{(a,b)\in M} |\vec{ab}|$ of the Euclidean distances between the matched points. Let $\mathcal{M}(\mathbb{A}, \mathbb{B})$ denote the set of all perfect matchings M of minimum cost between $\mathbb{A}$ to $\mathbb{B}$ such that for all distinct pairs (a, b), $(a', b') \in M$, the points a, a', b', b do not reside on the same line in that specific order. For example, M may not include the match shown in Figure 4.6(a), but may include the pairs shown in Figure 4.6(b). We call the matchings in this set *optimal*. It is easy to verify that $\mathcal{M}(\mathbb{A}, \mathbb{B}) \neq \emptyset$; note that there might be more than one optimal matching between $\mathbb{A}$ and $\mathbb{B}$.

We can compute a unique optimal matching, called *clockwise matching*, between two sets of n distinct points, A and B, as follows:

(1) First consider the bipartite graph $G[A, B] = (V, E)$ whose vertex set $V = A \cup B$ comprises the points of A and B, and where the edge set $E = \cup_{M \in \mathcal{M}(A,B)} M$ contains all pairs matched in at least one optimal matching.

(2) Consider now the connected components $G_1, G_2, ..., G_k$ of $G[A, B]$, and the periphery[4] C_i of component G_i; let A_i and B_i be the points of A in $G_i \setminus C_i$ and the points of B in $G_i \setminus C_i$, respectively.

(3) Consider next the subgraph $\hat{G}[A, B]$ of $G[A, B]$ recursively defined as follows: $\hat{G}[A, B] = \emptyset$ if $A = B = \emptyset$; otherwise $\hat{G}[A, B] = \cup_{1 \leq j \leq k}(C_i \cup \hat{G}[A_i, B_i])$. Note that each connected component Q of $\hat{G}[A, B]$ is either a cycle or a single edge.

(4) Finally, for each connected component Q_i of $\hat{G}[A, B]$, construct the matching W_i where $W_i = Q_i$ if Q_i is a single edge, otherwise, W_i is a clockwise tour $(a_1, b_1), (a_2, b_2), ..., (a_m, b_m)$ of Q_i.

The *clockwise matching* $W[A, B]$ between A and B is just the union of the matchings W_i of all the connected components Q_i of $\hat{G}[A, B]$.

---

[4]For a plane graph, the periphery is the boundary of the exterior face.

An important property is that the *clockwise matching* W so determined is unique and indeed optimal; i.e., $W[A, B] \in \mathcal{M}(A, B)$. But the crucial fact is that this property is invariant with respect to robots moving toward the matched landmarks. In fact,

Lemma 4.15 **[73]** *Let $A = \{a_1, ..., a_n\}$, $B = \{b_1, ..., b_n\}$, and $= \{c_1, ..., c_n\}$ be set of points which satisfy following:*
1. $\{(a_1, b_1), (a_2, b_2), ..., (a_n, b_n)\} \in W[A, B]$
2. $c_i \in \overline{a_i b_i}$
3. *if there exists $j \neq i$ such that $a_j \in \overline{a_i b_i}$ then $c_i = a_i$*
Then $\{(c_1, b_1), (c_2, b_2), ..., (c_n, b_n)\} \in W[C, B]$.

Thus, the (collision avoiding) solution protocol is simply [73]:

Algorithm LANDMARKCOVER
Assumptions: Visible Landmarks; Chirality.

1. Let $A = \{a_1, ..., a_n\}$ be the position of the robots (as returned by *Look*) and let $B = \{b_1, ..., b_n\}$ be the positions of the landmarks in my coordinate system.

2. Compute the clockwise matching $W[A, B]$. Let $a \in A$ be my position and $b \in B$ the landmark assigned to me in $W[A, B]$.

3. If $\forall a' \in A \setminus \{a\}$, $a' \notin \overline{ab}$, then move toward b.

Theorem 4.16 **[73]** *The LANDMARKS COVERING problem can be solved in ASYNC with minimal travel costs, provided there is Chirality.*

In other words, with Chirality, every *visible pattern* can be formed in ASYNC.

4.3   PATTERN FORMATION AND INITIAL CONFIGURATION

The proof of Theorem 4.4 shows that, with no agreement on the local coordinate systems, the ARBITRARY PATTERN FORMATION problem cannot be solved. Thus, an interesting question is what patterns could be formed, in absence of common coordinate system, starting from a *specific* configuration $\mathbb{E}$.

4.3.1   IMPOSSIBILITY

The patterns that the robots can or cannot form starting from configuration $\mathbb{E}$ at time $t = 0$ are strictly related to the classes of equivalence derived from the definition of views (seen in Section 4.1).

If the views of two or more robots are identical, in some executions (e.g., under a scheduler that activates them always at the same time) those robots will always perform the same actions, without being able to break their symmetry; so, the patterns that can possibly be formed must have the same or higher symmetricity, but always a multiple of the original one.

Theorem 4.17   [123]   *Starting from a configuration* $\mathbb{E}$ *with symmetricity* $\sigma(\mathbb{E})$, *it is* impossible *to form any pattern* $\mathbb{P}$ *with* $\sigma(\mathbb{P}) < \sigma(\mathbb{E})$, *or* $\sigma(\mathbb{P}) \neq k \cdot \sigma(\mathbb{E})$ *for some integer* $k > 1$.

In other words, if $\mathbb{E}$ is totally asymmetric (i.e., $\sigma(\mathbb{E}) = 1$), all patterns are potentially formable; on the other hand, if $\sigma(\mathbb{E}) = m > 1$, only patterns with the same symmetricity or with a symmetricity that is a multiple of m are candidate to be formable. Notice that this impossibility holds even if the robots are not oblivious. In the case of systems with chirality, by Lemma 4.2, we obtain the inability to form a pattern that cannot be partitioned, as the initial configuration, in $\frac{n}{m}$ regular m-gons.

Theorem 4.18   [123]   *In systems with* Chirality, *starting from a configuration* $\mathbb{E}$ *with symmetricity* $\sigma(\mathbb{E}) = m$, *it is* impossible *to form any pattern unless it is the union of* $\frac{n}{m}$ *regular m-gons all having the same center.*

4.3.2   POSSIBILITY

Once we know which are the only patterns that could be formed starting from a configuration $\mathbb{E}$, the questions become whether those patterns can be formed, and how. In ASYNC, no answers are known. In the case of SSYNC there are some conditional answers.

If the robots are *not oblivious* (recall that the impossibility holds even in this case), they can record all the snapshots in which they are active; the change of coordinates in two successive snapshots allows us to detect movement and to measure it; hence information can be communicated by moving appropriate distances [123]. In particular, they can communicate their own coordinate systems and unit of measures, so that the complete views can be locally constructed and examined; once this is done, forming the pattern is straightforward.

We are, however, interested in oblivious robots, for which there is *no* memory, and hence no tool to record information, to detect and measure movement, and thus to communicate. Interestingly, it is possible for oblivious robots to form all the formable patterns [131], if the robots have Chirality, move with *fixed mobility* (possibly different for each robot) and know the *maximum movement* $\hat{\delta}$.

Theorem 4.19   [131]   *A team of oblivious robots in* SSYNC *with* Chirality, *fixed mobility, and known maximum movement, starting from configuration* $\mathbb{E}$ *with* $\sigma(\mathbb{E}) = m$ *can form any pattern* $\mathbb{P}$ *decomposable into* $\frac{n}{m}$ *regular m-gons all having the same center.*

Notice that, since the robots do not agree on a common coordinate system, the level of symmetry perceived by the robots (given by their local views) might not correspond to the actual

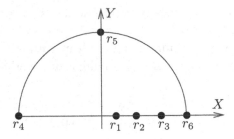

Figure 4.7: A T-stable configuration with six robots.

level of symmetry of the global view which, as defined earlier, takes into account also the coordinate systems.

Let $\mathbb{P} = p_1, \ldots, p_n$ be the pattern to be formed and let us assume that the robots start in n distinct positions. For simplicity we describe only the case when the pattern does not contain dense points. Moreover, we assume (again for simplicity) that each robot knows the origin of its own coordinate system, which does not change throughout the algorithm. The result still holds with some modifications also when these assumptions are removed. Also for simplicity we assume the unit distance of a robot coincides with $\hat{\delta}$.

The algorithm distinguishes the case when $\rho(\mathbb{E}) = 1$, and thus the initial configuration is totally asymmetric, even without considering the coordinate systems, from the case when $\rho(\mathbb{E}) > 1$.

Case $\rho(\mathbb{E}) = 1$.   In this case, the initial configuration $\mathbb{E}$ is perceived as asymmetric. This is the simplest case and also a building block possibly used in the other cases.

Since the symmetricity is 1 and there is chirality, a total order can be imposed on the robots, even in absence of a common coordinate system. The robots are in fact ordered in a non-decreasing order of their radii with respect to the center c of the smallest enclosing circle $SEC(\mathbb{E})$ (for points with the same distance, ties are broken by using chirality). Let this order correspond to $r_1, \ldots, r_n$, where the robots are aware of their own index. The algorithm is designed in such a way that SEC will never change until the pattern is "almost" formed.

Intuitively, the robots move from $\mathbb{E}$ to a special configuration, called a *T-stable configuration*, where SEC contains exactly three robots on the circumference: two opposite on a diameter and the third at 90 degrees from both, and no robots occupy the center (see Figure 4.7). The robots can then agree on a common coordinate system by selecting as X the line passing through the two robots positioned opposite on the diameter of SEC, and as Y the line passing through c and through the third robot placed at 90 degrees on the circumference.

The unit distance of this common coordinate system is chosen in a very specific way as $\frac{Rad}{2^l}$ where Rad is the radius of SEC, and l is the smallest positive integer such that $|r_j| < |p_j|$ for each $1 \leq j \leq n$, where $|r_j|$ (resp., $|p_j|$) indicates the distance from point r_j (resp., vertex p_j) to its own origin. This choice is made for the unit distance to be sufficiently small so that robots never move away from c while going toward their position to form the pattern. The robots now move one by one to their final destination following their order (which implies that robots closer to c move to their destination first). This order, combined with the fact that no robot has to move away from c in the process, guarantees that the magnitude of the unit distance does not change in the formation process, and that a robot that has reached its final position does not have to move anymore. The movements are performed without destroying the T-stable configuration, paying particular attention to the movements of the last three robots.

Case $\rho(\mathbb{E}) > 1$.   When the robots perceive $\rho(\mathbb{E}) > 1$, it does not necessarily mean that $\sigma(\mathbb{E}) > 1$, because the different coordinate systems might induce more asymmetry. In this general case, the robots perform two procedures. First they try to move from $\mathbb{E}$ to a configuration that reflects a symmetry m that divides $\rho(\mathbb{P})$. Once/if such a situation is reached, they proceed to form the pattern. If, while changing symmetricity, they happen to form a configuration $\mathbb{E}'$ with $\rho(\mathbb{E}') = 1$, they instead form the pattern using the algorithm described in the previous case.

Let us describe the first procedure that allows the robots to appropriately reduce the perceived symmetricity ρ until it divides the symmetricity of the pattern to be formed.

The idea is the following. First the center of the smallest enclosing circle c is identified. Point c is also the center of symmetry of $\mathbb{E}$; that is, the unique point such that the robots can be divided in $\frac{n}{\rho(\mathbb{E})}$ groups each forming a regular $\rho(\mathbb{E})$-gon with center c. Then each robot moves away from c in a straight line according to its coordinate system of a small amount. The amount is very carefully computed to guarantee that: 1) it is smaller than the robot's unit distance and thus can be reached instantaneously in one step; 2) if two robots are located symmetrically with respect to c and have non-symmetrical local coordinate systems, they will move of a *different* amount.

Depending on the activation schedule of the robots, the above procedure is shown to either completely break the symmetry in one step reaching a configuration $\mathbb{E}'$ where $\rho(\mathbb{E}') = 1$, or to reduce the symmetry, eventually reaching, after repeated applications of the procedure, a configuration $\mathbb{A}$ such that $m = \rho(\mathbb{A})$ divides $\rho(\mathbb{P})$.

Now both the pattern and the configuration can be partitioned into $k = \frac{n}{m}$ regular m-gons all having the same center so to have a correspondence between each m-gon with a group of m robots. Let $\mathcal{R}_1, \ldots, \mathcal{R}_k$ be the k sets of robots and let $\mathcal{R}_k = \{r_1, \ldots, r_m\}$. Set $\mathcal{R}_k$ is special and it is used to create consistent coordinate systems. In fact, in this case it is not possible for the robots to agree on a common coordinate system based on a T-stable configuration (like for the asymmetric case). Because of the rotational symmetry induced by the $\frac{n}{m}$ regular m-gons around c, each robot in one class of symmetry decides its destination individually. Each robot s_j in $\mathcal{R}_i$ chooses as X-axis the line passing through the common center c and the closest among the robots in $\mathcal{R}_k$; while the unit distance is chosen as described earlier. As for the destination point: each robot chooses the closest location among the m possible locations and ties are broken, for example, by chirality. In this way, the coordinate systems of robots belonging to the same class are rotational symmetric with respect to c and intervals $\frac{2\pi}{m}$, and the destinations form a regular m-gon with the same center that matches the one to be formed.

Notice that the algorithm described above works also for configurations and patterns with dense points, provided the robots have strong multiplicity detection. Indeed, it allows ut to form in SSYNC all patterns formable according to the strong *global* symmetricity $\sigma(\mathbb{E})$ of the initial configuration $\mathbb{E}$.

Possibility in ASYNC.   If we restrict ourselves to just plain patterns and initial configurations, and consider the weaker *local* symmetricity $\rho(\mathbb{E})$ of the initial configuration $\mathbb{E}$, then it is possible to form the patterns with symmetricity divisible by $\rho(\mathbb{E})$, even in ASYNC:

Theorem 4.20   **[72]**   *A team of oblivious robots in* ASYNC *with* Chirality, *starting from a plain configuration* $\mathbb{E}$ *with* $\rho(\mathbb{E})$ *can form any pattern* $\mathbb{P}$ *such that* $\rho(\mathbb{E})$ *divides* $\rho(\mathbb{P})$.

It is unknown whether this can be done without chirality.

4.4   CIRCLE FORMATION

A particular pattern extensively studied in literature is the *circle*: the robots, starting from arbitrary positions in the plane, have to arrange themselves in a circle (CIRCLE FORMATION problem). Notice that the formation of a circle provides a way for robots to agree on a common origin point and a common unit distance. One of the first discussions on circle formation by a group of mobile entities was by Debest [41], who introduced it as an illustration of self-stabilizing distributed problems, but did not provide an algorithm. The problem has been subsequently studied, as a preliminary step for resolution of other tasks, usually under restrictive assumptions in [21, 43, 94].

If the robots must be arranged at regular intervals on the boundary of a circle the problem is called UNIFORM CIRCLE FORMATION. This kind of formation can be usefully deployed in surveillance tasks: the robots are placed on the border of the area (or around the target) to surveil (e.g., see [76]). The related problem of *Converging To Uniform Circle* was first studied by Sugihara and Suzuki [121], and both problems have since been extensively investigated [21, 43, 44, 49, 50, 94, 117, 124].

Another related problem also investigated is the *Biangular Circle Formation* [94], whose goal is to have the robots placed on the boundary of a circle at intervals forming a biangular configuration (refer to Sections 2.9 and 3.3.2).

4.4.1   FORMING A CIRCLE

An algorithmic solution for the CIRCLE FORMATION problem that works in ASYNC without any additional restriction can be easily designed. It is sufficient that each robot computes the smallest circle *SEC* enclosing all the robots' positions (retrieved during the last *Look*), and then moves to the circumference of such a circle; clearly, if a robot is already on *SEC*, it does not move. Since *SEC* is

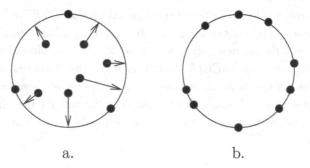

a.   b.

Figure 4.8: Example of circle formation.

defined by at least three points (on its circumference), or by two opposite points (i.e., that lie on the end points of one of its diameters), it follows that, while the robots strictly inside *SEC* move toward its circumference, *SEC* does not change; hence, in a finite number of cycles, all the robots will be on *SEC* (see Figure 4.8). The only technical problem consists in avoiding collisions while moving and not creating multiplicity points on *SEC*. Informally, this can be done as follows.

Protocol FORMCIRCLE
Assumptions: none

1. Consider the radiuses of *SEC* (i.e., rays from the center c of *SEC* to the boundary of *SEC*) which contain at least one robot; on each such ray, rank the robots according to their distance to *SEC*. Given a ray R, denote by $SEC[R]$ the point of *SEC* intersecting R (the ray where a robot r lies is denoted by $Rad(r)$).

2. A robot r inside *SEC* moves only if it is the robot on $Rad(r)$ inside *SEC* that is farthest from c:

   (a) If there is no robot at $SEC[Rad(r)]$, move there.

   (b) Otherwise, let R^+ be the first ray to the right of $Rad(r)$ (according to local compass); and let B be the ray bisecting the angle $\sphericalangle(Rad(r), c, R^+)$. Choose as destination a point p on *SEC* located between $SEC[Rad(r)]$ and $SEC[B]$, with $p \neq SEC[Rad(r)]$ and $p \neq SEC[B]$, and move there.

Theorem 4.21 *Protocol* FORMCIRCLE *solves the* CIRCLE FORMATION *problem in* ASYNC *without any additional assumption.*

Proof. Given any robot r, let A_r be the area delimited by $Rad(r)$, B, and SEC, with B as defined in Protocol FORMCIRCLE (B is not considered to be part of A_r). Note that, according to the protocol, given any ray R, only the farthest robot from c on R, say r, is allowed to move: if no robot is on $SEC[R]$, then it moves toward $SEC[R]$ (no other robots on R moves as long as r does not reach $SEC[R]$); otherwise, it moves inside A_r (no other robots on R moves as long as r does not leave R). The correctness of the Protocol FORMCIRCLE follows from the observation that the robots on SEC do not move, that any movement of r occurs always inside A_r, and that $A_r \cap A_s = \emptyset$, if $Rad(r) \neq Rad(s)$. □

4.4.2   CONVERGENCE TOWARD A UNIFORM CIRCLE IN SSYNC

An approach to *converging* toward a uniform circle in SSYNC consists of first moving all the robots on the smallest enclosing circle SEC, e.g., using Protocol FORMCIRCLE (see Section 4.4.1). Once this is achieved, the robots then use the following strategy, which requires guided trajectory:

Protocol UCIRCLECONV (for robot r)
Assumptions: SSYNC, guided trajectory

1. Consider the two direct neighbors $prev(r)$ and $next(r)$ on the boundary of SEC, and compute the midpoint p_m between them;

2. Move halfway toward p_m, remaining on SEC during the movement.

It can be shown that with procedure UCIRCLECONV, the robots converge toward a configuration wherein all robots are arranged at regular intervals on the boundary of SEC [43]. Note that, since we are in SSYNC, the assumption of *guided trajectory* (that guarantees that robots are always seen on the ring even if they do not reach their destination in that round) can be replaced by the assumption called *known fixed mobility* [43], that is, knowledge by each robot r of the guaranteed maximum distance $\hat{\delta}_r$ it travels in a move toward a further located destination (see Section 2.6). That is,

Theorem 4.22 **[43]** *In* SSYNC, *with* guided trajectory *or with* known fixed mobility, *it is possible to converge toward a uniform circle.*

Empirical evaluation of protocol UCIRCLECONV have been carried out through simulations [117]. With the additional assumption of `Chirality`, it is possible to have the robots converge toward a uniform circle with a different technique that does not separate the process of moving to SEC with that of converging toward a uniform circle [44]. However, if there is chirality, the robots can actually form (i.e., not just converge toward) the uniform circle even in ASYNC [65], as discussed in Section 4.4.6.

4.4.3   BIANGULAR CIRCLE FORMATION IN SSYNC

Before proceeding with the UNIFORM CIRCLE FORMATION problem, let us consider a less restricted version of that problem, the *biangular circle formation*: The robots must be placed on the boundary of a circle at intervals forming a biangular configuration (refer to Chapter 3). Notice that a uniform circle formation corresponds to the special *equiangular* case of the *biangular circle formation*.

The existing solution to this problem [94] requires guided trajectory; the process is divided into two main modules. In the first module, all robots are positioned to occupy distinct radiuses of *SEC*; the radius of *SEC* is used as common unit distance for the robots. A robot r can either move along its radius, or perform a *lateral* movement: in the latter case, the robot moves following the circular border of the circle centered in c and having radius $dist(c, r)$; hence guided trajectory is assumed. In particular, the first module is as follows:

MODULE I: PLACEMENT ON A CIRCLE
Assumptions: SSYNC, guided trajectory

1. If I am not on *SEC*, and I am the closest to *SEC* on the radius where I am, then move toward *SEC*.

2. If I am not the closest to c, then do not move.

3. If I am at c, then make a small movement away from c, so that after the movement I am the closest robot to c.

4. If I am the closest to c, then:

   (a) If I am at a distance greater than $1/2$ from c, move along the radius I am on at a distance $1/2$ from c.

   (b) If I am at a distance smaller than or equal to $1/2$ from c, then execute a *lateral* movement equal to $1/3$ of the angle between me and the radius closest to me where there are other robots; ties are broken according to my local clockwise orientation.

If on the radius $Rad(r)$ where r lies there is only robot r, $\forall r \in \mathcal{R}$, then, we say that the robots are on *distinct* radiuses. It is possible to show the following:

Lemma 4.23 [94] *After finite time, the robots are on distinct radiuses; hence, within finite time all robots are placed on the boundary of a circle.*

In the second module, the robots are uniformly placed on the boundary of a circle; here, it is assumed that the robots are already placed on distinct radiuses. In particular, this module first computes the *degree of symmetry* of the string of angles SA: the number of starting positions of the lexicographically minimum string, denoted by k. For instance, $k = 1$ means that the lexicographically minimum string starts only from one position in SA, and only according to one orientation (either clockwise or counterclockwise); if $k > 1$, then SA is either periodic or palindrome. Then, based on the value of k, a set of robots can be *elected*. For instance, if $k = 1$ it is possible to elect one robot: It is the robot from where the lexicographically minimum string starts. If SA is periodic, then it is possible to elect one robot for each period; if SA is palindrome, then it is possible to elect two robots for each period.

After the set of elected robots has been computed, all non-elected robots are moved toward SEC, and all elected robots are moved to a distance D from c that depends on the value k.

MODULE II: UNIFORM BIANGULAR CIRCLE
Assumptions: SSYNC, robots on distinct radiuses, guided trajectory

1. Compute the *String of Angles* SA (refer to Chapter 3).

2. Compute the *degree of symmetry* k of SA.

3. Compute the *elected* robots, based on SA and on k.

4. Let $D = 1/2 + 1/(4k)$.

   (a) If there exists a robot whose distance from c is strictly smaller than D, then move toward SEC.

   (b) If there exists a non elected robot that is not on SEC, then move toward SEC.

   (c) If I am not elected, then move toward SEC.

   (d) If there exists an elected robot that is not at distance D from c, then move at distance D from c.

   (e) Else, perform a *lateral* movement of a given angle α (see [94] for details on how α is chosen).

According to the definition of the second module, after all the elected robots are at distance D from c, they perform a lateral movement of a given angle α, chosen carefully in order to keep the robots on distinct radiuses: the consequence of these movements will be either to form the final regular circle, or to decrease the value k of symmetry. About the behavior of this module, there is the following property:

Lemma 4.24 [94] *In* SSYNC, *during the execution of* MODULE II, *the degree of symmetry never increases.*

And the following conjecture:

Conjecture 4.25 [94] In ASYNC, during the execution of MODULE II, the degree of symmetry never increases.

According to the conjecture, the behavior of the robots executing MODULE II is as follows. Let k be the degree of symmetry at the beginning. Within finite time, the k elected robots move on a circle (smaller than SEC) having radius $D = 1/2 + 1/(4k)$. Now, as soon as one of them executes a lateral move, the degree of symmetry lowers (let it $k' < k$), hence the set of elected robots changes. Therefore, MODULE II starts over again, by having the non-elected robots on SEC, and the new set of elected robots on a circle having radius $D' = 1/2 + 1/(4k') > D$. Hence, by previous claim, MODULE II can start over only a finite number of times. When $k = 1$, the final uniform bi-angular placement on SEC is achieved by a particular algorithm [94].

There are a few things still to be noted: first, any movement of the robots has to be performed in order to never change SEC. Second, if the robots always move in a synchronous way, the degree of symmetry never decreases. In this case, the procedure described for $k = 1$ would be executed independently in each period of SA, however, no details are available [94].

Third, in the case that at the beginning the robots are not on distinct radiuses, MODULE II cannot be applied directly. In this case, it is necessary to execute MODULE I first (see Lemma 4.23). The only aspect to be carefully checked is that the combination of the two models work correctly in ASYNC. In particular, the lateral movements performed in MODULE I needs to be kept distinct from the lateral movements of MODULE II: in other words, when executing MODULE II, it is crucial to avoid the situation when a robot starts executing a lateral movement while there is still a robot executing a lateral movement from MODULE I. Here, the trick is given by two factors: a lateral movement in MODULE I is performed only by the closest robots to c, and a robot can perform a lateral movement in MODULE I only if it is at a distance smaller than or equal to $1/2$ from c. This implies that, in MODULE I, when the last robot performs a lateral movement all the others can either be still or moving toward SEC. Furthermore, in MODULE II no lateral movement is executed before all robots are at least at distance $D = 1/2 + 1/(4k) > 1/2$ from c: hence, when in MODULE II a robot starts a lateral movement, the algorithm ensures that no lateral movement from MODULE I is going on.

Theorem 4.26   *In* SSYNC, *with* guided trajectory, *it is possible to move from an arbitrary configuration to a biangular configuration.*

4.4.4   FROM BIANGULAR TO UNIFORM CIRCLE

The following algorithm transforms any biangular configuration with all robots on SEC, into a uniform configuration along the circle; the solution works in ASYNC [49].

The idea of the algorithm is based on the definition of a particular kind of strings, the *swing words*. Let A be a finite set of letters; given a non-empty string (or *word*) w over A, $w = < a_0, \ldots, a_{l-1} >$, the jth *rotation* of w, denoted by $R_j(w)$, is defined by

$$R_j(w) = \begin{cases} \emptyset & \text{if } w = \emptyset \\ a_j, \ldots, a_{l-1}, a_0, \ldots a_{j-1} & \text{otherwise.} \end{cases}$$

Let $u = <a_0, a_1, \ldots, a_{l-1}> (l \geq 2)$ be a finite word over A. Denote by Λ_u the set of words $v = b_0, b_1, \ldots, b_{l-1}$, where $b_i \in \{0, 1\}$ and, for every $i \in \{0, \ldots, l-1\}$:

$$b_i = \begin{cases} 0 & \text{if } a_{i \mod l} \preceq a_{(i+1) \mod l} \\ 1 & \text{if } a_{i \mod l} \succeq a_{(i+1) \mod l}, \end{cases}$$

where $\preceq$ and $\succeq$ denote the *lexicographically smaller* and *greater* relation, respectively. Note that, if $a_{i \mod l} = a_{(i+1) \mod l}$, b_i can be either 0 or 1, giving rise to different words in Λ_u. To better understand the above definitions, consider the following example.

Example 4.27   Assume that $A = \{1, 2\} (1 \prec 2)$. Then, $\Lambda_{11} = \Lambda_{22} = \{00, 01, 10, 11\}, \Lambda_{12} = \{01\}$, $\Lambda_{112} = \{001, 101\}$, $\Lambda_{1112} = \{0001, 1001, 0101, 1101\}$, and $\Lambda_{1221} = \{0110, 0111, 0010, 0011\}$. For instance, since both $1 \succeq 1$ and $1 \preceq 1$ are true, $\Lambda_{112} = \{001, 101\}$, because both $a_0 \preceq a_1 \preceq a_2 \succeq a_0$ and $a_0 \succeq a_1 \preceq a_2 \succeq a_0$ are true.

Next, we introduce the formal definition of a *swing word*:

Definition 4.28 Swing word   A finite non-empty word $w = a_0, a_1, \ldots, a_{l-1} (l \geq 1)$ made over A is a *swing word* if and only if the following two conditions are true: (1) $w \neq a_0^l$, and (2) there exists $u \in \Lambda_w$ such that $u \in \{(01)^{l/2}, (10)^{l/2}\}$. u is called an *associate swing word* of w.

For instance, in Example 4.27 above, 1112 is a swing word, since $0101 \in \Lambda_{1112}$. Note that, even if Λ_{11} and Λ_{22} contain 01, both 11 and 22 are not swing words because they are equal to 1^2 and 2^2, respectively. The following properties on swing words hold:

Lemma 4.29 [49]   *If a word $w = a_0, a_1, \ldots, a_{l-1}, (l \geq 1)$, is a swing word, then: (i) $l = 2p$, $(p \geq 1)$; (ii) $\overline{w}$ is a swing word, with $\overline{w} = a_{l-1}, \ldots, a_1, a_0$; (iii) for every $j \in 0, \ldots, l-1$, $R_j(w)$ is a swing word; and (iv) w has a unique associate swing word.*

The above definitions and properties of swing words are applied to a specific set of strings built over the edges of the convex hull of the robots' positions. In particular, let $H(\mathcal{R})$ be the convex hull of the robots, and let us assume that all robot are on the vertexes of $H(\mathcal{R})$. First, observe the following geometric property:

Observation 4.30   It is possible to *associate* a unique regular $2k$-gon to a regular k-gon ($k \geq 3$) centered in O, by applying the following construction (refer to Figure 4.9):

1. Consider one edge of $[p_1, p_2]$ of the regular k-gon, and place two points x_1, x_2 on this edge such that $\sphericalangle(x_1, O, x_2) = \pi/2k$ and the distance between x_1 and p_1 is equal to the distance between x_2 and p_2.

2. Reiterate with the other edges of the regular k-gon.

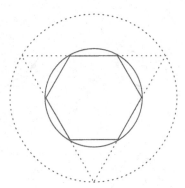

Figure 4.9: An example showing a regular $2k$-gon associated to a regular k-gon, with $k = 3$.

These adding points form a regular $2k$-gon.

Note that, given a k-gon ($k \geq 3$), its associated $2k$-gon, and their respective smallest enclosing circles $\mathcal{C}_1$ and $\mathcal{C}_2$, then $\mathcal{C}_1$ and $\mathcal{C}_2$ are concentric circles.

Let r_0 be any arbitrary robot, and $r_1, \ldots, r_{n-1}$ be the other robots, where the indices are given starting from r_0 and proceeding in clockwise order on the vertexes of $H(\mathcal{R})$. Note that the system does not necessarily have chirality; the clockwise direction is used here only for notation purposes. Let $A = \{x_0, \ldots, x_{n-1}\}$ be the alphabet formed by the length of the edges of $H(\mathcal{R})$. For each robot r_i, let us define the word $SE(r_i)$ over A (where SE stands for *string of edges*) as follows:

$$SE(r_i) = dist(r_i, r_{i+1}), \ldots, dist(r_{n-2}, r_{n-1}), dist(r_{n-1}, r_0), \ldots, dist(r_{i-1}, r_i).$$

The reverse of $SE(r_i)$ is denoted by $\overline{SE(r_i)}$. Note that, for every robot r_i, $|SE(r_i)| = |\overline{SE(r_i)}| = k$. Moreover, if the configuration is a regular n-gon, then for every robot r_i, $SE(r_i) = \overline{SE(ri)} = u^n$, where u is the common length of all the edges of $H(\mathcal{R})$. In the following, H will always refer to $H(\mathcal{R})$.

Definition 4.31   Swing convex hull   A Convex Hull H is said to be a *swing convex hull* (denoted by *Swing-CH*) if and only if there exists a robot r_i on H such that $SE(r_i)$ is a swing word.

The following lemma directly follows from Lemma 4.29:

Lemma 4.32   [49]   *If $SE(r_i)$ is a swing word, then for every r_j on H, $SE(r_j)$ and $\overline{SE(r_j)}$ are swing words. Moreover, if a H is a swing convex hull, then each robot r_i on H can determine that H is a swing convex hull by locally computing its string of edges, regardless of the local clockwise direction of r_i.*

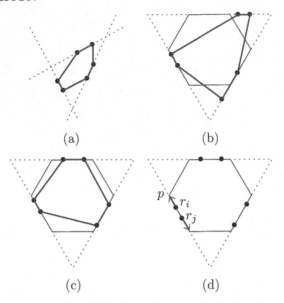

Figure 4.10: (a) A *Swing-CH* which is not perfect: *IL* is not a regular 3-gon. (b) A *Swing-CH* which is not perfect: There exist robots that are not on the edges of the regular 6-gon associated to *IL*. (c) A perfect convex hull. (d) An example describing Procedure FROM-BIANG-TO-EQUI.

Let $SE(r_0) = s_0, s_1, \ldots, s_{l-1}$ be a swing word built on a *Swing-CH* and $u = u_0, u_1, u_{l-1}$ its associate swing word. The edge $\overline{r_i r_{i+1}}$ is an *up-edge* (respectively, a *down-edge*) iff $u_i = 1$ (respectively, $u_i = 0$). From Lemma 4.29, we can easily deduce that the up-edges and down-edges are the same for all the robots on a *Swing-CH*.

Given two adjacent robots r_i and r_{i+1} on a *Swing-CH*, we say that they form a *couple* if and only if the edge, linking r_i and r_{i+1} is a down-edge. In a *Swing-CH*, we denote by *SetLines* the set of all lines passing through both robots of the same couple. Also, *IntersectionLines* (denoted by *IL*) is the set of intersection points between the line passing through r_i and r_{i+1}, and the line passing through r_{i+2} and r_{i+3}, for $i = 0, \ldots, n - 1$ (all operations are modulo n).

Definition 4.33 Perfect Convex Hull H is said to be *perfect* if the following four conditions hold:
1) $n = 2k$ and $k \geq 3$;
2) H is a *Swing-CH*;
3) *IL* is a regular k-gon; and,
4) all the robots are on the edges of the regular $2k$-gon associated to *IL*.

We say that the set of robots $\mathcal{R}$ is in perfect convex hull if $H(\mathcal{R})$ is perfect and all the robots are located at distinct positions on it (refer to Figure 4.10(a)–(c), where non-perfect and perfect convex hulls are shown). Also, two perfect convex hulls are said to be *equivalent* if they share the same regular k-gon *IL* in a system configuration.

The following observation is central in the circle formation protocol, and it is based on all the previous lemmas:

Observation 4.34 If all the robots are in a biangular configuration, and all of them are on *SEC*, then they form a perfect convex hull.

The overall idea of the protocol is then very simple: starting from a configuration where the robots are all located on *SEC* and form a biangular configuration, they compute H (which is a perfect convex hull) and *IL*; then, each pair moves toward the vertexes of *IL*.

FROM-BIANG-TO-EQUI
Assumptions: $n \geq 5$.

1. Let H be the convex hull of $\mathcal{R}$.

2. Compute *IL* (forming the $n/2$-gon).

3. Let r_j be r_i's neighbor such that (r_i, r_j) is a couple of H.

4. Let p be the position on the associated n-gon on the opposite direction of r_j on the line passing through r_i and r_j (refer to Figure 4.10(d)).

5. Move toward p.

Lemma 4.35 **[49]** *In* SSYNC, *using Protocol* FROM-BIANG-TO-EQUI, *if all the robots are in a perfect convex hull at time t_j, then at time t_{j+1}, either the configuration is an equivalent perfect convex hull, or the n-gon is formed.*

Proof. From Lemma 4.32, all the perfect convex hulls computed by the robots are equivalent. Let *Unit* denote the distance between two adjacent vertexes on the associated n-gon. Using Protocol FROM-BIANG-TO-EQUI, at time t_{j+1}, the distance between two H-adjacent robots forming a couple is lower than or equal to *Unit*, whereas the distance between two H-adjacent robots, not forming a couple, is greater than or equal to *Unit*. So, at time t_{j+1}, if for every pair of adjacent robots (r_i, r_k), the distance between (r_i, r_k) is equal to *Unit*, then the n-gon is formed. Otherwise, the up-edge and the down-edge are the same ones as at t_j, because $|down - edge| \leq Unit \leq |up - edge|$. Furthermore, each robot moves only on the edge of the associated regular n-gon without collisions. So, each robot can recompute the same *IL* and the same associated regular n-gon. □

From the previous lemma, we have the following:

Lemma 4.36 [49]   *In SSYNC, Protocol FROM-BIANG-TO-EQUI is a deterministic algorithm transforming a perfect convex hull into a regular n-gon if $n \geq 5$.*

The previous Lemma 4.35 shows that Protocol FROM-BIANG-TO-EQUI guarantees that the regular $n/2$-gon *IL* and the associated regular n-gon are preserved for every robot while they are moving toward the regular n-gon; therefore, even assuming ASYNC, the perfect convex hull computed by the robots remains equivalent for every pair of robots, while the regular n-gon is not formed. Hence,

Theorem 4.37 [49]   *In ASYNC, it is possible to move $n \geq 5$ robots from a biangular configuration to a uniform circle.*

4.4.5   UNIFORM CIRCLE FORMATION IN SSYNC

Uniform circle formation can be reached in SSYNC, relying on lemma 4.24. In fact, starting from an arbitrary configuration, exploiting the protocol presented in Section 4.4.3, the system is eventually in a biangular configuration, with all robots on *SEC*. If n is odd, then the robots form a regular n-gon and the uniform circle configuration is reached (a biangular configuration is defined only for n even). Otherwise (n is even), after executing the protocol described in Section 4.4.3, the robots form either a regular n-gon or a biangular configuration with all robots on *SEC*. At this point, algorithm FROM-BIANG-TO-EQUI from Section 4.4.4 could be used to conclude the protocol, implying that the problem is solvable for $n \geq 5$ [49]. Since there are specific solutions that work in SSYNC for $n \leq 4$ robots [51], we have:

Theorem 4.38 [49, 51]   *In SSYNC, the UNIFORM CIRCLE FORMATION problem is solvable for all n.*

4.4.6   UNIFORM CIRCLE FORMATION IN ASYNC

In ASYNC, the only provably correct technique available so far requires `Chirality` and uses guided trajectory. The technique first moves all the robots on the smallest enclosing circle *SEC* using the protocol described in Section 4.4.1. Once all the robots are on *SEC* the algorithm is very simple [65]. For robot r let r^+ be the neighboring robot on *SEC* in the clockwise direction (also called the successor); and let d be the desired final robot inter-distance on the uniform circle.

Protocol UCircleForm (for robot r)
Assumptions: chirality, guided trajectory

1. Let d^+ be the distance to r^+

2. If $d^+ > d$ move toward the point p on *SEC* at distance d from r^+, remaining on the circle *SEC* during the movement.

The difficulty is not in the protocol but in the proof of its correctness.

We now introduce some terminology needed for the proof. We say that a robot is *white* if its distance to the clockwise closest robot is greater than or equal to d. We say that a robot is *grey* if such a distance is smaller than d. Moreover, we say that a white robot is *good* if its distance to the clockwise neighbor is exactly d, it is *large* if its distance is strictly greater than d. To prove that the algorithm is correct, we must prove that, within finite time, all robots become *good*. Let a *white bubble* be a sequence of consecutive white robots delimited by grey robots. Let $W = r_i, r_{i+1}, \ldots, r_{i+m}$ be a white bubble. Robot r_{i-1} is said to be the predecessor of the bubble, robot r_{i+m+1} is the successor. Clearly, predecessors and successors of a white bubble are grey, unless the ring contains white robots only; notice that in this case all robots are good. The size of W, indicated as $|W|$, is the number of white robots composing the bubble (in this example m); its length, indicated by $l(W)$, is the length of the ring between the predecessor of the white bubble and its successor (assuming not all robots are white), i.e., $l(W) = \sum_{j=-1}^{m} d_{i+j}$. Similarly, a *grey bubble* $G = r_i, r_{i+1}, \ldots, r_{i+m}$ is a sequence of consecutive grey robots delimited by white robots. Its size $|G|$ is the number of grey robots in G; the length $l(G)$ is defined as the length of the ring between the first and the last grey robot in G (note that this definition is different from $l(W)$). It can be easily shown that:

Lemma 4.39 [65] *At each point in time, if there are grey nodes, then the number of white bubbles equals the number of grey bubbles. Moreover, there must be at least one bubble.*

Another useful property toward formation is that:

Lemma 4.40 [65] *A white robot cannot become grey.*

The following are the main lemmas on which the correctness proof is based:

Lemma 4.41 [65] *Let $W = r_i, r_{i+1}, \ldots r_{i+m}$ be a white bubble in the ring at time t. If $l(W) \geq d \cdot (|W| + 1)$, in finite time, say at time t', the size of the bubble increases.*

Proof. We prove by induction on the robots in W that, by time t', all robots in the white bubble are good, and the predecessor r_{i-1} is white (which means that the bubble has become bigger).

By definition of protocol UCircleForm, in finite time, say at time t_1, r_{i+m} becomes good placing itself at distance d to the successor of W. Let us assume that at time $t_j < t'$ all robots $r_{i+m}, r_{i+m-1} \ldots, r_{i+m-j}$ are good. Let us consider now robot $r_{i+m-j-1}$. If this robot is not already good, by definition of the algorithm and since by hypothesis the successor of W does not become white, $r_{i+m-j-1}$ will move to place itself at distance d to r_{i+m-j}, thus becoming good at time t_{j+1}.

Thus, in finite time, say at t', all robots in the bubble are good, which means that the distance between robot r_i and robot r_{i+m+1} is equal to $d \cdot m = d \cdot s(W)$. Since, by hypothesis, $l(W) \geq d \cdot (s(W) + 1)$, it follows that the distance between r_{i-1} and r_i becomes greater than or equal to d, which means that r_{i-1} has become white. $\square$

Lemma 4.42 **[65]** *Let $W_1, \ldots W_z$ be the white bubbles present in the ring at time t. At least one of these bubbles W_k is such that $l(W_k) \geq d \cdot |W_k| + 1$.*

Proof. By contradiction, let $l(W_i) < d \cdot (|W_i| + 1)$, for all W_i. The length L of the ring is the sum of the lengths of all white bubbles and all grey bubbles. That is, from Lemma 4.39, $L = \sum_{i=1}^{z} (l(W_i) + l(G_i))$. By hypothesis, $\sum_{i=1}^{z} l(W_i) < d \sum_{i=1}^{z} |W_i| + d \cdot z$. Moreover, by definition of grey bubble, $\sum_{i=1}^{z} l(G_i) < d \sum_{i=1}^{z} (|G_i| - 1) = d \sum_{i=1}^{z} |G_i| - d \cdot z$. Summing up, we have $L < d \sum_{i=1}^{z} (|G_i| + |W_i|) = d \cdot n$, a contradiction. $\square$

By Lemmas 4.41 and 4.42, we have that:

Lemma 4.43 **[65]** *The number of grey robots decreases.*

Finally, by Lemmas 4.40 and 4.43 it follows that in finite time all robots are *good*, and we can conclude:

Theorem 4.44 **[65]** *With guided trajectory and chirality, the* Uniform Circle Formation *problem is solvable in* Async.

Finally, note that, if Conjecture 4.25 holds, then the algorithm described in Section 4.4.3 would work also in Async with guided trajectory; thus, by Theorem 4.37, the combination of the two could possibly solve Uniform Circle Formation in Async with guided trajectory, and without chirality.

4.5 FORMING A SEQUENCE OF PATTERNS IN SSYNC

In this chapter we have discussed, under a variety of assumptions about the robots' capabilities and features, how to form a (possibly arbitrary) pattern given in input. A natural question is whether the robots can form not just a single pattern but a *series of distinct patterns*, given in a particular order, or, more generally of characterizing the series that can be formed. To enable a series of patterns to be formed, a protocol must guarantee that a robot that wakes up in an arbitrary configuration can, in spite of its obliviousness, figure out what pattern in the sequence is being formed to join the others in performing the required tasks. In other words, a solution must provide, through the robots' movement, some form of memory in an otherwise memoryless system.

In this section we consider oblivious robots with chirality, in Ssync under unlimited mobility (i.e., all robots always reach their destinations when performing their move). The focus is on *infinite* series: *periodic* (or cyclic) series $\mathbb{S}^{\infty} = \langle \mathbb{P}_1, \mathbb{P}_2, \ldots, \mathbb{P}_m \rangle^{\infty}$, i.e., the periodic repetition of a finite series $\mathbb{S}$ of distinct patterns. The results are then generalizable to infinite *aperiodic* series. Three different scenarios are analyzed, depending on the level of anonymity of the robots: completely anonymous robots, a visibly indistinguishable but ordered set of robots, and distinctly labeled robots.

Before describing the three scenarios, we introduce some special patterns needed in the rest of the section: 1) POINT is the pattern consisting of a single point; 2) TWO-POINTS is the pattern consisting of exactly two points; 3) POLYGON(k), for any $k \geq 3$, is the pattern consisting of points $p_1, p_2, \ldots, p_k$ that are vertexes of a regular convex polygon of k sides.

4.5.1 ANONYMOUS ROBOTS

Consider n identical robots starting from distinct locations. Central to the anonymous case is the notion of symmetry in a configuration, which is quantified using the concept of *centered view*, and *centered symmetricity*, $\hat{\rho}$, a slight modification of the notion of local view and of symmetricity ρ discussed in Section 4.3.

If r_i is not located at the center of the smallest enclosing circle, its centered view $CV_i(t)$ contains the coordinates of all the other robots considering as origin $(0, 0)$ its own position and as $(1,0)$ the position of the center. On the other hand, if r_i is in the center of the smallest enclosing circle, the origin is still the location of r, but any robot r_j whose view $CV_j(t)$ is minimum among all the other robots is thought to be at coordinate $(1, 0)$. Finally, no information about the coordinate system of the robots is available in these views because they are assumed unknown and not necessarily consistent.

Notice that, given any arbitrary configuration $\mathbb{E}$, there is a total order of the distinct centered views of the robots in $\mathbb{E}$, in spite of their anonymity. The elements of CV_i can be ordered lexicographically to obtain an ordered sequence $Q(CV_i)$, for each robot $r_i \in \mathbb{E}$. For any two robots r_i and r_j, the ordered sequences $Q(CV_i)$ and $Q(CV_j)$ contain the same number of elements and these sequences can be ordered lexicographically. So, $CV_i < CV_j$ if and only if $Q(CV_i)$ is lexicographically smaller than $Q(CV_j)$.

An obvious consequence of anonymity is that from a configuration $\mathbb{E}$ consisting of anonymous robots at w distinct locations, a configuration $\mathbb{E}'$ where the robots occupy more than w distinct locations might not be reachable, which restricts the size of patterns in any formable series of patterns. To form repetitively any series $\mathbb{S}$ of patterns, all the patterns in $\mathbb{S}$ should be of the same size. Thus, only patterns of size n are considered, where n is the number of robots. Each robot starts from a distinct location and during the pattern formation algorithm, no two robots should occupy the same location (i.e., no dense points are allowed). Moreover, those patterns are indeed formable.

The formation algorithm is based on the identification of special configurations: the *bi-circular* and the *q-symmetric-circular* configurations. Before giving an intuition of the technique employed, we define these special configurations (see Figure 4.11 for an example of a bi-circular configuration).

Definition 4.45 BCC   A configuration is called *bi-circular* (denoted by BCC) if: (i) there is a unique location (called the *pivot*), such that the smallest enclosing circle *SEC* containing all the robots has a diameter more than three times the diameter of the circle C containing all robots except those at the pivot; (ii) *SEC* and C intersect at exactly one point: the point directly opposite the pivot (called the *base point*).

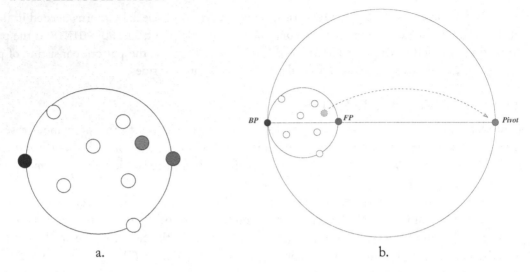

Figure 4.11: (a) An arbitrary configuration of robots and the smallest enclosing circle. (b) A bi-circular configuration.

Definition 4.46 SCC   A configuration containing n robots is called q-*symmetric-circular* or, SCC(q), $1 < q < n$, if: (i) the smallest enclosing circle *SEC* has exactly q points on its circumference that are occupied by robots; (ii) all the other robots lie on or in the interior of a smaller circle $\mathcal{C}$ that is concentric to *SEC* such that $Diameter(SEC) \geq (5 + \sin^{-1}(\pi/q)) \cdot Diameter(\mathcal{C})$; ($iii$) there are no robots in the center of *SEC*.

In both configurations, the former circle (*SEC*) is called the *primary enclosure* while the latter ($\mathcal{C}$) is called the *secondary enclosure*. The point on the secondary enclosure directly opposite the base-point is called the *frontier-point*. The ratio of the diameter of the primary enclosure over the diameter of the secondary enclosure is called the *stretch* of the configuration.

An interesting property of the bi-circular configuration is that in such a configuration the robots can agree on a coordinate system and define a unique way to order the robots. It can also be shown that from an arbitrary initial configuration either a particular type of BCC configuration or a particular type of SCC(q) configuration can always be formed. More precisely:

Lemma 4.47   [39]   *Starting from any configuration* $\mathbb{E}$ *with symmetricity* $\hat{\rho}(\mathbb{E}) = q$, *and for any* $k \geq (5 + \sin^{-1}(\pi/q))$ *we can reach a configuration* $\mathbb{E}'$ *such that either (i)* $\mathbb{E}'$ *is SCC(q') having stretch k, where $q' > 1$ is a factor of q, or, (ii)* $\mathbb{E}'$ *is BCC having stretch $k' = (k + 1)/2$.*

It can also be shown that, once a bi-circular configuration containing n robots is formed, any pattern $\mathbb{P}$ of size n can be formed.

Lemma 4.48 **[39]** *(i) In any bi-circular configuration, the robots can agree on a unique coordinate system. (ii) Starting from a bi-circular configuration with $n \geq 4$ robots in distinct locations, any pattern $\mathbb{P}$ of size n can be formed.*

Similarly, it can be shown that:

Lemma 4.49 **[39]** *Starting from a configuration of type SCC(q), $q > 1$, with n robots occupying distinct locations, any pattern $\mathbb{P}$ such that the symmetricity $\hat{\rho}(\mathbb{P}) = q \cdot a, a \geq 1$ and size($\mathbb{P}$)$= n$ can be formed.*

Based on the above properties, the idea of the algorithm for forming a cyclic series of distinct patterns $\langle \mathbb{P}_1, \mathbb{P}_2, \dots, \mathbb{P}_m \rangle^{\infty}$ by n anonymous robots is the following.

Let F be a function that maps each pattern $\mathbb{P}_i$ to a real number $t_i = F(\mathbb{P}_i)$ that satisfies the condition of Lemma 4.49. To signal the formation of pattern $\mathbb{P}_i$, one of the following configurations is unambiguously used: either SCC(x) with stretch k_i, where x is any factor of q or, configuration BCC with stretch $k_i' = (k_i + 1)/2$. Due to Lemma 4.47 it is possible to form one of these configurations starting from an arbitrary configuration of symmetricity q. By computing the stretch of the configuration, the robot can then identify which pattern $\mathbb{P}_i$ is being formed. The robots can then form, by Lemmas 4.48 and 4.49, pattern $\mathbb{P}_i$. During the formation of pattern $\mathbb{P}_i$, at each intermediate configuration, each robot can uniquely identify which pattern is being formed. Once the pattern has been completed the resulting configuration has symmetricity q. Hence, by Lemma 4.47, it is again possible to form a SCC or BCC configuration having the appropriate stretch for the next pattern $\mathbb{P}_{i+1}$ in the sequence. Using this technique, the robots can move from one pattern to the next, and thus they can form the required sequence of patterns.

Theorem 4.50 **[39]** *In SSYNC with unlimited mobility and chirality, n anonymous robots starting from distinct locations in an arbitrary configuration $\mathbb{E}$, can form a cyclic series of distinct patterns $\langle \mathbb{P}_1, \mathbb{P}_2, \dots, \mathbb{P}_m \rangle$, each of size n, if and only if $\hat{\rho}(\mathbb{P}_i) = \hat{\rho}(\mathbb{P}_j) \geq \hat{\rho}(\mathbb{E}) \; \forall i, j \in \{1, 2, \dots m\}$.*

4.5.2   ROBOTS WITH DISTINCT VISIBLE IDENTITIES

Let us consider now the case when each robot r_i has a unique identity ID_i (w.l.g, $ID_i = i$) and any other robot can see this identity. During the *Look* operation, a robot r_i obtains a snapshot containing (j, x_j, y_j) tuples where $j \neq i$ and (x_j, y_j) is the location of the j-th robot, with respect to the local coordinate system of robot r_i. In this case, even in absence of agreement on directions, the symmetry among the robots can be broken by the use of distinct labels. The view of each robot is unique as it contains information about both the identities and locations of the other robots. Thus, there are no symmetric configurations. Moreover, as opposed to the anonymous case, robots can be allowed to form dense points, since the robots can be separated later, if required.

When there is only one robot, the only pattern that can be formed is obviously POINT. With $n = 2$ robots, only two patterns can be formed: POINT and TWO-POINTS and it is easy to form the sequence (POINT, TWO-POINTS)$^\infty$, by movement of a single robot (say r_2). The more interesting cases occur when there are at least three robots (i.e., $n \geq 3$); in this case any sequence of distinct patterns $\mathbb{S} = \langle \mathbb{P}_1, \mathbb{P}_2, \ldots \mathbb{P}_m \rangle$ can be formed, with the only restriction that each pattern $\mathbb{P}_i$ has at most n points. A description of the algorithm is given below.

Robots r_1, r_2, and r_n have special roles. In particular, r_1 and r_2 remain fixed in distinct locations for the entire algorithms serving as fixed points of reference for the other robots. The idea is to apply a known function F to each pattern $\mathbb{P}_j$ so to obtain a real number $w_j = F(\mathbb{P}_j)$, $w_j \in (1, \infty)$ (distinct for every pattern). Before forming pattern $\mathbb{P}_j$, robot r_k moves to a location between r_1 and r_2 such that the ratio of distances $dist(r_1, r_2)/dist(r_1, r_n)$ is equal to w_j. This is the signal for the other robots to indicate which pattern is being formed. Each robot r_i, $2 < i < n$ can compute the location where it should move to in order to form pattern $\mathbb{P}_j$. Once each of these robots has moved into the correct positions, robot r_n moves to complete the pattern. During the execution of the algorithm every configuration of the robots (excluding at most the first two configurations) either corresponds to some pattern $\mathbb{P}_l \in \mathbb{S}$, or is an intermediate configuration which signals the formation of $\mathbb{P}_l$ (i.e., where r_1, r_2, and r_n maintain a ratio of $w_j = F(\mathbb{P}_l)$. The function F must be chosen in such a way that the ratio $dist(r_1, r_2)/dist(r_1, r_n)$ in an actual pattern never matches any values in the range of F. Thus, each robot can unambiguously determine the location that it needs to move to, by looking at the current configuration.

This algorithm works for any sequence of patterns not containing the POINT pattern. In order to include the POINT pattern in the sequence of patterns formed, small modifications must be done to the algorithm in the behavior of robots r_2 and r_n. Based on the algorithm above, the authors conclude that:

Theorem 4.51 [39]   *In* SSYNC *with* unlimited mobility *and* chirality, $n \geq 2$ *robots having distinct visible identities can form any cyclic sequence of distinct patterns* $\langle \mathbb{P}_1, \mathbb{P}_2, \ldots, \mathbb{P}_m \rangle$ *provided that* $\forall i$, *size*$(\mathbb{P}_i) = n_i \leq n$.

4.5.3   ROBOTS WITH INVISIBLE DISTINCT IDENTITIES

In this case the identities of the robots are not visible to other robots. The robots are assumed to be ordered with labels $1, 2, 3, \ldots, n$ and each robot r_i knows its own label i, but it cannot visibly identify the label of other robots. In this case, the information contained in the views of the robots is similar to the anonymous case. Thus, two robots may have identical views (in particular, robots at the same location have identical views). However, since the robots have distinct identities, they can execute different algorithms depending on their own labels.

Consider first the case when there are at least four robots. The BCC configuration, defined for the anonymous case, is used here as well to signal the formation of specific patterns in a series. As already mentioned, dense points are allowed and the algorithm must ensure that there is at least one robot at the pivot and one at the base-point of the bi-circular configuration.

From any arbitrary configuration $\mathbb{E}$ with more than 3 robots, a bi-circular configuration of any given stretch $k > 3$, can be formed by the movement of a single robot (this single robot will place itself in a pivot position).

The technique for forming any given pattern $\mathbb{P}$ starting from a bi-circular configuration of stretch k_i is as follows: As mentioned before, the bi-circular configuration can be formed by robot r_n jumping to the pivot location. Once the robots are in bi-circular configuration BCC with stretch k_i, robot r_1 and robot r_{n-1} occupy the base-point and the frontier-point. These three robots remain in their location while the other robots move to the required positions for forming pattern $\mathbb{P}$. The positions are assigned in the following manner. The points in the pattern $\mathbb{P}$ are mapped to locations in the bi-circular configuration such that the smallest enclosing circle of pattern $\mathbb{P}$ coincides with the secondary enclosure of the configuration and the base-point coincides with the lexicographically smallest point p_i on the smallest enclosing circle of $\mathbb{P}$, i.e., $p_i \in SEC(\mathbb{P})$ and $p_i \leq p_j$, for any $p_j \in SEC(\mathbb{P})$. Notice that this mapping is unique. Let $\Gamma(\mathbb{P})$ be the unique mapping obtained by each robot (i.e., the locations that correspond to points in the pattern $\mathbb{P}$). The elements of $\Gamma(\mathbb{P})$ are sorted in such a way that the first point is the base-point of the current BCC configuration of the robots, and all points which lie on the secondary enclosure $\mathcal{C}$ precede those that are located in the interior of $\mathcal{C}$. For $1 \leq i \leq size(\mathbb{P}_i)$ robot r_i is assigned the ith location in $\Gamma(\mathbb{P})$ and for $size(\mathbb{P}_i) < j \leq n$ robot r_j is assigned the n-th location in $\Gamma(\mathbb{P})$.

During the formation of a pattern $\mathbb{P}_i$ of size $size(\mathbb{P}_i)$, the algorithm ensures that the BCC configuration is maintained by keeping robots r_1, r_{n-1}, and r_n stationary at the base-point, at the frontier-point, and at the pivot positions respectively. Only when all the other robots have moved to their assigned location, robot r_{n-1} moves to its own assigned location, and this is also done ensuring that BCC is preserved with the appropriate stretch so that robot r_n can unambiguously move to the required position to complete the pattern.

The remaining cases are when there are exactly two or three robots. For $n = 2$, the case of invisible identities is the same as that of visible identities. The case of $n = 3$ has been studied in [13], and an algorithm for forming any sequence of patterns of at most three points has been given. As mentioned before, the transformations between any two patterns of size 3 is straightforward and requires the movement of a single robot (say r_3). The only challenging scenario involves the formation of POINT and TWO-POINTS, where the intermediate configurations before and after forming POINT must be distinguished from the configuration forming TWO-POINTS. In conclusion:

Theorem 4.52 [39] *In* SSYNC *with unlimited mobility and chirality, n robots having distinct invisible identities can form any cyclic sequence of distinct patterns $\langle \mathbb{P}_1, \mathbb{P}_2, \ldots, \mathbb{P}_m \rangle$ where $\forall i$, size($\mathbb{P}_i$) $\leq n$.*

CHAPTER 5

Scatterings and Coverings

In this chapter we consider *Scattering* problems where the goal is to have the robots occupy the space each in a distinct position, satisfying certain criteria, starting from arbitrary configurations possibly containing dense points. In the simplest problem of this class, the robots are simply required to *break the multiplicities* and to terminate in a plain configuration (i.e., one that does not contain any dense points). The more advanced scattering problems refer to robots, randomly dispersed in a *bounded* region of space, that must then scatter themselves throughout the region so to "cover" it satisfying some optimization criteria. For example, *uniform covering* of a region requires an "equi-distribution" of the robots in the region (i.e., an equi-partitioning of the region, with a robot assigned to each partition); *maximum coverage* with a given "sensing range" s, requires the robots to scatter so to maximize the part of the region covered by the circles of radius s centered in the robots' locations; etc. These *covering* (or *self-deployment*) problems are important in many applications, and come in many flavors; the majority of the studies use robots provided with memory, explicit communication devices, global localization capabilities (e.g., GPS), etc. In this chapter, we discuss what is known in the case of scattering of oblivious and finite-state robots; agreement on the coordinate systems and unit of distance is sometimes required.

5.1   REMOVING DENSE POINTS

In most of the problems discussed in the previous chapters, one of the assumptions that the initial configuration has to satisfy is that the robots occupy distinct positions (e.g., the plain configuration for the GATHERING problem); in other words, the robots need to be scattered in the plane in an arbitrary plain configuration. Actually, the problem of deploying the robots in the area where they operate on distinct positions is interesting on its own, and is known as the SPLIT problem.

The SPLIT problem is to design a protocol for n mobile autonomous robots so that, if two robots are in distinct positions at some time, they will stay in distinct positions thereafter and, from an arbitrary initial configuration of the robots, the system converges toward a plain configuration.

It is clear that no deterministic algorithm can solve the SPLIT problem. In fact, if initially all the robots are located at the same position, and they all have the same orientation and direction of the local coordinate axes, they all clearly have the same view of the world. If they would execute a deterministic protocol $\mathcal{A}$ according to a synchronous schedule, they would continue being on the same location. Therefore,

Lemma 5.1 *There exists no deterministic algorithm that solves the* SPLIT *problem in* FSYNC *(and thus in* SSYNC *and* ASYNC*).*

As a consequence, any solution must be probabilistic. Two such algorithms are described below, in the unlimited and in the limited visibility settings. Both algorithms are based on the well-known concept of Voronoi diagram.

5.1.1 REMOVING DENSE POINTS: UNLIMITED VISIBILITY

A probabilistic algorithm that solves SPLIT in SSYNC, in the unlimited visibility setting, is described below (for robot r) [52].

Algorithm PROBSPLIT
Assumptions: SSYNC, probabilistic

- Compute the Voronoi Diagram of set of points occupied by the robots.

- Choose randomly a value over $\{0, 1\}$: 0 with a probability 3/4 and 1 with a probability 1/4.

- If the randomly chosen value is 0, then move toward any point inside my Voronoi cell.

Both closure and convergence properties hold for the above algorithm, as stated by the following:

Lemma 5.2 [52] *For any two robots in distinct positions, by executing the* PROBSPLIT *protocol the robots remain at distinct positions thereafter; also, for every pair of robots r and s in the same position at time t_j $(r(t_j) = s(t_j))$, we have that $\lim_{k \to \infty} Pr[r(t_{j+k}) \neq s(t_{j+k})] = 1$.*

Without assuming multiplicity detection, the above protocol never terminates, and the robots never stop moving inside their Voronoi cells, even if no two robots are located at the same position. In order to have a terminating protocol, the robots need to be equipped with multiplicity detection; in this case, the robots stop if there exists no position with more than one robot. Thus,

Theorem 5.3 [52] *In the unlimited visibility setting there exists a perpetual probabilistic algorithm that solves* SPLIT *in* SSYNC *with probability 1; there exists a terminating probabilistic algorithm in the same setting if the robots have* multiplicity detection.

Note that, with multiplicity detection, the output of the PROBSPLIT protocol provides a valid initial configuration for any protocol that in SSYNC needs to start in a plain configuration, such as the SSYNC protocols to solve to the ARBITRARY PATTERN FORMATION and the GATHERING problem.

5.1.2   REMOVING DENSE POINTS: LIMITED VISIBILITY

The SPLIT problem can be solved probabilistically in SSYNC also under limited visibility [87]. The probabilistic algorithm that we describe below solves the problem by preserving the connectivity of the initial visibility graph, assuming that the robots have *multiplicity detection* (a robot can detect whether a point is occupied by one or more robots but cannot know the exact number).

The overall idea of the protocol (Algorithm PROBSPLIT -LIMITED) is as follows. A robot is said to be *blocked* if it cannot move without breaking some of the edges of the visibility graph. For instance, a robot that can see two robots collinear with itself, both on the border of its visibility range (i.e., at distance V) is clearly blocked. So, any blocked robot cannot move.

At the beginning the configuration is clearly assumed to be not already scattered; so, there exists at least one non-blocked robot. The protocol has two main rules: (i) The non-blocked robots move in a way that at least one blocked robot becomes non-blocked; thus, repeating this process, all robots will eventually become non-blocked; (ii) If a group of robots that occupy the same location (i.e., these robots needs to be scattered) is non-blocked, it is divided into single ones in a probabilistic way, thus achieving the scattering.

To analyze the time-complexity of the protocol, let a round be the shortest fragment of an execution in which each robot in the system executes at least once its cycle. Then we have:

Theorem 5.4   [87]   *Algorithm* PROBSPLIT -LIMITED *solves the connectivity-preserving* SPLIT *problem within* $O(min\{n, D^2 + \log n\})$ *expected rounds, where D is the diameter of the initial visibility graph.*

We finally have:

Theorem 5.5   [87]   *There exists a probabilistic algorithm that solves* SPLIT *in* SSYNC *with limited visibility and* multiplicity detection.

5.2   UNIFORM COVERING OF THE LINE

In this section we consider the uniform covering of a very special space: a *line* $\mathcal{L}$, on which the robots are initially located at random distinct points. The goal is for the robots to self-deploy evenly in the segment of the line delimited by the positions of the two extreme robots (that, alternatively, could represent some perimeter marks rather than robots) [19, 30, 106].

If the robots have unlimited *unobstructed* visibility, uniform covering of the line is very simple to reach.

Algorithm PROBSPLIT -LIMITED
Assumptions: SSYNC, multiplicity detection

Let r be any non-blocked robot, and let RAND be any random oracle that generates a random bit. Also, let $\mathcal{R}(r)$ be the set of robots in the visibility range of r.

1. If no robot in $\mathcal{R}(r)$ is on the boundary of the visibility range of r, then r computes its maximum travel distance d. This distance is bounded by two factors: (i) the minimum distance between the boundary of r's visibility range and the robots in $\mathcal{R}(r)$; and (ii) the distance between r and its closest neighbor. In other words, the value of d is the *safety margin* for preserving connectivity and avoiding collisions: r chooses as destination a point at distance $d/3$ from its current position, along an arbitrary chosen vector; let p be this destination point.

2. If some robot in $\mathcal{R}(r)$ is on the boundary of the visibility range of r, then let $\mathcal{R}'(r)$ be the robots that are on this boundary, and let arc be the minimal arc on the visibility boundary that contains all robots in $\mathcal{R}'(r)$. Also, let w be the chord of arc; l be the half-line bisecting the center angle of arc; and q be the intersection between l and w. Then, the direction of movement of r is given by $\overline{rq}$, and the length of its movement is given by distance d computed as in the previous case; let p be this destination point.

3. If there are robots in my visibility range, or the position where I am is dense:

   (a) If RAND $= 1$ then move toward point p' on $\overline{rp}$ at distance $1/4$ from my current position;

   (b) Else, move toward point p' on $\overline{rp}$ at distance $1/2$ from my current position.

Less simple is to achieve that goal if visibility, although unlimited, is *obstructed*: In each direction, a robot r sees the closest robot s (if it exists), regardless of its distance, but r's visibility of any other robot in that direction is blocked by s. The robots visible from r are usually called its *neighbors*; for this reason, when the universe is a line, unlimited obstructed visibility is also called *neighbor visibility*. The following is a remarkably simple uniform covering algorithm [30].

Protocol CORRIDORSPREAD (for robot s_i)
Assumptions: SSYNC, neighbor visibility

  • If no other robot is seen on the left or on the right, then do nothing.

  • Otherwise, move to point $x = \frac{1}{2}(s_{i+1} + s_{i-1})$, where s_{i+1} and s_{i-1} denote the two neighbors of s_i.

Let us show the idea of the convergence proof in the FSYNC model. Let $s_0, \ldots, s_{n-1}$ be the robots, and let us assume them to be arranged from left to right on the line: clearly, the robots have no knowledge of the identifiers, that here are used only for presentation purposes. Note that, since the robots operate in one dimension, any coordinate system will give the same resulting destination. Therefore, in order to analyze the protocol, an external global coordinate system is used, of which the robots clearly have no knowledge. In the following, the coordinate system where $s_0(t) = 0$ and $s_{n-1}(t) = 1$ is chosen as the global coordinate system. The goal is to spread the robots uniformly; that is, at the end, robot s_i should occupy position $\frac{i}{n-1}$. Let $\mu_i[t]$ be the *shift* of the s_i's location at time t from its final position. According to the protocol, the position of robot s_i changes from $s_i(t)$ to

$$s_i(t+1) = \tfrac{1}{2}\left(s_{i-1}(t) + s_{i+1}(t)\right).$$

for $2 \leq i \leq n-1$, while robots s_1 and s_n never move. Therefore, the shifts change with time as

$$\mu_i[t+1] = \tfrac{1}{2}\left(\mu_{i+1}[t] + \mu_{i-1}[t]\right).$$

Consider the following *progress* measure:

$$\psi[t] = \Sigma_{i=1}^{i=n}\, \mu^2[t].$$

It can be shown that $\psi[t]$ is a decreasing function of t, unless the robots are already equally spread. Finally,

Theorem 5.6 [30] *In the* FSYNC *model, every $O(n^2)$ cycles, $\psi[t]$ is at least halved; furthermore, the robots converge to equidistant positions.*

The idea of the convergence proof in SSYNC is similar; in fact, first a non-decreasing quantity is defined, and its monotonicity proven. Then, by relating this quantity to the non-constant terms of the cosine series, it is proven that it decreases by a constant factor on every round, proving convergence.

Theorem 5.7 [30] *With* neighbor visibility, *convergence toward a uniform covering of the line is achievable in* SSYNC.

5.3 UNIFORM COVERING OF THE RING

Another important class of spatial regions is represented by *circular borders* or *circular rims*. Covering in these spaces should occur for example when the robots have to surround a dangerous area and can only move along its outer perimeter. This situation is modeled by describing the space as a *ring C*. Starting from an initial arbitrary placement on the ring, the robots must, within finite time, position themselves along the ring at (approximately) equal distance; see Figure 5.1.

The covering of a ring is related to the problem of UNIFORM CIRCLE FORMATION (discussed in Section 1.1), in which the robots are required to uniformly place themselves on the circumference of a circle not determined in advance (i.e., the entities do not know the location of the circle to

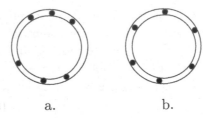

a.   b.

Figure 5.1: Starting from an initial arbitrary placement (a), the robots must move to a uniform cover of the ring (b).

form). The main difference between the uniform circle formation and the uniform covering of the ring is that in uniform circle formation the entities can freely move on the two-dimensional plane in which they have to form the circle; in contrast, here the robots can move only *on* the ring, which is the entire environment.

5.3.1   DEFINITIONS

Let $\mathcal{R} = \{s_1, \ldots, s_n\}$ be the n robots initially arbitrarily placed on the ring $\mathcal{C}$ (see Figure 5.1). Initially no two robots are placed at the same location; the algorithms should avoid *collisions*, i.e., having two robots simultaneously occupying the same point; without loss of generality, let s_i be the robot immediately before s_{i+1} in the clockwise direction, with s_n preceding s_1. Let $d_i(t)$ be the distance between robot s_i and robot s_{i+1} at time t; when no ambiguity arises, we will omit the time and simply indicate the distance as d_i. Let $d = L/n$, where L denotes the length of the ring $\mathcal{C}$. The robots have reached an *exact* covering at time t if $d_i(t) = d$ for all $1 \leq i \leq n$. Given $\epsilon > 0$, the robots have reached an ϵ-*approximate* covering at time t if $d - \epsilon \leq d_i(t) \leq d + \epsilon$ for all $1 \leq i \leq n$.

An algorithm $\mathcal{A}$ correctly solves the *exact* (resp. ϵ-*approximate*) covering problem if, in any execution of $\mathcal{A}$ by the robots in $\mathcal{C}$, regardless of their initial position in $\mathcal{C}$, there exists a time t' such that the robots have reached an *exact* (resp. ϵ-*approximate*) covering at time t' and are in a quiescent state.

5.3.2   IMPOSSIBILITY WITHOUT CHIRALITY

There is a strong negative result for the SSYNC (and thus for the ASYNC) model. In fact, *exact* self-deployment is actually *impossible* if the robots do not share a *common orientation* of the ring (i.e., there is no chirality); notice that this is much less a requirement than having global coordinates or sharing a common coordinate system [65]. This impossibility result holds even if the robots have unlimited memory of the past computations and actions (i.e., unlimited persistent memory), and their visibility radius is unlimited.

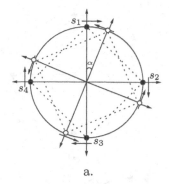
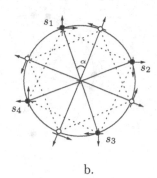

a.   b.

Figure 5.2: (a) An example of starting configuration for the proof of Theorem 5.8. The black robots are in S_1, while the white ones are in S_2. (b) Theorem 5.8: the adversary moves only robots in S_1.

Theorem 5.8   *Let the robots be on a ring C. In absence of common orientation of C, there is no deterministic exact covering algorithm even if the robots have unbounded persistent memory, their visibility radius is unlimited, and the scheduling is* SSYNC.

To see why this is the case, consider the following setting. Let n be even; partition the robots in two sets, $S_1 = \{s_1, \ldots, s_{n/2}\}$ and $S_2 = S \setminus S_1$, and place the robots of S_1 and S_2 on the vertexes of two regular $(n/2)$-gons on *Circle*, rotated of an angle $\alpha < 360°/n$. Furthermore, all robots have their local coordinate axes rotated so that they all have the same view of the world (refer to Figure 5.2(a) for an example). In other words, the robots in S_1 share the same orientation, while those in S_2 share the opposite orientation of C. Denote a configuration with such properties by $Y(\alpha)$. A key property of $Y(\alpha)$ is the following.

Property 5.9   Let the system be in a configuration $Y(\alpha)$ at time step t_i.

1. If activating only the robots in S_1, *no* exact self-deployment on C is reached at time step t_{i+1}, then also activating only the ones in S_2 *no* exact self-deployment on C would be reached at time step t_{i+1}; furthermore, in either case the system would be in a configuration $Y(\alpha')$ for some $\alpha' < 360°/n$

2. If activating only the robots in S_1 an exact self-deployment on C is reached at time step t_{i+1}, then also activating only the robots in S_2 an exact self-deployment on C would be reached at time step t_{i+1}.

3. If activating only the robots in S_1 an exact self-deployment on C is reached at time step t_{i+1}, then if activating both sets no exact self deployment on C would be reached at time step t_{i+1}, and the system would be in a configuration $Y(\alpha')$ for some $\alpha' < 360°/n$.

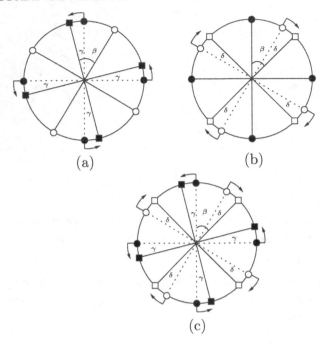

Figure 5.3: Theorem 5.8. (a) If only the robots in S_1 are activated at t, all robots would be uniformly placed at time $t + 1$, with $\beta + \gamma = 45°$. (b) If only the robots in S_2 are activated at t, all robots would be uniformly placed at time $t + 1$, with $\beta + \gamma = 45°$. (c) Therefore, if all robots would be activated at t, they would not be in an exact self-deployment on $\mathcal{C}$, having $\gamma + \beta + \delta \neq 2\pi/n = 45°$. In all figures, the squares represent the destination of the active robots.

Using this property, it is easy to design an adversary that will force any self-deployment $\mathcal{A}$ to never succeed in solving the problem: the adversary will choose $Y(\alpha)$ as the initial configuration, and behave as follows:

(Step a) If activating only the robots in S_1 no exact self-deployment on $\mathcal{C}$ is reached: then activate all robots in S_1, while all robots in S_2 are inactive; otherwise, activate all robots. Go to (b).

(Step b) If activating only the robots in S_2 no exact self-deployment on $\mathcal{C}$ is reached: then activate all robots in S_2, while all robots in S_1 are inactive; otherwise, activate all robots. Go to (a).

By Property 5.9, if the configuration at time $t_i \geq t_0$ is $Y(\alpha)$ for some $\alpha < 360°/n$, then, regardless of whether the adversary executes step (a) or (b), the resulting configuration is $Y(\alpha')$ for some $\alpha' < 360°/n$, and hence *no* exact self-deployment on $\mathcal{C}$ is reached at time step t_{i+1}. Hence, there exists an infinite execution of $\mathcal{A}$ in which no exact self-deployment will ever be reached. The alternating between steps (a) and (b) by the adversary ensures the feasibility of this execution: every robot will in fact become active infinitely often.

5.3.3   UNIFORM COVERING WITH LIMITED VISIBILITY

Since the impossibility result of Theorem 5.8 holds in absence of common orientation of the ring, to solve the exact covering of a ring, the ring must be oriented (i.e., there must be Chirality).

Let d indicate the distance that the robots must have in their final configuration (i.e., $d = \frac{size}{n}$, where $size$ is the size of the wrong, and n the number of robots).

Interestingly, the same technique described in Section 4.4.6 for uniform circle formation once the robots are on SEC, can produce an exact covering of the ring if the robots know the desired final inter-distance d between any two robots (alternatively, they have to know the size of the ring and the number of robots). Moreover, even though the protocol of Section 4.4.6 for uniform circle formation assumed unlimited visibility, it can be executed for covering of the ring by robots with limited visibility, provided that the visibility radius V is greater than $2d$. For completeness we describe the protocol in this context.

Protocol RingCoveringExact
Assumptions: chirality, knowledge of d, $V > 2d$

1. Let d^+ be the distance to the next robot s^+ (if no robot is visible clockwise, $d^+ = 2d$).

2. If $d^+ > d$ move toward the point p at distance d from s^+ (if visible, otherwise at distance d from current location).

Theorem 5.10   [65]   *With limited visibility and $V > 2d$, the exact covering of the ring problem is solvable in* ASYNC, *with* Chirality *and knowledge of the final inter-distance.*

5.3.4   CONVERGENCE TO UNIFORM COVERING

Consider now the case with chirality but with no knowledge of the final inter-distance d. An ϵ-approximate covering is still possible for any $\epsilon > 0$ assuming that the visibility radius V is greater than $2d$.

The algorithm is very simple: the robots asynchronously and independently *Look* in both directions at distance V (the visibility radius), then they position themselves in the middle between the closest observed robots (if any) [65].

Algorithm RINGCOVERINGCONVER
Assumptions: Chirality, $V > 2d$

- Let d_i be the distance to next robot, d_{i-1} the distance to the previous (if no robot is visible clockwise, $d_i = V$, analogously for counterclockwise).

- If $d_i \leq d_{i-1}$ do not move.

- If $d_i > d_{i-1}$ move to $\frac{d_i + d_{i-1}}{2} - d_{i-1}$ clockwise.

This algorithm converges to a uniform deployment. The crucial property is that:

Lemma 5.11 **[65]** *For any $\epsilon > 0$ there exists a time t, such that $\forall t' > t, \forall i: |d_i(t') - d| \leq \epsilon$.*

Hence, by adding to the protocol a test on whether both d_i and d_{i-1} are within ϵ from d (in which case no move is performed by s_i), it follows that ϵ-*approximate* self-deployment is possible even if the scheduling is ASYNC, if the robots share a common orientation of the ring C and the visibility radius is greater than $2d$.

Theorem 5.12 **[65]** *With limited visibility and $V > 2d$, the convergence toward a covering of the ring with* Chirality *is achievable in* ASYNC.

5.4   FILLING OF ORTHOGONAL SPACES

In the traditional covering problem it is assumed that the robots are already in the space, in arbitrary positions, and must then scatter themselves throughout the region to "cover" it, satisfying some optimization criteria.

The FILLING problem has the same overall goal as the other covering problems: the entire region must be "covered" by robots. However, the robots are not yet in the region; instead, they enter the space, one by one, from a point called *door*. When a robot enters the region, it must disperse itself in the space. This process continues until the entire region is covered.

In this section we consider the filling problem when the space is a simple *orthogonal* region of space; i.e., a polygonal region, without holes, with sides either parallel or perpendicular to one another (e.g., see Figure 5.4(a)).

The robots enter from a single door, have ConsistentCompass, and agree on the unit of distance. Because of this, we can superimpose on the space a logical *orthogonal grid* of the appropriate size, which divides the space into cells of fixed size (see Figure 5.4(b)). The resulting cellular space $\mathcal{M}$ can be completed to become a bicolored cellular rectangle A (the smallest cellular rectangle enclosing $\mathcal{M}$), where each cell, called *pixel*, is colored *white* if it is part of $\mathcal{M}$, *black* otherwise (see Figure 5.4(c)). The filling problem is then reduced to the task of having a robot in each of the white pixels of A.

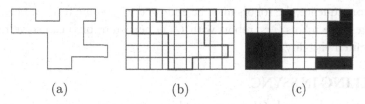

(a)   (b)   (c)

Figure 5.4: (a) A simple orthogonal space; (b) the superimposed grid; (c) the corresponding black and white rectangular cellular space.

5.4.1 IMPOSSIBILITY WITHOUT MEMORY

A basic impossibility result states that, for solving the filling problem successfully, the robots must have some form of persistent memory of the past.

To see why this is the case, consider the space consisting of a single line of $w = 2m + 1$ pixels of which one of them is a door. By contradiction, let $\mathcal{A}$ be a correct filling protocol. Since the robots have no memory of past, each step taken by a robot depends only on the current configuration (i.e., which cells are filled and which are empty). We can represent each empty cell by 0 and each filled cell by 1; the door would be represented by D; however note that it is not distinguishable from a filled cell. A configuration can thus be represented by the sequence $< d_1 \ldots d_w >$ of the values of the cells left-to-right. If algorithm $\mathcal{A}$ is correct then the penultimate configuration (i.e., the final configuration before the space is completely filled), must have exactly one empty cell and this cell should be adjacent to the door. So, if the door is the leftmost cell then the only possible final configuration is $< D011 \ldots 11111 >$. Notice that this is indistinguishable from the configuration $< 10D11 \ldots 1111 >$ and the algorithm must make the same move in both cases. In the former situation, the leftmost robot (from the door) must move to the right, but the same move will leave the space unfilled in the latter scenario. So the configuration $< 10D11 \ldots 1111 >$ must be avoided by the algorithm; this implies that the only correct penultimate configuration when the door is the third cell is $< 11D01 \ldots 1111 >$. Extending this argument inductively, the only correct penultimate configuration when the door is the $2i + 1$-th cell ($0 \leq i < m$), is the one where $d_{2i+1} = D$, $d_{2(i+1)} = 0$, and all other d_j's are 1. Hence, the only correct penultimate configuration when the door is the $2(m - 1) + 1$-th cell, must be $< 11111 \ldots 1D01 >$. Notice that this configuration is indistinguishable from $< 11111 \ldots 110D >$ which thus must be avoided by the algorithm. However, this is the only possible penultimate configuration when the door is the rightmost cell. A contradiction.

Theorem 5.13 **[40]** *The FILLING problem cannot be solved by oblivious robots, even if they have unbounded visibility. This result holds even in SSYNC.*

As a consequence, the robots must be endowed with some form of persistent memory. As we will see, finite-state robots (i.e., robots with $O(1)$ persistent bits) can solve the problem in SSYNC even with limited visibility.

5.4.2   FILLING IN SSYNC

We consider now robots with $O(1)$ persistent bits of memory and limited visibility. When in a cell c, a robot is capable of seeing completely only the neighboring cells. A solution to the filling problem by such finite-state robots is described below for SSYNC.

Let the bicolored cellular $l \times h$ rectangle A containing $\mathcal{M}$ be formed of pixels $p_{i,j}$, $1 \le i \le l$, $1 \le j \le h$; we say that the robots have *discrete* visibility radius 1 if they see all eight neighboring cells in the eight directions (North, NorthEast, East, SouthEast, South, SouthWest, West, NorthWest) indicated with $N(c), NE(c), E(c), SE(c), S(c), SW(c), W(c), NW(c)$. In other words, $V \ge \sqrt{2}q$, where q is the cell length.

The structure of $\mathcal{M}$ can be represented by a graph $G = (V, E)$ defined as follow: First partition each column into segments of consecutive white pixels ended by a black pixel in both extremes and numbered from top to bottom. Each segment is a node of G. Denote by $v_j^k \in V$ the node corresponding to the $k - th$ segment of column j, and by d_j^k the bottom-most pixel of the segment v_j^k. There is an edge $(v_j^k, v_{j'}^{k'}) \in E$ if and only if one of the cells of the $k - th$ segment of column j and one of the ones of the $k' - th$ segment of column j' are adjacent. That is if: (a) $j = j' + 1$ or $j = j' - 1$ and (b) there is a pixel $p_{i,j'} \in v_{j'}^{k'}$ neighbor to d_j^k or there is a pixel $p_{i,j} \in v_j^k$ neighbor to $d_{j'}^{k'}$. It is easy to see that the graph G so obtained is an acyclic connected graph (i.e., a tree).

The idea of the algorithm (FILLINGSINGLEDOOR) [40] is to move the robots along the links of G, starting from the node containing the door, in a depth-first fashion. To achieve that, the local rules are quite simple.

Let $block^+(c) \equiv (c \text{ is empty}) \wedge (S(c) \text{ is black}) \vee (SE(c) \text{ is black}))$ and let $block^-(c) \equiv (c \text{ is empty}) \wedge (S(c) \text{ is black}) \vee (SW(c) \text{ is black}))$.

Protocol FILLINGSINGLEDOOR for robot s in cell c:

Assumptions: SSYNC, finite-state, common coordinate systems

Meta-Rule: A robot remembers where it came from and it never backtracks

  If ($N(c)$ is empty) **Then** s moves north.

  Else If ($S(c)$ is empty) **Then** s moves south.

  Else If (($block^-(W(c))$)) **Then** s moves to west.

  Else If (($block^+(E(c))$)) **Then** s moves east.

  Else s does not move.

Note that the only persistent memory used in the above algorithm is for a robot to remember where it came from, so to avoid oscillating behaviors. Since algorithm FILLINGSINGLEDOOR is collision free, it terminates in finite time, and completely fills the space.

Theorem 5.14 [40] *In* SSYNC, *the* FILLING *problem can be solved with limited visibility, for any simple orthogonal space with a single door, by* finite-state *robots with a* common coordinate system *and* common unit of distance.

CHAPTER 6

Flocking

The problem of a team of robots forming a given pattern was examined in Chapter 4. A more complex task is that of having the robots move in the spatial universe, forming a given pattern, and maintain it while moving. This problem is called FLOCKING, and its study is part of the more general investigation in multi-robot systems on how to make mobile robots *move together* as a group, behaving as a single entity [130].

There are two versions of the FLOCKING problem, depending on whether or not there is a special entity that decides the movement of the group.

In the more common version of the FLOCKING problem, the direction of the movement of the group is given by an exogenous source: There is a distinguished mobile entity, called the *leader* or *guide*, possibly controlled by an external operator, that the group of robots (the *flock*) is required to follow while keeping a predetermined formation (i.e., they are required to move in formation, like a group of soldiers). Furthermore, the robots (in this context the term *vehicle* is also used) do not know beforehand the path the guide will take: Their task is just to follow the guide wherever it goes, and to keep the formation while moving. This version of the problem, which we shall call *guided flocking*, has been extensively studied in robotics (e.g., [108, 110, 127, 130]) with several applications (e.g., military [6], or in factories, where robots can be asked to move in cooperation to carry heavy loads).

In the other version of the problem, there is no exogenous source (i.e., no guide) and every robot knows the trajectory: The path along which the flock has to move is known in advance to every robot (e.g., [17, 119, 120]). Notice that this version of the problem, which we shall call *homogeneous flocking*, is the one closer to the original natural phenomena in biological systems of animals and insects; indeed, the first work about artificial flocking was a computer graphic animation of a group of birds [115]. In the solutions to homogeneous flocking, a leader might be elected among the robots to coordinate the computation; the presence of visible distinguished identifiers/markings, if assumed (e.g., [4, 23]), is only to simplify the computation. In both versions of the problem, almost all existing solutions require direct communication. In this chapter we examine how FLOCKING can be solved obliviously without direct communication. Notice that, unlike GATHERING and PATTERN FORMATION, FLOCKING is a *continuous* task: the movement of the flock is not assumed to ever terminate.

We saw in Chapter 4 that which patterns can be formed depend on which assumptions are made about the environment (e.g., chirality, consistent compasses, etc.). Clearly, with the same assumptions, fewer patterns can be formed and maintained while moving, as required in FLOCKING. Thus, an important parameter in the study of FLOCKING is the class of patterns that a protocol allows us to form and keep while the flock continues to move.

6.1 DEFINITIONS AND GENERAL STRATEGY

In spite of the differences between homogeneous flocking and guided flocking, we can use a common terminology and solution strategy.

A *formation* $\mathbb{F} = \{p_L, p_1, \ldots, p_{n-1}\}$ is a set of points with a distinguished point, p_L, called *leader* of the formation, while the remaining points are called *followers*.

The formation whose points are the current positions of the robots (including the leader) is called the (current) *fleet* (denoted by $\mathbb{E}$), while the formation given in input to the robots, and whose points represent the desired position of the robots once the flock is formed, is the *pattern* $\mathbb{P}$.

Notice that while we allow a pattern to be translated (to follow the leader) and rotated (to be oriented according to the leader's current direction), we do not allow it to be scaled. This is in keeping with the idea of a "flock" as a mobile formation of fixed size. In other words, we do not want the followers to simply scale the pattern instead of actually following the leader, as in Figure 6.1, with the pattern becoming bigger and bigger as the leader goes farther away. This implies that all the followers must have an *agreement on the unit of measure* (since they must be able to know when the pattern has been formed at the right scale).

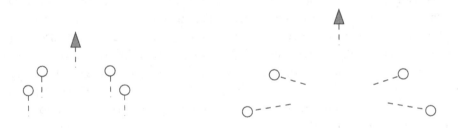

Figure 6.1: (a.) Flocking versus (b.) scaling the pattern.

We can consider that the desired pattern is reached when the robots place themselves in the desired shape, with no regard for the orientation, or we can ask, in addition, for a specific orientation (typically, corresponding to the current heading of the leader). These two alternatives are defined formally in the following.

Definition 6.1 Target Given a pattern $\mathbb{P}$ and a fleet $\mathbb{E}$, we call an *undirected target* of the robots any formation that is obtained by translating $\mathbb{P}$ so that its leader point coincides with the leader of $\mathbb{E}$, and rotating it by an arbitrary angle. We denote such a formation with $\mathcal{T}_{\mathbb{P},\mathbb{E}}$.

Given, in addition, an angle θ, we call the *directed target* of the robots the particular undirected target that is rotated by θ. We denote this formation with $\mathcal{T}_{\mathbb{P},\mathbb{E}}^{\theta}$. We call the followers' positions in a target the *slots* of the target.

Given a fleet $\mathbb{E}$ and a pattern $\mathbb{P}$, we say that the followers in $\mathbb{E}$ *exactly form* an undirected target $\mathcal{T}_{\mathbb{P},\mathbb{E}}$ if $\mathcal{D}(\mathbb{E}, \mathcal{T}_{\mathbb{P},\mathbb{E}}) = 0$, where the *distance* $\mathcal{D}()$ between two configurations $\mathbb{C} = \{c_1, \ldots, c_n\}$ and $\mathbb{G} = \{g_1, \ldots, g_n\}$ is defined as follows:

$$\mathcal{D}(\mathbb{C}, \mathbb{G}) = \min_{\pi \in \Pi} \sum_{i=1}^{|\mathbb{C}|} dist(c_i, g_{\pi(i)}),$$

where Π is the set of all the possible permutations of $1 \ldots |\mathbb{C}|$. Moreover, if ψ is the heading of the leader, we say that the followers exactly form the directed target if $\mathcal{D}(\mathbb{E}, \mathcal{T}_{\mathbb{P},\mathbb{E}}^{\psi}) = 0$. Similarly, we say that the undirected (resp., directed) target is *formed up to* ξ if $\mathcal{D}(\mathbb{E}, \mathcal{T}_{\mathbb{P},\mathbb{E}}) \leq \xi$ (resp. $\mathcal{D}(\mathbb{E}, \mathcal{T}_{\mathbb{P},\mathbb{E}}^{\psi}) \leq \xi$).

Finally, we are ready to introduce the formal definition of the FLOCKING problem:

Definition 6.2 The FLOCKING Problem Let $f_1, \ldots, f_{n-1}$ be a group of robots, and let L be an additional distinguished leader robot, with heading ψ, and let $\mathbb{P}$ be a pattern given in input to $f_1, \ldots, f_{n-1}$. The robots solve the exact (resp. approximate) FLOCKING problem with pattern $\mathbb{P}$ if, starting from an arbitrary formation, for all $t \geq 0$ there exists $t' \geq t$ such that the configuration at t', $\mathbb{E}$, is such that the robots exactly (resp. up to ξ) form $\mathcal{T}_{\mathbb{P},\mathbb{E}}^{\psi}$.

In general, any strategy that solves the FLOCKING problem can be divided in two main steps: (i) identify a unique leader robot r_l; (ii) move in a flock following r_l.

In the case of *homogeneous flocking* (e.g., [17, 119, 120]), no a priori leader exists in the group. In this case, the solving strategy needs to include a leader election phase, in order to identify the leader; after r_l has been identified as the leader, the robots can move in a flock following r_l; since the leader is dynamically elected, and it is no different from the other robots, the path followed by the leader must be known to all robots.

In the case of *guided* flocking (e.g., [75]), the guide is distinguished robot r_l in the system: in this case, the leader can be uniquely identified during the *Look*, and acts independently from the other robots. Hence, in this case, there is no real step (i) in the strategy; step (ii), instead, is the same as in the first case: the followers move in a flock while keeping up with r_l.

In the case of homogeneous robots, it is assumed that all robots know the trajectory and have the same capabilities and properties, including velocity. In the case of guided flocking, since the guide is the only one that knows the trajectory and is potentially different from the other robots, a number of conditions must be met for the problem to be solvable. Let v_L and ω_L be the maximum absolute linear and angular velocity of the guide, respectively, and let v_f be the maximum absolute linear velocity of follower f. Firstly, the guide must not move too fast, otherwise the followers will lag behind it and will not be able to maintain the formation. Formally, $v_L < \min_i v_{f_i}$. Moreover, the slots must not move too fast for the followers, as a consequence of the guide changing direction; the angular velocity of the guide must also be limited, thus obtaining the stronger condition: $v_L + \omega_L \cdot Rad(\mathbb{P}) < \min_i v_{f_i}$, where $Rad(\mathbb{P})$ denotes the *radius* of $\mathbb{P}$, that is the maximum distance between the distinguished point of $\mathbb{P}$ and the other points in $\mathbb{P}$.

6.2   GUIDED FLOCKING IN ASYNC

The existing solution for the ASYNC model is for guided flocking [75]: There is a distinguished leader that acts completely independently and does not behave according to the followers' algorithm; all the robots in the flock do not know the path of the leader in advance, and they cannot derive it (e.g., by observing the orientation of the leader's prow, or by deriving it by observing the leader in different positions). It makes no assumptions on the local coordinate system or on chirality. The solution works for formations that are symmetric with respect to the (estimated) direction of movement of the leader L (refer to Figure 6.3 for a few examples). It is assumed that the pattern is expressed in a coordinate system having the leader as origin and oriented according to the heading of the leader.

Since there is the necessity to model robots that "continuously" move, here it is assumed that the time spent in looking and computing is negligible compared to the time spent in moving. Also, note that the exact flocking variants cannot be solved in general in ASYNC, since we assume that the leader moves continuously and arbitrarily, while the followers only have discrete opportunities for observing the position of the leader and adjust their course accordingly. Hence, while exact flocking can be considered an ideal reference problem, in the following we will concentrate on the approximate variant of the problem.

6.2.1   THE FLOCKING ALGORITHM

The intuition behind the solution is described in the following: Every follower f_i is given in input a pattern $\mathbb{P}$ described as a set $p_1, \ldots p_{|\mathbb{P}|}$ of points, relative to the leader robot, L; we clearly assume to have $|\mathbb{P}| - 1$ followers arbitrarily placed on distinct positions at the beginning (this defines a *valid* initial configuration for this problem; see also Figure 6.2).

First, the generic follower f computes the baricenter B of the followers' positions, and a shared vertical axis Y given by the line passing through L and B, and oriented according to $\overrightarrow{BL}$ can be derived.[1] Then S_0, S_1, and S_2, containing, respectively, robots whose positions are exactly on Y, to its left, and to its right, are computed (according to the local concept of *left/right of Y*).

At this point, f rotates the points in $\mathbb{P}$, assuming that the leader is moving according to the direction and orientation of Y, and translates them into the observed leader's position. The positions returned by this operation are the *slots* that the followers will try to reach. After having computed the baricenter B_F of the slots, these positions are partitioned in three subsets: those exactly on Y (say F_0), to the left of Y (say F_1), and to its right (say F_2). Then, F_j, $j = 0, 1, 2$, are sorted in decreasing order with respect to the distances from L and B_F, and S_j, $j = 0, 1, 2$, are sorted in decreasing order with respect to the distances from L and B. In particular, after the sorting, it is guaranteed that

$$\forall i, j, i < j \quad \Rightarrow \quad (dist(l, p_i) > dist(l, p_j)) \vee$$
$$(dist(l, p_i) = dist(l, p_j) \wedge dist(b, p_i) > dist(b, p_j)),$$

[1]If $L = B$, the followers can simply wait for the leader to move away from B, or for some fellow follower that is already moving to break the tie.

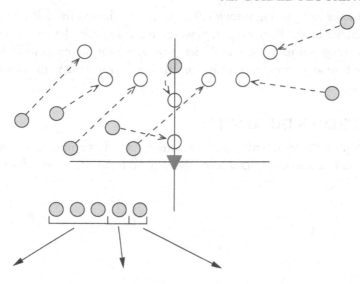

Figure 6.2: Examples of the behavior of the Basic Algorithm. The filled triangle is the leader, the filled circles are the followers, and the empty circles the slots the followers want to reach.

where p_i and p_j are points in P. Next, the rank k of f in the subset it belongs to is computed (i.e., the position that f occupies in the sorting).

Now, if f is the k-th follower in S_1, and $k \leq |F_1|$, then it moves toward the k-th position in F_1. Otherwise, if there are slots *available* in S_0 (i.e., $|F_0| > |S_0|$ and $k - |F_1| \leq |F_0| - |S_0|$), f is directed toward S_0. In particular, the set H containing the robots in S_1 and S_2 whose rank is, respectively, bigger than $|F_1|$ and $|F_2|$ is computed; H is then sorted, and the rank k' of f in H is computed. Then, f is directed toward the $(k' + |S_0|)$-th slot in F_0, that is toward a slot in F_0 that is not a target of robots in S_0. If no position in S_0 is available, f moves toward the $(|F_2| - (k - |F_1| - |F_0| + |S_0|) + 1)$-th position in F_2, that is toward one of the slots in F_2 that is not a destination point of either a robot in S_1 whose rank is smaller than k, or of a robot in S_2.

If f is in S_2, the algorithm behaves symmetrically to the case when f is in S_1, provided that the indices 1 and 2 are swapped in the description above.

If f is in S_0, and its rank k is smaller than $|F_0|$, then it simply moves toward the k-th slot in F_0. Otherwise, it chooses to move toward the side that has fewer robots (note that if $|S_1| = |S_2|$, then it chooses to move toward a slot in F_1). In Figure 6.2, an example of how the followers choose their slots is depicted.

Clearly, since the robots cannot remember p in the next cycle, this implies that it is possible that f changes its destination point in the next cycle, because its ranking can change. Also, the robots cannot be sure of the direction of movement of L. They only assume that the leader is going away from B (i.e., according to $\overrightarrow{BL}$). Furthermore, the followers assume that the direction of movement of L is given by the axis passing through B and L, and oriented from B toward L, hence they can reach an agreement on Y. They cannot, however, reach in general a similar agreement on X, that is on an axis orthogonal to Y that would let them agree on the concept of *left* and *right*. Hence, the basic algorithm applies only to formations that are symmetric with respect to the direction of movement of L.

6.2.2   EXPERIMENTAL RESULTS

The algorithm given above does not guarantee convergence. Experimental results, based on computer simulations[2] conducted to assess its efficacy, show that the algorithm provides statistical convergence in most cases [75].

Figure 6.3: Fleet formations used in the simulations.

The fixed formations used in the experiments are shown in Figure 6.3. To give the reader an idea of the actual behavior of the algorithm, Figure 6.4 shows the courses of the robots in two simulation runs.

The basic algorithm suffers from a number of problems, and is subjected to somewhat restrictive conditions. In particular:

1. The basic algorithm converges rapidly only for approximate undirected flocking, while convergence in the case of approximate directed flocking is typically slower. This is caused by the followers' inability to observe the real heading of the leader and by their obliviousness, since they cannot remember the previous position of the leader and thus cannot compute its movement vector.

2. The followers can assume and maintain for an unpredictably long time a wrong formation. For instance, the followers can assume a formation that is specular to the correct one, and placed "in front" of the leader instead of behind it. In such a situation, as long as the leader maintains a heading that coincides with the $\overrightarrow{BL}$ axis, the followers will compensate any movement of

[2]The simulator developed and used for the experiments is publicly available at http://www.di.unipi.it/~gervasi/FlockSim

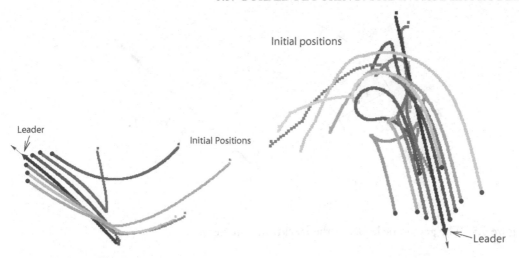

Figure 6.4: Trace of the robots while forming and keeping a wedge shaped formation (left), and the spread formation with ten robots (right). In the figure to the right, note the circular trajectory of the robots at the beginning, while trying to align the formation with the course of the leader.

the leader toward them by moving farther away, while keeping the formation on the wrong side and thus reproducing the same situation.

Problems 1 and 2 can be solved by observing the heading of the leader (i.e., by being able to distinguish the prow of the leader from the back), or — with a better approximation w.r.t. the baricenter — by having enough memory to store the previous position of the leader.

(3) In certain situations, two or more robots could continue changing the slots they have to reach, causing instability and slowing down or impeding altogether the convergence of the algorithm.

Some suggestions to help fixing some of these problems have been proposed [75].

6.3 GUIDED FLOCKING: THE INTRUDER PROBLEM

A special case of guided FLOCKING is an interesting problem called INTRUDER.

In the INTRUDER problem, the team of robots, called *cops*, must continuously keep encircled a distinguished mobile entity, called *intruder*, regardless of the movements of the intruder. The robots do not know the path followed by the intruder.

The problem is formally defined as follows. Given $f_1, \ldots, f_n$ cops and the intruder I, let $\mathcal{C}_1$ and $\mathcal{C}_2$ be the two circles centered in I and having radius l_1 and l_2, respectively, where l_1 and l_2 are given constants of the problem, with $l_2 > l_1$. The cops must place themselves in the *capture area* $\mathcal{K} = \mathcal{C}_2 \setminus \mathcal{C}_1$. In other words, the cops have to reach positions in the plane such that

$$\forall 1 \leq i \leq n, \, l_1 \leq dist(f_i, I) \leq l_2. \tag{6.1}$$

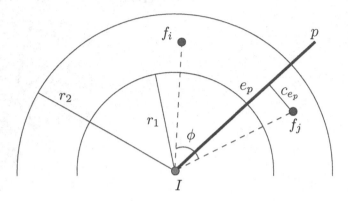

Figure 6.5: The geometric layout of the INTRUDER problem.

Moreover, the cops must evenly foreclose any escape route to the intruder. In formal terms, let p be a point on the plane such that $dist(I, p) > l_2$ (i.e., p lies outside of C_2, and hence outside of K). An *escape route* e_p for I to p is the segment $\overline{I, p}$. The *capture distance* c_{e_p} for e_p is

$$c_{e_p} = \min_{1 \leq i \leq n} dist(e_p, f_i),$$

where we have extended $dist()$ to segments in the usual way.

Intuitively, the capture distance c_{e_p} is the minimum distance that the intruder would place between itself and the nearest cop, if it tried to escape K along e_p. Hence, the goal of the cops is to place themselves such that

$$\max_p c_{e_p} \text{ is minimal.} \tag{6.2}$$

It is easy to see that this condition is satisfied when the cops place themselves spaced evenly on the inner border of the region allowed by Condition (6.1), thus forming a regular polygon of characteristic angle $\phi = 2\pi/n$ and radius l_1 (refer to Figure 6.5).

At this point it should be clear that the INTRUDER problem is the special case of the *guided* FLOCKING problem: The intruder is the guide, and the formation the robots have to keep while moving is that of a regular n-gon with the guide at the center.

6.3.1 LIMITATIONS

Since the intruder keeps moving, it is impossible for the cops to maintain a perfect solution, hence sub-optimal solutions are considered acceptable, as long as they are indefinitely maintained once first reached at time t_0. In this context a sub-optimal solution is defined as having, at each time $t > t_0$,

$$\forall \, 1 \leq i \leq n, \, l_1 - \epsilon_1 \leq dist(f_i, I) \leq l_2 + \epsilon_2,$$

and

$$\frac{\max_p c_{e_p}}{\tilde{c}} \leq 1 + \epsilon_3,$$

where $\tilde{c}$ is the minimal value from Condition (6.2) above.

The constants ϵ_1, ϵ_2 and ϵ_3 are also tied to the temporal features of the asynchronous behavior of the cops. In fact, the longer the time between two consecutive *Look*s of a cop, the more outdated the snapshot taken of the other agents' positions becomes. Hence, computationally slow cops will only be able to guarantee a sub-optimal solution for relatively large values of ϵ_1, ϵ_2 and ϵ_3, while faster cops will be able to better approximate the optimal solution.

Finally, it is worthwhile to observe that the cops have no hope of reliably capturing an intruder faster than themselves. Therefore, as for the FLOCKING problem, a necessary condition for the solvability of the problem is that the intruder is slower than the slowest of the cops.

6.3.2   AN ALGORITHMIC APPROACH

With unlimited visibility and no agreement on the robots' coordinate systems, a solution for the ASYNC model does exist, and it is described below [76].

The idea of the algorithm is as follows. First, the closest cop to the intruder is identified (call it *chief*). The chief simply moves toward the intruder, trying to maintain a distance l_1 from it. All the other cops aim to reach the vertexes of the regular n-gon inscribed in the circle C_r of radius $r = \max(l_1, dist(I, Chief))$ and centered in the observed intruder's position. Once they reach such vertexes, and $l_1 \leq r \leq l_2$, the cops' task is achieved. In order to reach an agreement on which vertex is assigned to each cop, the cops are sorted. In particular, the chief is considered to be the first cop in the order; the other cops are sorted, in increasing order, according to the angle each of them forms with the intruder and the chief. At this point, the targets (i.e., the positions they have to reach in order to complete the task) of the cops are computed: These are the vertexes of the regular polygon having characteristic angle $\phi = 2\pi/n$, with the first vertex being on the chief's position, and inscribed in the circle C centered in I and having radius $r' = r(1 + \epsilon)$. The target of the i-th cop in the ordering is the i-th vertex of the polygon. The angle between the half-line $[I, Chief)$ and the x axis in the local coordinate system of the executing cop is used to rotate the polygon to be formed so that the first vertex coincides with the *Chief*. The reason for the targets being computed with respect to C and not with respect to C_r is to reduce cases where another cop becomes chief, displacing the previous chief: in fact, such displacements would introduce some instability in the algorithm, slowing down convergence.

Also, it is possible that a cop f, to reach its target, crosses C. This too would introduce instability in the algorithm, since in so doing f could come closer to I than the current chief, thus becoming chief itself. To avoid this effect, the algorithm forces f to take a route outside C, so that no crossing is possible: f moves sideways until a straight path from its current position to its assigned target does not cross C (see the example depicted in Figure 6.6). The cop will keep stepping sideways until necessary to reach its real target without crossing C.

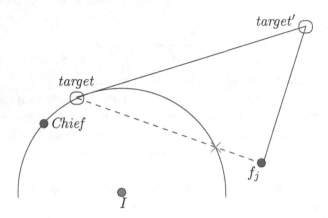

Figure 6.6: Sideway stepping.

6.3.3   A HEURISTIC APPROACH

We now consider a simpler heuristic approach to solve the INTRUDER problem [77]: All robots are subject to a force, attracting them toward the enemy if they are farther than l_1 from it, or repulsing them if they are nearer. Moreover, when two robots come closer to each other than a certain distance *cord*, they repel each other. The distance *cord* is computed as the side of an n-gon of radius l_1.

   While the algorithm by itself does not coordinate the behavior of each robot with that of its fellows, like the previous algorithm does when establishing a shared assignment of robots to vertexes, it has a lowest-energy equilibrium in a configuration where the robots do evenly surround the enemy. In this sense, the behavior of this mode of heuristic algorithm is truly *emergent*, in that no explicit and direct solution to the problem is provided in the code (see [4, 6]).

6.3.4   EXPERIMENTAL RESULTS

The effectiveness of both approaches was assessed using numerical simulations [76, 77]. Each run included a random[3] number of cops between 2 and 50; the intruder and the cops were initially placed at random in a 256×256 units square. The cops had their axes orientation and direction assigned randomly, and linear speed v_f between 0.5 and 5 space units per time units.

   The intruder's course was determined as follows. At all times, the intruder would move forward according to its linear velocity. At each move, with a probability of 1/10, the intruder could start turning to its left or right, with random angular velocity less than its maximum angular velocity. If already turning, with probability 1/100 the intruder could stop and continue its course as a straight line (these parameters ensured curved, irregular trajectories).

---

[3]In all cases, random values were obtained from a linear distribution.

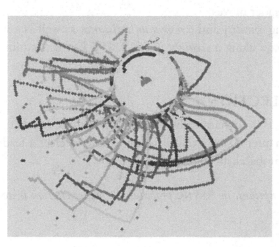
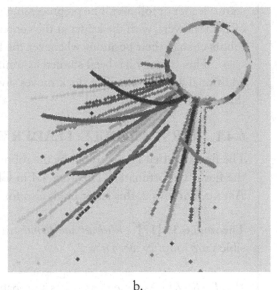

a.   b.

Figure 6.7: Traces of the behavior of the robots according to (a) the algorithmic approach, and (b) the heuristic solution. The camera is fixed on the enemy, that thus appears static.

Note also that the proposed solutions are self-stabilizing. In particular, any external intervention (e.g., if one or more of the cops are stopped, slowed down, knocked out, or simply faulty) does not prevent the completion of the task.

Simulations in the case of faults were done for both solutions: in particular, the case of transient faults and of faults that occur indefinitely were studied [76, 77]. As an example, Figures 6.7(a) and 6.7(b) show the traces of two runs of the two algorithms.

6.4   HOMOGENEOUS FLOCKING IN ASYNC

In the previous sections, the FLOCKING problem was approached assuming that the leader is a distinguished unit (possibly controlled by an external operator). In the case of homogeneous flocking, all robots are identical and a leader of the team, if needed, is elected during the execution.

Homogeneous flocking has been examined in ASYNC when the target formation is not a specific pattern, but any pattern that satisfies the property of being a *circular arrangement* of all the robots but one, located inside *SEC* (refer for instance to the example reported in Figure 6.8(a)). Unlike the case of the INTRUDER problem, here there is no restriction on uniformity of the followers on the circle.

The solution strategy has been to divide the task into three modules: a leader election module, a preprocessing module, and a motion module. The leader election module returns to each robot its status: leader or follower. The preprocessing module aims to arrange robots in a circular arrangement of the followers, with the leader at the center. The motion module provides the rules that will make robots change their positions whenever the leader moves.

This strategy has been studied assuming *chirality* and *common unit distance*, as well as a strong additional assumption: The flock moves always along a *straight line* [17, 18]. Let us examine the three modules in more detail.

6.4.1   FIRST MODULE: LEADER ELECTION

The first step that is carried out by the robots is to (dynamically) elect a leader whose task is to lead the flock. Unfortunately, Theorem 4.4 in Chapter 4 states that it is impossible to elect a leader in ASYNC. For $n = 2$, this result holds also for probabilistic algorithms:

Theorem 6.3 [17]   *Without additional assumptions, in* ASYNC *probabilistic leader election is* impossible *with chirality when $n = 2$.*

Proof. (*Sketch*) Assume there exists a probabilistic algorithm that solves the problem. Since the two robots do not share the same reference system, and do not know the system of the other robot, they can never know when the algorithm conditions are verified for the other robot. Therefore, the system will contain executions where the two robots may think that the other robot is the leader or executions where the two robots will change infinitely their state (position) in order to become leader. The set of executions verifying the above scenario has probability 1. □

Because of these negative limitations, the first module can only be carried out by $n \geq 3$ robots via a probabilistic protocol. A solution to the first module is as follows [17]:

LEADER ELECTION Module.
Assumptions: `Chirality`.

1. For $n = 3$, the robots are the vertexes of a triangle. The leader is the robot with the smallest angle, or the robot different from the other two robots in the case of an isosceles triangle. Randomization is used to break the symmetry of equilateral triangles.

2. For $n > 3$, the leader is the robot whose position is the one closest to the center of SEC; randomization is used to break any symmetry. To give the other robots the possibility of inferring the heading of the flock, the leader has to define a second reference point (in addition to the center of SEC). Therefore, the leader should not be placed on the center: If initially a robot is positioned on the center, that robot first moves to a free position inside SEC chosen non-deterministically.

Thus, the robots randomly change their positions until only one of them is the closest to SEC, and no robot is on its center.

The following lemma holds:

Lemma 6.4 [17, 18] *In* ASYNC, *the* LEADER ELECTION *module let $n \geq 3$ homogeneous robots converge in a finite number of steps to a configuration with a unique leader.*

6.4.2 SECOND MODULE: SETTING A MOVING FORMATION

After a leader r_l has been selected, the robots arrange themselves in the flocking formation. This step is composed of two sub-steps: First, all the robots reach an *oriented configuration*: all robots, with the exception of the leader, are on the SEC, and no robot is at c, the center of SEC. In particular, once the leader r_l has been elected, the robots (but r_l) move toward SEC following the radius they are on. In particular, the robots closest to the rim of SEC are placed on the circle. Then, recursively, all the other robots, with the exception of the leader, are placed on the border of SEC. The movements are performed in order to avoid collisions.

Lemma 6.5 [17, 18] *In* ASYNC, *the* MOVING FORMATION *module let $n \geq 3$ robots with chirality converge in a finite number of steps and avoiding any collision to a configuration where all robots but r_l are on SEC.*

Once an oriented configuration is achieved, the robots arrange themselves to form a specific pattern, where a robot r_1 is placed on the intersection between SEC and $\overrightarrow{c, r_l}$, with c the center of SEC (recall that r_l is the only robot inside SEC; also, it is not on c), and the other robots are uniformly disposed on the half circle that does not contain r_1 and that is delimited by the intersection between SEC and the perpendicular to $\overline{c, r_l}$ (see the example depicted in Figure 6.8(a)); this particular formation is called *circular moving formation*. Here, the robots use their agreement on the chirality in order to achieve an agreement on a *global* coordinate system: specifically, the common Y axis is given by the line passing through r_l and r_1, with the positive side given by $\overrightarrow{r_l, r_1}$. This axis and the common chirality allow the robots to achieve the agreement also on the orientation and direction of the X axis: in particular, the X axis is given by the line orthogonal to Y, with the positive side being to the right of Y, according to the clockwise orientation. The leader r_l occupies position $(0, 0)$ in the global X-Y coordinate system (see also Figure 6.8(b)). More formally,

Definition 6.6 Circular Moving Formation   A set of $n > 4$ robots, $r_0, \ldots, r_{n-1}$, is a *circular moving formation* if:

- r_1 and r_0 define the Y axis of the system such that the Y-coordinate of r_0 is 0, and the positive values are in the r_1 direction;

- the X axis is perpendicular to Y in r_0, and has positive values to the right of Y, according to the clockwise orientation;

- all the other robots are such that:

  1. $\forall r_i \neq r_1$ and $r_i \neq r_0, r_i.y < 0$;

  2. $\forall r_i, r_j, r_i.x \neq r_j.x$;

  3. $\forall r_i$ such that $r_i.x \neq 0, \exists r_j$ such that $r_i.x = -r_j.x$;

  4. if $|r_i.x| > |r_j.x|$, then $|r_i.y| < |r_j.y|$;

  5. there exists at most one (unique) robot with $x = 0$ and $y < 0$.

First, the following lemma holds:

Lemma 6.7 [17, 18]   *If there is chirality, the circular moving formation is unique when $n > 4$.*

Thus, by the previous lemma, once the robots are in an oriented configuration, they can uniquely compute the final positions to reach in order to achieve the moving formation. All movements must clearly be only on the border of *SEC*; if a robot is blocked by some other robot, it will wait until its way is free; it can be shown that no deadlock can occur (i.e., no robot can be blocked infinitely) [18].

Lemma 6.8   *In* ASYNC, *the* MOVING FORMATION *module let $n > 4$ robots with* Chirality *and* guided trajectory *to achieve a circular moving formation within finite time.*

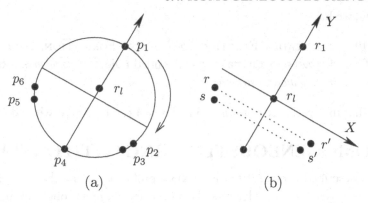

Figure 6.8: The circular moving formation.

6.4.3 THIRD MODULE: FLOCKING

Once the moving formation is achieved, the robots are ready to move while keeping this formation. In particular, there is only one robot inside SEC, the leader r_l, and one robot r_1 on the intersection between the center c of SEC and $\overrightarrow{cr_l}$; this second robot is the *head* of the flock, and will lead the others. The path the head follows is strictly along the positive side of the common Y the robots agreed upon in the second module; also, each robot r is allowed to move only straight on the line parallel to Y and passing through r. The obvious constraint that needs to be satisfied is that the head cannot move more quickly than the slowest robot in $\mathcal{R} \setminus \{r_1\}$; also, as already noted, the robots need a common unit of measure.

Note that, according to Definition 6.6, the robots in $\mathcal{R} \setminus \{r_l, r_1\}$ can be paired according to their X-coordinate. The algorithm idea is as follows. The head of the group always moves along the positive side of Y. When the head moves, it is followed within a distance ϵ (a parameter of the algorithm) by the leader robot. In other words, the leader moves to point $(0, -\epsilon)$, then, the pair of most external robots closest to the leader moves within a distance ϵ' toward the leader: That is, if r is one of these robots, it moves to point $(r.x, -\epsilon')$. Then the second external pair of robots moves within a distance ϵ' toward the pair of most external robots closest to the leader; that is, if (r, r') is the pair of most external robots closest to the leader, and (s, s') the second one (with $r.x, s.x < 0$ and $r'.x, s'.x > 0$), then s will move to $(s.x, r.y - \epsilon')$ and s' will move to $(s'.x, r'.y - \epsilon')$ (refer to the example depicted in Figure 6.8(b)). The following holds:

Lemma 6.9 [17, 18]   *The circular moving formation is preserved during the movements of the robots, provided that the head always moves along the positive side of Y.*

Summarizing, we have:

Theorem 6.10 *The* LEADER ELECTION, *the* MOVING FORMATION, *and the* FLOCKING *modules allow a set of* $n > 4$ *robots with* Chirality *and guided trajectory to form and keep a circular moving formation, while moving along a straight line.*

Note that the special cases for $n = 3$ and $n = 4$ can be solved with ad-hoc solutions [17].

6.5 HOMOGENEOUS FLOCKING WITH OBSTACLES

All solutions described above for the FLOCKING problem assume that the area where the robots move is free of obstacles. Consider now the case when there are obstacles in the environment; in particular, the obstacles are convex and compact sets, and can in general have different sizes; a robot can distinguish the robots from obstacles. Flocking in these conditions is clearly a very complex task.

However, in contrast to the solutions for the FLOCKING problem considered in the previous sections, here the robots are not required to form and maintain any specific formation while moving: They are only required to move on a straight line, following a common *flocking vector* they are given in input, with the only requirement of avoiding collisions among them and with the static obstacles placed in the environment.

In this section we will present two solutions that deal with the presence of static obstacles in the environment where the robots operate: the first deals with the usual 2D space considered so far; the second study extends the protocols to the 3D space.

6.5.1 THE 2D CASE

The 2D case has been investigated for homogeneous robots in FSYNC with ConsistentCompass; here, the robots are assumed to move toward a *destination* defined by a *flocking vector* $\vec{F}$, known to all robots [132]. The robots however have *limited visibility*.

Borrowing ideas from work in engineering and AI (e.g., [4, 115, 125]), the solution is based on an attractive force between robots in order to keep the formation, and a repulsive force in order to avoid collisions with other robots and obstacles.

The first force a robot is subject to is an attractive one toward the other robots it sees in its range of visibility; the desired distance between robots is denoted by d, with d smaller than the sensor range s of the robots. In particular, the movement vector $\vec{M}_i$ of robot r_i is given by $\vec{M}_i = \vec{N}_i + \vec{F}$, where $\vec{N}_i$ denotes the movement vector of r_i with respect to all its *neighbors*, that is, the robots in its range of visibility, denoted by N_i; in particular,

$$\vec{N}_i = \sum_{j \in N_i} \frac{1}{2} \frac{r_j - r_i}{|r_j - r_i|} ((|r_j - r_i|) - d). \tag{6.3}$$

In the previous equation, $\frac{r_j - r_i}{|r_j - r_i|}$ is the unit vector whose direction is given by $\overrightarrow{r_i, r_j}$; and $(|r_j - r_i|) - d$ is the distance deviation between the actual distance and the desired distance between two robots: thus, if r_i and r_j are closer than d, they will move away from each other; otherwise, they will get closer. Also, the size of $\vec{N}_i$ must not be larger than the visibility range of r_i; so, the algorithm normalizes $\vec{N}_i$ according to the sensor range s: when $\vec{N}_i > s$, then $\vec{N}_i = \vec{N}_i / |\vec{N}_i| * s$.

If there are obstacles in the environment, the moving vector expressed by Equation (6.3) needs to be adjusted. In particular, let l be the *safety margin* between a robot r and an obstacle O: if the distance between r and O is larger than l, then no repulsive force will be applied to r, and its movement is defined by Equation (6.3) above. Otherwise, r is subjected to a repulsive force in order to avoid collisions with O (and with the other robots in its sensing range); let us denote by Ob_i the set of obstacles in the sensor range of r_i, by O_k any object in Ob_i, and by o_k the position of O_k. The repulsive force is described by the following equation:

$$\vec{O}_i = \sum_{k \in Ob_i} \frac{o_k - r_i}{|o_k - r_i|} \mathrm{Safe}(l - (|o_j - r_i|)), \qquad (6.4)$$

where $\mathrm{Safe}(z) = max\{0, z\}$. The property expressed by the previous equation is that the closer a robot is to an obstacle, the larger is the repulsive force. Thus, combining Equations (6.3) and (6.4), the final vector movement of r_i (given by $\vec{N}_i + \vec{O}_i$) is normalized with respect to the distance d_i^* of the closest object to r_i; that is:

$$\vec{M}_i = \frac{(\vec{N}_i + \vec{O}_i)}{|\vec{N}_i + \vec{O}_i|} \min\{d_i^*, |\vec{N}_i + \vec{O}_i|\}. \qquad (6.5)$$

That is, in order to avoid the obstacles, the distance that a robot moves is no more than d_i^*; the direction of the final movement vector of r_i is the same as that of the vector $\vec{N}_i + \vec{O}_i$.

Thus, summarizing, the movement of a robot is determined by three forces: from its neighbors, from obstacles (if any), and from the flocking vector. The above described algorithm has been tested by computer simulation. In particular, the simulation setting included twenty units with sensor range of 2.0m, and three obstacles. Initially, the robots are randomly positioned in different places. The flocking movement vector $\vec{F}$ is $(0.1, 0)$: That is, the direction of the whole flock is along the X axis. The desired distance between robots is 1.5m. In all simulations, despite the fact that different robots may clearly choose different routes to flock, they all can effectively avoid collisions with obstacles [132].

6.5.2 THE 3D CASE

A similar approach can be adopted to study the problem with obstacles in a 3D space where the robots operate independently and asynchronously [101]. The robots are modeled as dynamic points in 3D space and have, as in the 2D case, ConsistentCompass; also in this case, they have a limited sensing range. The idea of the algorithm is that each robot r_i determines the magnitude and orientation of its movement vector in each time step based on the distances from three of its neighbors' robots.

More specifically, the first of these reference robots, say r_1, is the closest to r; that is,

$$r_1 = \arg[\min_{r_j \in N_i} \{dist(r_i, r_j)\}].$$

The other two reference robots are defined as follows:

$$r_2 = \arg[\min_{r_j \in N_i \setminus \{r_1\}} \{dist(r_i, r_j) + dist(r_i, r_1)\}],$$

$$r_3 = \arg[\min_{r_j \in N_i \setminus \{r_1, r_2\}} \{area(r_i, r_1, r_2, r_3))\}].$$

where $area(r_i, r_1, r_2, r_3)$ denotes the surface area of the tetrahedrons configuration formed by the four robots r_i, r_1, r_2, and r_3.

The basic behavior of each individual robot is then to maintain distance d with the other three specific neighbors, thus forming a regular tetrahedron. Consequently, the idea is to have the team to form a network which is made of multiple regular tetrahedrons in the space. In particular, the movement vector of robot r_i is similar to that defined by Equation (6.3), but here the computation is referred only to the three selected neighbors[4]. Each robot is also subject to a repulsive case when it approaches an obstacle, that is quite similar to the one described by Equation (6.4).

The algorithm has been tested by computer simulation, by enabling the robots to move toward a target in a 3D environment: When a large group is flocking toward a target in an environment filled with multiple obstacles, if the size of the obstacles is larger than d, the group will possibly adapt its shape to fit the gap between the obstacles and pass through. Otherwise, if the size of the obstacle is much smaller than the distance d, the group maintains its shape and directly flocks through the obstacles. As in this study calculations involve only three other neighbors' positions, the control strategy has less computation and becomes less influenced by other robots.

---

[4]More precisely, since the basic control principle employed in this study is inspired from virtual physics of spring mesh, the formula is also tied to two other constants, modelling the *spring stiffness* and the *damping coefficient*.

CHAPTER 7

Other Directions

The model we have considered (with all its variations of assumptions) is the standard one in the research. As questions generate investigations, continuously creating newer research branches, the model evolves in different directions. In particular, other research directions have emerged from questions on robots' memory and on the spatial universe in which robots move.

7.1 COMPUTING WITH COLORS

The focus of the research, and thus of this book, has been on oblivious robots. We have also (to a lesser extent) considered *finite-state* robots, i.e., robots with $O(1)$ bits of persistent memory (see Section 5.4).

An interesting new question is what happens if these $O(1)$ persistent bits are externally *visible* [38]. For example, each robot is equipped with a light bulb that can display a constant number of different colors; the colors are visible to all other robots, and are persistent, that is, the light bulbs are not automatically reset at the end of each cycle. Thus, they can be used to remember states and to communicate. Apart from these lights, the robots are oblivious in all other respects.

7.1.1 COLORED ASYNC VERSUS SSYNC

The presence of lights with visible colors is undoubtedly a very powerful computational tool even if just constant in number. Indeed, it can overcome the limitations of ASYNC making the robots strictly more powerful than traditional SSYNC robots, as we see in the following.

The proof that asynchronous robots with lights are *at least as powerful as* semi-synchronous ones consists of a protocol (SIM) that allows us to execute any semi-synchronous algorithm $\mathcal{A}$ in an asynchronous setting, each robot using a light with a constant number of colors [38]. A version using five colors is described below. The five colors are: T(rying), M(oving), S(topped), F(inished), W(aiting). At the beginning, all lights are set to T.

The protocol is a sequence of Mega-Cycles, each of which starts with all robots trying to execute protocol $\mathcal{A}$ (color T) and ends with all robots finishing the Mega-Cycle having executed $\mathcal{A}$ once (color F). All robots with light F then eventually turn their lights to T; when this process is completed, a new Mega-Cycle starts.

During a Mega-Cycle every robot executes $\mathcal{A}$ once. Each Mega-Cycle is composed of a sequence of *stages*; at each stage, some robots are allowed to execute $\mathcal{A}$, and protocol SIM ensures that they have the *same* view of the world (i.e., they observed the same snapshot).

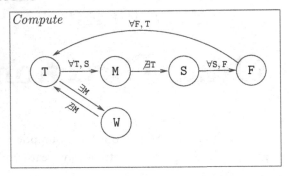

Figure 7.1: The transition diagram of the SIM protocol.

At the beginning, all the robots that during their *Look* phase see only robots with light T are allowed to enter the first stage by turning their own lights to M before executing $\mathcal{A}$. Any other robot with light T that performs its *Look* operation when some robots' lights are M (and thus the robots are potentially moving), is prevented from entering the current stage, loses its turn, changes color to W and waits for another turn. While the robots are changing from color T to M or to W, none of the other robots is allowed to perform protocol $\mathcal{A}$. Only when no robot has color T, the M robots are allowed to change color to S. While the M robots are changing to color S, the other robots are not allowed to perform $\mathcal{A}$ and they do not change their color. Once no robot has color M anymore (i.e., all robots are either S or W), the W robots can change color to T. Note that, while the robots are changing from W to T, those that are already colored T are not allowed to do anything. Only when there are no more W robots (i.e., all robots are either T or S), the next Mega-Cycle can start. For a diagram representing the change of colors during the *Compute* phase, see Figure 7.1.

There are problems that robots cannot solve *without* visible bits, even if they are semi-synchronous, but can be solved with $O(1)$ visible bits even if the robots are asynchronous [38]. One such a problem is *rendezvous*, i.e., the gathering of two robots; from Chapter 3, we know that this problem is not solvable in SSYNC. We now see how the problem can be solved if the robots have $O(1)$ colors.

The idea of Algorithm TWOGATHERLIGHT is described below (for the transition diagram of this algorithm see Figure 7.2). Let r and s be the two robots. The protocol uses four colors: OFF, RED, GREEN, and BLUE; initially, the light of both r and s are set to OFF.

If, after the beginning of the execution, both robots observe OFF as the color of the other robots' light, then they both try to reach the point halfway between the two robots. On the other hand, if one robot begins execution earlier than the other it will move toward the midpoint, turning its light RED before moving. If the second robot now performs a *Look* operation, it will see the RED light and know that the other robot is potentially moving. In this case, the second robot waits for the first robot to change colors from RED to BLUE. When the robot sees the BLUE light on the other

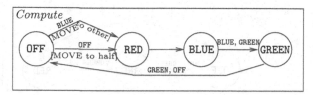

Figure 7.2: The transition diagram of the TwoGatherLight protocol.

robot it will try to move directly toward it. A robot with BLUE light waits until the second robot has also turned its light to BLUE. When both robots have BLUE lights, they turn their lights to GREEN to signal the end of one round of the algorithm (i.e., the robots synchronize with each other at the end of each round). At this point, the robots turn their lights to OFF to start the next round.

Algorithm Sim together with protocol TwoGatherLight for the rendezvous problem lead to the following result:

Theorem 7.1   [38] *Asynchronous robots endowed with $O(1)$ visible lights are strictly more powerful than semi-synchronous robots without any light.*

7.1.2   COLORED ASYNC VERSUS FSYNC

The relationship between Fsync and *Colored* Async is less understood. What is known is that asynchronous robots, if empowered with both a constant number of lights and the ability to remember a single snapshot from the past, become at least as powerful as synchronous robots.

There is a simple protocol (SyncSim) that simulates, using three lights and one snapshot, a fully synchronous execution of any asynchronous algorithm. Protocol SyncSim uses three colors: OFF, GREEN, and RED; initially, all lights are OFF (see Figure 7.3 for the transition diagram). Similarly to Protocol Sim, this protocol enforces a sequence of Mega-Cycles $mc_0, mc_1, \ldots$: the difference here is that *all* robots execute $\mathcal{A}$ in each Mega-Cycle based on the same snapshot (we are simulating Fsync). Each Mega-Cycle mc_i starts with all robots being OFF; within finite time, all OFF robots become GREEN; when a robot becomes GREEN in a Mega-Cycle, it stores in a local array Perm[] the configuration it just observed: this is necessary to ensure that all robots will compute on the same configuration in this Mega-Cycle. After all robots become GREEN, the destination point is computed, using as configuration the one locally stored in Perm[] and the robot starts to perform the *Move* operation, turning its light to RED. After a robot has completed the *Move*, it changes its light to OFF. When the lights of all robots are OFF, the current Mega-Cycle ends and the next one begins.

In other words, asynchronous robots endowed with $O(1)$ visible lights, and able to remember a single snapshot, are at least as powerful as traditional fully synchronous robots.

Interestingly, there are problems that can be solved in Async with three colors and one past snapshot, but are not solvable in Fsync without additional information [38]. This is the case, for

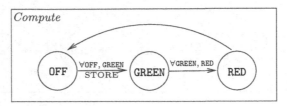

Figure 7.3: The transition diagram of the SyncSim protocol.

example, of the Blinking problem, which requires $n > 2$ robots to perform subtasks T_1 and T_2 repeatedly in alternation. In T_1, the robots must form a circle, i.e., each robot lies on a distinct point on the same circle C of radius $Rad > 0$; while in T_2, the robots must gather at a single point.

The simulation algorithm, together with the example of a problem not solvable in Fsync but solvable in Async with lights and one past snapshot, leads to the following result:

Theorem 7.2 [38] *Asynchronous robots, endowed with $O(1)$ visible lights and able to remember a single snapshot, are strictly more powerful than fully synchronous oblivious robots without any lights.*

This is to be contrasted with the fact that, without lights, Async robots are not even as powerful as Ssync, even if they remember an unlimited number of previous snapshots [113].

7.2 SOLID ROBOTS

In the standard model, the robots are viewed as points, i.e., they are *dimensionless*. An interesting variant of the model is to consider entities that occupy a physical space of some size; that is, the entities have a solid dimension. These robots, called *solid* or *fat*, are assumed to have a common unit distance and are viewed as circular disks of a given diameter. The disks of two robots can touch but cannot overlap. Moreover, it is assumed that, if during its movement a robot collides with another, its movement stops (*fail–stop collision*).

The robots' visibility is clearly affected by their solid dimension and it is defined as follows. Two robots r_1 and r_2 can see each other if there exist points x and y in the visibility radius of r_1 and r_2 respectively, such that the segment $\overline{xy}$ does not contain any point of any other robot. Note that if a robot r_1 can see robot r_2, it can see some non-zero arc of its bounding circle and thus it can always compute its center.

In the following, whenever we refer to distance between a robot and some point (or some other robot), we refer to the distance from (or to) the center of the corresponding circular disks.

7.2.1 GATHERING SOLID ROBOTS

Solid robots have been studied in the context of the Gathering problem. Obviously, in the case of solid robots, the definition of gathering has to be modified.

The robots are said to form a connected configuration in the plane if between any two points of any two robots there exists a polygonal line each of whose points belongs to some robot. Gathering is accomplished if the robots form some connected configuration and they are all visible to each other (and thus are aware that a connected configuration is achieved).

Adding a physical dimension to the robots significantly complicates the task, mainly because of the fact that their "body" can obstruct visibility. An example that shows one of the difficulty is given by a team of four robots whose centers are situated on two intersecting non-perpendicular lines, one robot in each of the four half-lines (a bi-angular configuration). The obvious algorithm that would work if the robots were points would be to have them move toward the center of bi-angularity, which is invariant under straight moves. However, it is easy to see that an adversary might have two robots meet in their move toward the center, thus obstructing the view to the other two, without forming a connected configuration. In general, the lack of full visibility due to obstruction, prevent the robots from being able to compute easily an invariant point.

For the gathering of solid robots, currently there are only solutions for very small teams; in fact, no gathering algorithm is known for $n > 4$ solid robots.

Furthermore, these algorithms are not collision-free and they rely on the fail-stop collision assumption to work.

Gathering $n = 3$ *Solid Robots.*   In the case of $n = 3$, there is a simple algorithm that allows the three robots, which know n, to gather in Async. The main idea of the algorithm is to force the robots to either form a triangle (in which case, full visibility of all three robots is assured), or collinearity (in which case all robots are aware of it, although two of them do not have full visibility) [33]. Several rules regulate the robots' behavior once one of these cases occur. The algorithm is as follows:

Algorithm THREESOLIDROBOTS (for robot r)
Assumptions: fail-stop collisions, common unit distance, $n = 3$ known.

If Robots form a triangle with all angles $\leq 120°$ **Then**
    $c :=$ center of equiangularity;
    If $dist(r, c) > 2\frac{\sqrt{3}}{3}$ **Then**
        $p :=$ point such that $dist(p, c) = 2\frac{\sqrt{3}}{3}$;
        Move(p).
    End If
Else
    If Robots are collinear (forming line l) **Then**
        If I am the central robot **Then**
            $p :=$ point at distance 1 perpendicular to l;
            Move(p).
        End If
    Else %*The largest angle in the triangle is strictly between* $120°$ *and* $180°$%
        $s :=$ robot corresponding to the largest angle of the triangle;
        If I am not s **Then**
            $p :=$ point at distance 2 from s on $\overrightarrow{sr}$;
            Move(p).
        End If
    End If
End If

Theorem 7.3   **[33]**   *Three solid robots can gather in* ASYNC *with common unit distance and* fail-stop collisions.

Gathering $n = 4$ ***Solid Robots.***   The case of $n = 4$ solid robots is significantly more complicated.

Nine situations which form a partition of all possible positions in which robots can find themselves are identified: 1. *gathering*, 2. *four aligned*, 3. *partial visibility*, 4. *locking*, 5. *leaving line*, 6. *three aligned*, 7. *sliding*, 8. *quadrilateral*, and 9. *triangle*. These situations, when they occur, are not necessarily seen by all the robots because of obstructions. The general idea is that, if a robot cannot understand what situation the system is in, it does not move; otherwise, when recognizing situation i, it follows a specific routine TREAT-SITUATION i.

FOURSOLIDROBOTS
Assumptions: fail-stop collisions, common unit distance, $n = 4$ known.
    If Situation i and $i \neq 1$ **Then** TREAT-SITUATION i

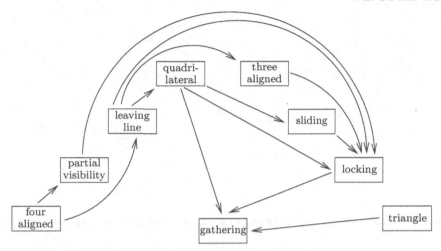

Figure 7.4: Diagram of transitions between situations for Procedure FOURSOLIDROBOTS. Rectangles depict Situations 1–9 and arrows depict possible transitions between them.

Because of the solid dimension of the robots and of asynchrony, many technical details complicate the various rules. As usual with asynchronous solutions, the most difficult problem in the design of the algorithm is on one hand to prevent robots from "unexpectedly" transiting to an unwanted situation and, on the other, to take care of a possible switch of situations whenever they can potentially occur. In the following we describe at high level the actions taken in the various cases.

1. *Gathering*: the robots have gathered.

2. *Four aligned*: the centers of the robots belong to the same line. Let the external robots be the pair of robots whose visibility is obstructed. This situation is broken by the movement of the internal robots. The idea is that the external robots do not move while the internal robots (or one of them) move a small distance perpendicularly to the line of their alignment. Clearly, because of lack of orientation, it is impossible to predict the directions of movement so, depending on their choice, different situations arise. Moreover, in the case when the two internal robots move in the same direction, in view of asynchrony, the robots could reach a quadrilateral or triangle situation. All these possibilities have to be taken care of.

3. *Partial visibility*: the robots form a convex quadrilateral and two robots collectively obstruct visibility of two other robots (see, for example, Figure 7.5(a)). In this case, the external robots do not move, while the internal ones move in different directions depending on geometric considerations (in Figure 7.5(a) a possible sequence of movements is indicated). In all cases it is shown that they reach a situation when they form a convex quadrilateral with two robots that are very close to each other and other two that can see each other (*Locking*).

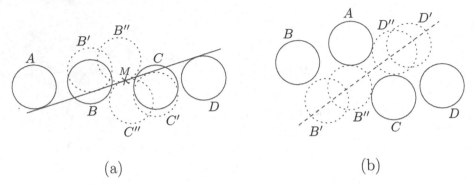

Figure 7.5: Some configurations occurring in situations *Partial Visibily* (a) and *Locking* (b).

4. *Locking*: robots form a convex quadrilateral, Situation 3 does not hold, and one of the diagonals has length $d \leq 8$. The robots corresponding to the larger diagonal appropriately move to touch the other two thus reaching gathering (see, for example, Figure 7.5(b) where the movement of robots B and D to reach gathering is indicated).

5. *Leaving line*: robots form a convex quadrilateral in a very specific way (with none of the previous situation occurring). This is an intermediate situation arising only from Situation 2. The external robots do not move, while the internal ones, having full visibility, can move without obstructing the others in such a way to reach either *Locking* or a situation where three of the four robots are aligned.

6. *ThreeAligned*: the centers of three robots (r_1, r_2, r_3) belong to the same line, the center of r_4 does not, and none of the previous situations occur. Only robot r_4 is allowed to move; it does so avoiding situations *leaving line* and *four aligned*, to reach *locking*.

7. *Sliding*: the bounding circles of the four robots are tangent to a line s (sliding line), two on one side, two on the other. The two pairs of robots on opposite sides of s (r, r_2, r_3, r_4) are such that the distance of their tangency points with s is at most $\frac{1}{3}$. In this situation there is full visibility. Each pair of robots carefully slides toward the other never losing tangency to s, to reach *Locking*.

8. *Triangle*: robots form a triangle with a robot inside and none of the previous situations occur. In this case, the idea is to gather the robots forming the triangle around the robot that is inside. The corresponding routine makes the robots at the vertexes of the triangle move toward the internal robot until they touch it, while the internal robot does not move.

9. *Quadrilateral*: robots form a quadrilateral and none of the previous situations occur. The robots are made to move along the diagonals of the quadrilateral until they form a rectangle consisting

of two symmetric pairs tangent to the same line l and tangent to the other robot in the pair. Note that for some angles between diagonals and some positions of the robots this may be complicated by mutual obstructions of robots on their way. Different actions are required in case of perpendicular and non-perpendicular diagonals; the perpendicular case is relatively simple, while the other case involves several technicalities to guarantee correctness and to reach *Sliding Locking* or *Gathering*.

The proof of correctness is quite involved. The difficulty is to show that only certain transitions from a situation to another are possible (see the diagram of Figure 7.4). The correctness then follows by observing that the diagram is acyclic and has a unique sink at situation *gathering*.

Theorem 7.4   [33] *Four solid robots can gather in* ASYNC *with common unit distance and* fail-stop collisions.

Other Gatherings by Solid Robots.   A few other studies exist on gathering fat robots. All of them are, however, designed under stronger assumptions. For example, an algorithm that works under certain conditions is described in [22] for $k \geq 5$ robots that are solid but transparent (i.e., they are considered not to obstruct each other's view) and have unlimited visibility. The robots must be initially placed in an asymmetry configuration (so that a leader can be elected) and the desired gathering pattern is a circular layered structure of robots with the elected leader in the center. The idea is to have the robots gather around the center of the smallest enclosing circle of the robots; a leader moves to the center of the smallest enclosing circle, and the other robots, one at a time, join it in the desired pattern. The algorithm is not guaranteed to succeed: in fact, it fails if at some point the configuration becomes symmetric. In such a case, in fact the leader election algorithm that would determine which new robot can join the pattern fails.

In [31] gathering by solid robots is considered in a different setting. Each robot is given in input the position of the gathering point in its own coordinate system. All robots have the same dimension dim, and they are said to be gathered when they form a sphere with minimum radius around the predefined gathering point. Robots have *limited visibility*, large enough to avoid collisions (thus, a visibility radius $V \geq 2dim$ is sufficient) and they operate in FSYNC. An algorithm is described and experimentally evaluated that either allows the robots to gather, or, if they end up blocking each other's view, make them spin around the center of the sphere.

7.2.2   UNIFORM CIRCLE OF SOLID ROBOTS

Solid robots have been also studied in the context of circle formation, where simulation results exists.

Convergence toward a Circle.   The first attempt at solving the UNIFORM CIRCLE FORMATION problem by oblivious robots [121] was a heuristic that allowed the robots to form an approximation of a non-degenerated circle (i.e., with finite radius greater than zero) having a given diameter $D \leq v$ in ASYNC with the additional assumption of common unit of distance. For robot s, let $s_f(t)$ and

$s_c(t)$ denote the position of the farthest and of the closest robots at time t, respectively; and let $\epsilon > 0$ be an arbitrarily small predefined quantity. The protocol is rather simple:

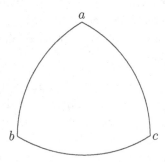

Figure 7.6: Reuleaux's triangle. It is obtained by drawings arcs $arc(a, b), arc(b, c)$, and $arc(c, a)$, with radii equal to D, from the vertexes c, a, and b, respectively, of an equilateral triangle $\triangle(a, b, c)$ with sides equal to D.

Protocol CIRCLE CONVERGENCE (for robot s at time t)
Assumptions: common unit distance

1. If $|s_f(t) - s(t)| > 2D$, then move toward $s_f(t)$.

2. If $|s_f(t) - s(t)| < 2D - \epsilon$, then move away from $s_f(t)$.

3. If $2D - \epsilon \leq |s_f(t) - s(t)| \leq 2D$, then move away from $s_c(t)$.

Experiments have shown that sometimes the robots converge toward a configuration similar to a *Reuleaux triangle* rather than a circle (see Figure 7.6). A better approximation of the circle can be obtained with some modifications [124].

Convergence toward a Circle with directional vision. The problem of arranging in circular shapes mobile robots whose vision is not only limited (i.e., within the visibility range v) but also *directional* has also been studied [109]. The vision function of each robot detects another robot within distance v with the center of the robot assumed to be the origin and the direction of movement the reference angle ($0°$); however the detection occurs only within three areas: forward (FV), and its left (LV) and right (RV) sides; the backward area is that not detecting a robot (see Figure 7.7).

Furthermore, the robots can only detect the presence of other robots within their visibility areas, and not the exact number of robots in their surrounding. In particular, each robot can distinguish two scenarios for the forward area: zero robots (FV= 0), or ≥ 1 robots (FV= 1); for the left area, each robot can distinguish three scenarios: zero robots (LV= 00), one robot (LV= 01), or more than one robot (RV= 10); symmetrically, three scenarios can be detected for the right area as well. Based on this simple information, each robot acts as described in the following protocol.

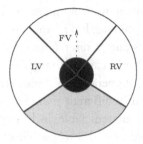

Figure 7.7: The vision model for the emergent approach to circle formation. The black circle represents the robot; the dark area is the blind zone of the robot.

Protocol EMERGENT CIRCLE (for robot s_i)
Assumptions: solid.

If FV= 0, LV= 01, and RV= 00 **Then** Turn left.
If FV= 0, LV= 00, and RV= 01 **Then** Turn right.
If FV= 0, LV= 01, and RV= 01 **Then** Turn to the last previous direction.
For the others scenarios, proceed straight.

Experimental results [109] show that the formation of the circle depends on the number of robots and the front and side view angles of local vision, demonstrating that the front view angle must be between 15° and 75°, while the side view angles between 60° and 120°. Another interesting observation arising from the simulations is that the circle formation rate decreases the larger the number of robots is; that is, an excessive number of robots affects negatively the formation process.

7.3   OBLIVIOUS COMPUTATIONS IN DISCRETE SPACES

The oblivious robots model has been recently employed also in *discrete* spaces, i.e., when the spatial universe $\mathcal{U}$ in which the robots operate is a graph.

Let $G = (N, E)$ be an undirected connected simple graph where N is the set of vertexes and E the set of edges, with $|N| = n$; let $E(x)$ be the edges incident to $x \in N$.

The vertexes are unlabeled (i.e., the graph is anonymous), while the edges might or might not be labeled. If the graph is edge-labeled, let $\lambda_x : E(x) \to \mathcal{L}$ be an injective local labeling function that associates a label from a set $\mathcal{L}$ to each edge incident on x. Let $\lambda = \{\lambda_x : x \in N\}$ be the global labeling function and let (G, λ) denote the resulting edge-labeled graph.

Let Ψ be the placement function describing the position of the robots in the graph. Let (G, Ψ) (resp. (G, λ, Ψ)) denote the graph (reps. edge-labeled graph) with the placement of the robots.

We say that (G, λ, Ψ) is *symmetric* if there exists an automorphism of (G, λ, Ψ) that preserve the labels and the placement; *asymmetric* otherwise. Analogous definition holds for (G, Ψ).

In discrete spaces, the robots move from node to neighboring node still following the *Look-Compute-Move* cycle. The ASYNC, SSYNC, FSYNC models can be defined similarly to the continuous space case, with some distinctions due to discreteness. In particular, the *Look* operation provides a snapshot of the graph (or part of it in case of limited visibility), showing the presence or absence of robots on the nodes. The *Move* operation is considered instantaneous in all three models. In ASYNC the robots look in arbitrarily different moments and the time to complete both *Compute* and *Move* operations is finite but unpredictable; in FSYNC all robots simultaneously perform each of the operations; while in SSYNC in each cycle a subset of the robot is active, and those robots simultaneously perform each of the operations.

Like in the case of continuous spaces, the robots might have *limited visibility* (i.e., see only up to a certain distance given in terms of number of hops), they may have *multiplicity detection* capabilities and be able to distinguish nodes containing more than one robots. In these settings also *local multiplicity* detection has been considered, where a robot can detect multiplicity (or strong multiplicity) only on the node it resides.

The only problems that have been studied in the discrete setting are *gathering*, *exploration*, and *deployment*. These problems (especially exploration) have been extensively investigated in graphs where the robots (typically called agents) are *not oblivious*. In this short section, we briefly outline only the results for *oblivious* robots.

7.3.1   GATHERING

Gathering is defined analogously to the case of continuous spaces. An initial placement (or configuration) of agents (G, Ψ) (or (G, Λ, Ψ) in the case of edge-labeled graphs) is called *gatherable* if there exists an algorithm that gathers all the agents in one node in finite time. The gathering problem in the discrete setting consists in determining which initial configurations are gatherable and in designing an algorithm that gathers all gatherable configurations.

Unless otherwise stated, all results described below hold for anonymous graphs in the ASYNC model.

Unlabelled ring, unlimited visibility, multiplicity detection.   Even in this specific setting, the problem turns out to be surprisingly complicated, and different solutions have been devised for different cases, depending on the number of robots and on their initial placement. In [97], the authors show that gathering is not solvable for periodic configurations, and for configurations that are symmetric with respect to an axis that passes through edges. Moreover, they also prove that multiplicity detection is necessary for the problem to be solved. Two algorithms have been shown to achieve gathering with multiplicity detection respectively, (*i*) for any starting configurations with an odd number of robots, and (*ii*) for any asymmetric configurations. In [96] another solution is described that works for the symmetric cases with an even number of robots when gathering is possible, provided that there are more than eighteen robots. Yet another paper describes the specific case of six robots symmetrically placed [35]. Finally, a general algorithm that works for all gatherable configurations is shown in [36] providing the complete characterization.

Theorem 7.5   [36]   *In unlabelled rings, with unlimited visibility and multiplicity detection, gathering $k > 2$ robots can be done if and only if the initial configuration of robots is aperiodic, or it is symmetric but does not admit an edge–edge axis of symmetry.*

Unlabelled ring, unlimited visibility, local multiplicity detection.   Multiplicity detection has been shown to be necessary to solve gathering in [97]. In [85] the authors show that, under some circumstances, *local multiplicity* detection actually suffices for the problem to be solvable and they provide a solution algorithm. All the results reported below assume unlimited visibility.

Theorem 7.6   [85]   *In unlabelled rings, gathering $2 < k \leq \lfloor \frac{n}{2} \rfloor - 1$ robots can be done with* local multiplicity detection *if the initial configuration of robots is neither periodic nor symmetric.*

The constraints that $k \leq \lfloor \frac{n}{2} \rfloor - 1$ and that the initial configuration is not symmetric have been subsequently removed and the problem solved for an odd number of robots.

Theorem 7.7   [90]   *In unlabelled rings, gathering an odd number of $2 < k < n - 3$ robots can be done with* local multiplicity detection *if the initial configuration of robots is not periodic.*

Finally, the particular case of an even number of robots in an odd size ring has been also studied.

Theorem 7.8   [99]   *Gathering an even number of $k > 8$ robots in unlabelled rings of odd size $n > k + 3$, can be done with* local multiplicity detection *if the initial configuration of robots is not periodic.*

Self-stabilizing Probabilistic Gathering in Unlabelled rings.   An assumption common to the previous gathering results is that the robots start from different nodes. Gathering in the ring has been recently investigated by probabilistic algorithms assuming that the initial configuration might contain multiplicity points. A solution in such a case would be *self-stabilizing*. In this setting multiplicity detection and strong multiplicity detection have the usual meaning, *local* (resp. *local-strong*) multiplicity detection indicates the capability of a robot to determine multiplicity in the node it resides (resp. the exact number of robots sharing its node).

Theorem 7.9   [111]   *In unlabelled rings: (i) self-stabilizing probabilistic gathering is impossible in* ASYNC, *even with strong multiplicity detection, (ii) self-stabilizing probabilistic gathering is impossible in* SSYNC *if only local-strong or weak multiplicity detection are available, (iii) probabilistic gathering is possible in* SSYNC *with strong multiplicity detection.*

Unlabelled grid, unlimited visibility.   Interestingly, in the case of grids of dimension greater than 2, multiplicity detection (global or local) is shown not to be necessary. A full characterization of gatherable configurations is provided in [34] where it is shown that, even if the robots have multiplicity detection, a configuration is ungatherable if it is periodic (i.e., the same view can be obtained by rotating the grid around its geometric center of an angle smaller than 360°) on a grid with at least an even side, or it is symmetric with the axis of symmetry passing through edges. For all the other cases, a gathering algorithm is provided which does not require any multiplicity detection.

Theorem 7.10 [34]   *In unlabelled grids with unlimited visibility, a configuration of robots is ungatherable if and only if it is periodic and the grid has at least an even side, or it is symmetric with the axis of symmetry passing through edges.*

Unlabelled regular bipartite graph, limited visibility, multiplicity detection.   The only result assuming *limited visibility* applies to regular bipartite graphs [80] where a robot can see only its neighbors. Necessary and sufficient conditions for gatherability are given determining a very small class of gatherable configurations; in fact, the class of gatherable initial configurations consists only of "stars" (an agent with all other agents adjacent to it) of size at least 3.

Theorem 7.11 [80]   *In unlabelled regular bipartite graphs, with limited visibility and multiplicity detection, gathering $k > 2$ robots can be done if and only if the initial configuration of robots forms a star.*

Labelled arbitrary topology, unlimited visibility, multiplicity detection.   Gathering in arbitrary topologies has been investigated in [20] assuming that the edges of the graph are labeled. In other words, a robot at a node can distinguish the incident links and can "see" the edge labels of the entire graph when performing its Look operation. The presence of the labels partially compensate for the difficulty due to the arbitrary topology.

   In [20] it is shown that if (G, λ, Ψ) is *symmetric, Gathering* cannot be solved. Conversely, if (G, λ) is *asymmetric Gathering* is of simple resolution. When (G, λ) is *symmetric* but (G, λ, Ψ) is *asymmetric (asymmetric placement)* it is shown that any odd number of robots can gather in any connected graph. As for an even number of robots: it is shown that four robots asymmetrically placed can gather and it is conjectured that any number of asymmetrically placed robots can.

Theorem 7.12 [20]   *With unlimited visibility and multiplicity detection: gathering cannot be performed if (G, λ, Ψ) is symmetric. Moreover, gathering of $k = 2l + 1 > 1$ and $k = 4$ robots can be done if (G, λ, Ψ) is asymmetric.*

Finally, a complete characterization for rings and trees is given showing that, in these special topologies, gathering can be achieved if and only if (G, λ, Ψ) is asymmetric, regardless of the number $k > 2$ of robots.

Theorem 7.13 **[20]** *In labeled rings and trees gathering of $k > 2$ robots with unlimited visibility and multiplicity detection can be done if and only if (G, λ, Ψ) is asymmetric.*

7.3.2 EXPLORATION WITH STOP

To explore a graph, a team of oblivious robots must visit all the nodes of the graph and terminate in finite time. All solutions devised in the literature apply to anonymous topologies. Whenever not specified, we assume the robots operate in the ASYNC model. A particular issue common to all the investigations is the determination of the minimum number of robots necessary to perform exploration and the conditions under which exploration is possible for any starting configuration.

Unlabelled line, unlimited visibility, multiplicity detection. The case of the unlabelled line with unlimited visibility has been investigated in [62], where a complete characterization has been given in terms of sizes of teams of robots capable of exploring an n-node line. For $k < n$, exploration by k robots is possible if and only if either $k = 3$, or $k \geq 5$, or $k = 4$ and n is odd. For all values of k for which exploration is possible, an exploration algorithm is given. For all others, impossibility results are provided.

Theorem 7.14 **[62]** *The exploration of an unlabelled line by k oblivious robots with unlimited visibility and multiplicity detection can be performed if and only if $k = 3$, or $k \geq 5$, or $k = 4$ and n is odd.*

Unlabelled tree, unlimited visibility, multiplicity detection. In [63] it is shown that, in general, $\Theta(n)$ robots are necessary to explore any arbitrary tree with n nodes. If the maximum degree of the tree is 3 then it is possible to explore it with only $O(\frac{\log n}{\log \log n})$ robots and this size is asymptotically optimal. The algorithm that allows a team of $O(\frac{\log n}{\log \log n})$ robots to explore the tree and terminate is quite complex. In this setting, the major difficulty in the design of a terminating exploration algorithm comes from the fact that, because of obliviousness, the robots must always form different configurations until the task is completed (otherwise the adversary will force the robots in an endless cycle without being able to terminate). To achieve this goal without communication and without persistent memory, the robots implement a distributed memory with several counting modules that enable them to perform the task and to terminate.

In [63] it is also shown that, in order to explore trees that do not have any non-trivial automorphisms (called rigid trees), four robots are always sufficient and often necessary. This stresses the fact that the difficulty in tree exploration stems from the symmetries of the tree. Summarizing:

Theorem 7.15 **[63]** *With unlimited visibility and multiplicity detection, $\Theta(n)$ robots are necessary to explore an arbitrary unlabelled n-nodes tree.*

Theorem 7.16 [63] *With unlimited visibility and multiplicity detection, $O(\frac{\log n}{\log \log n})$ robots are necessary and sufficient to explore n-node unlabelled trees of maximum degree 3, starting from any initial configuration.*

Theorem 7.17 [63] *Any rigid unlabelled tree with $n \geq 7$ nodes can be explored by four robots with unlimited visibility and multiplicity detection, starting from any initial configuration. Moreover, four robots are required to explore any rigid tree with at least four leaves.*

Unlabelled ring, unlimited visibility, multiplicity detection.   In the case of the ring, it is shown in [64] that no deterministic exploration is possible when the number of robots k divides n. The algorithm to achieve exploration employs at least seventeen robots (provided that n and k are coprime). The minimum number $\rho(n)$ of robots that can explore a ring of size n is also analyzed and it is shown that $\rho(n)$ is $O(\log n)$ and $\rho(n) = \Omega(\log n)$ for infinitely many n.

Theorem 7.18 [64] *With unlimited visibility and multiplicity detection, the exploration of an n-node unlabelled ring with $k < n$ robots is not possible if $k|n$. Moreover, let $17 \leq k < n$. A team of k robots with unlimited visibility and multiplicity detection, can explore an n-node ring and enter a terminal state within finite time, provided $gcd(n, k) = 1$.*

Theorem 7.19 [64] *With unlimited visibility and multiplicity detection, the minimum number $\rho(n)$ of robots that can explore an n-node unlabelled ring has the following properties:*
1) $\rho(n) \in O(\log n)$;
2) there exists a constant c such that, for infinitely many n, we have $\rho(n) \geq c \log n$.

The ring has been studied further with the focus on probabilistic algorithms, and on the minimum number of robots necessary to solve the problem in SSYNC. In particular, in [48] the authors have shown that in a probabilistic setting four robots are necessary and sufficient to perform exploration without any constraint on the relationship between number of nodes and number of robots, and they have given an optimal algorithm for any ring size greater than eight. This result is in contrast with the fact that, in SSYNC, $\Theta(\log n)$ robots are instead necessary and sufficient for obtaining a deterministic solution.

Theorem 7.20 [48] *There exists no exploration protocol (even probabilistic) of an n-node ring by $k < 4$ robots with unlimited visibility and multiplicity detection. On the other hand, in SSYNC with unlimited visibility and multiplicity detection, there exists a probabilistic exploration protocol for four robots in n-nodes unlabelled rings with $n > 8$.*

An optimal algorithm for the probabilistic exploration of rings of size smaller than eight in SSYNC is given in [46].

Another result on the relationship between the number of robots and the size of the ring for exploration has been given in [100] where it is shown that no deterministic exploration is possible in SSYNC (and thus in ASYNC) with less than five robots whenever the size of the ring is even, and that five robots are sufficient for any n that is co-prime with five.

Unlabelled grid, unlimited visibility, multiplicity detection.   The grid has been investigated in [47] with the focus on the number of robots necessary and sufficient for exploration. Impossibility results for both deterministic and probabilistic solutions are given an optimal deterministic algorithms designed. The main results obtained are summarized in the following theorem:

Theorem 7.21   **[47]**   *A $x \times y$ grid with $x, y > 3$ cannot be explored in* SSYNC *(and thus in* ASYNC*) with less than three robots, even by probabilistic algorithms. Moreover, it can be explored in* ASYNC *with three robots.*

Labelled arbitrary topology, unlimited visibility, multiplicity detection.   Conditions of solvability and generic algorithms that allow a team of robots to explore an arbitrary topology have been given in [20], where the graph is assumed to be edge-labeled. The presence of the labels partially compensate for the difficulty due to the arbitrary topology.

Like in the case of GATHERING, in [20] it is shown that if (G, λ, Ψ) is *symmetric*, exploration cannot be done. Conversely, if (G, λ) is *asymmetric*, exploration can be easily performed. Exploration is then investigated in the most complex situation when (G, λ) is *symmetric* but (G, λ, Ψ) is *asymmetric* (*asymmetric placement*).

Explorability heavily depends on the number of robots. When the team is composed by $k = 3$ robots, not all connected graphs with asymmetric placement can be explored. A complex necessary and sufficient condition for the graph to be explorable is given and an algorithm that performs the exploration when the condition is verified is described. On the other hand, when $k = 2l + 1 > 3$ all graphs with asymmetric placement can be explored and the exploration algorithm is based on gathering. Exploration can be solved in any graph also in the even case of $k = 4$ robots with asymmetric placement. The general even case is left as an open problem.

As for the case of gathering, a complete characterization for exploration in rings and trees is shown. It is in fact proven that both problems can be solved if and only if (G, λ, Ψ) is asymmetric, regardless of the number $k > 2$ of robots. The only exception is the case of three robots in the tree where slightly different, necessary, and sufficient conditions are given.

7.3.3   PERPETUAL EXPLORATION

A variant of exploration has been studied in the discrete setting where the robots perpetually explore all nodes of a graph, without ever stopping. An additional requirement is that no two robots may occupy the same node at any time. The ring [9] has been investigated in the ASYNC model with unlimited visibility, and it has been shown that three deterministic robots are necessary and sufficient for rings of size at least ten, while no algorithm with three robots exists for rings of size smaller than ten. It is also shown that $n - 5$ robots are necessary and sufficient for rings of size n when n is co-prime with k. The perpetual exploration problem has also been studied in a partial grid topology (i.e., a grid with missing edges) [7] in FSYNC, with limited visibility and sense of direction (the edges are labeled with *north*, *south*, *east*, and *west*). In this setting, the authors study the relationship between the visibility radius and the number of robots that are necessary and sufficient to solve the problem. The solution was later generalized [11] in ASYNC with unlimited visibility to complete grids without sense of direction. Finally, in a recent study [10], a generic method for obtaining all possible protocols for a swarm of mobile robots operating in a particular discrete space is proposed and is applied to perpetual exploration in rings as a case study.

7.3.4 UNIFORM DEPLOYMENT IN THE RING

The *uniform deployment* problem in a ring is defined similarly to the case of the continuous setting of the circle discussed in Section 5.3. The k robots are initially placed in arbitrary nodes of a ring of size n and they have to move until they reach a situation where the distance between any two adjacent robots is either $\lceil n/k \rceil$ or $\lfloor n/k \rfloor$ (this situation is also called balanced configuration). From this moment on, the robots must stay in a balanced configuration. Note that, since a balanced configuration is not unique, the robots might still be moving from balanced configuration to balanced configuration once deployment is reached. A stronger form of uniform deployment is when the agents are required to stop moving as soon as they form a balanced configuration (*uniform deployment with stop*). The robots have visibility radius V, and obstructive vision. In other words, the visibility is limited to the minimum between V and the next robot.

The uniform deployment problem has been studied in [60], where several impossibility and possibility results are shown depending on the presence of an orientation, on the visibility radius, and on the level of synchronicity. First of all, it is shown that in unoriented rings no deterministic oblivious algorithm can achieve a uniform deployment, even in FSYNC (and even with full visibility). The impossibility holds also in oriented rings if the robots' visibility radius V is strictly less than $\lfloor n/k \rfloor$. On the other hand, a solution exists in SSYNC, and an algorithm is described for $V > \lfloor n/k \rfloor$. It is then shown that uniform deployment with stop is impossible even in oriented rings, with obstructed visibility.

Bibliography

[1] N. Agmon and D. Peleg. Fault-tolerant gathering algorithms for autonomous mobile robots. *SIAM Journal on Computing*, 36:56–82, 2006. DOI: 10.1137/050645221 Cited on page(s) 14, 25, 55, 57, 58, 59, 60, 61

[2] H. Ando, Y. Oasa, I. Suzuki, and M. Yamashita. A distributed memoryless point convergence algorithm for mobile robots with limited visibility. *IEEE Transactions on Robotics and Automation*, 15(5):818–828, 1999. DOI: 10.1109/70.795787 Cited on page(s) 1, 38, 39, 40, 48

[3] H. Ando, I. Suzuki, and M. Yamashita. Formation and agreement problems for synchronous mobile robots with limited visibility. In *Proceedings of the 1995 IEEE Symposium on Intelligent Control*, pages 453–460, 1995. DOI: 10.1109/ISIC.1995.525098 Cited on page(s) 38, 65

[4] R. C. Arkin. Motor Schema-Based Mobile Robot Navigation. *International Journal of Robotics Research*, 8(4):92–112, 1989. DOI: 10.1177/027836498900800406 Cited on page(s) 1, 117, 126, 132

[5] C. Bajaj. The algebraic degree of geometric optimization problems. *Discrete and Computational Geometry*, 3:177–191, 1988. DOI: 10.1007/BF02187906 Cited on page(s) 28

[6] T. Balch and R. C. Arkin. Behavior-based Formation Control for Multi-robot Teams. *IEEE Transaction on Robotics and Automation*, 14(6):926–939, December 1998. DOI: 10.1109/70.736776 Cited on page(s) 1, 117, 126

[7] R. Baldoni, F. Bonnet, A. Milani, and M. Raynal. On the solvability of anonymous partial grids exploration by mobile robots. In *Proceedings of 12th International Conference on Principles of Distributed Systems (OPODIS)*, pages 428–445, 2008. DOI: 10.1007/978-3-540-92221-6_27 Cited on page(s) 152

[8] L. Barrière, P. Flocchini, E. Mesa-Barrameda, and N. Santoro. Uniform scattering of autonomous mobile robots in a grid. *International Journal of Foundations of Computer Science*, 22(3):679–697, 2011. DOI: 10.1142/S0129054111008295 Cited on page(s) 3, 12

[9] L. Blin, A. Milani, M. Potop-Butucaru, and S. Tixeuil. Exclusive perpetual ring exploration without chirality. In *Proceedings of 24th International Symposium on Distributed Computing (DISC)*, pages 312–327, 2010. DOI: 10.1007/978-3-642-15763-9_29 Cited on page(s) 151

[10] F. Bonnet, X. Défago, F. Petit, M. Gradinariu Potop-Butucaru, and S. Tixeuil. Brief announcement: Discovering and assessing fine-grained metrics in robot networks protocols. In *Proceedings of the* 14th *International Conference on Stabilization, Safety, and Security in Distributed Systems (SSS)*, 2012. Cited on page(s) 152

[11] F. Bonnet, A. Milani, M. Potop-Butucaru, and S. Tixeuil. Asynchronous exclusive perpetual grid exploration without sense of direction. In *Proceedings of* 15th *International Conference on Principles of Distributed Systems (OPODIS)*, pages 251–265, 2011. DOI: 10.1007/978-3-642-25873-2_18 Cited on page(s) 152

[12] Z. Bouzid, S. Das, and S. Tixeuil. Wait-free gathering of mobile robots. Technical Report arXiv:1207.0226v1, arXiv.org, 2012. Cited on page(s) 58

[13] Z. Bouzid and A. Lamani. Robot networks with homonyms: The case of patterns formation. In *Proceedings of* 13th *International Symposium on Stabilization, Safety, and Security of Distributed Systems (SSS)*, pages 92–107, 2011. DOI: 10.1007/978-3-642-24550-3_9 Cited on page(s) 101

[14] Z. Bouzid, M. Gradinariu Potop-Butucaru, and S. Tixeuil. Byzantine convergence in robot networks: The price of asynchrony. In *Proceedings of* 13th *International Conference Principles of Distributed Systems (OPODIS)*, pages 54–70, 2009. DOI: 10.1007/978-3-642-10877-8_7 Cited on page(s) 61, 63

[15] Z. Bouzid, M. Gradinariu Potop-Butucaru, and S. Tixeuil. Optimal Byzantine-resilient convergence in uni-dimensional robot networks. *Theoretical Computer Science*, 411:3154–3168, 2010. DOI: 10.1016/j.tcs.2010.05.006 Cited on page(s) 61, 62, 63

[16] F. Bullo, J. Cortes, and S. Martinez. *Distributed Control of Robotic Networks*. Princeton University Press, 2009. Cited on page(s) 1

[17] D. Canepa and M. Gradinariu Potop-Butucaru. Stabilizing flocking via leader election in robot networks. In *Proceedings of* 9th *International Symposium on Stabilization, Safety, and Security of Distributed Systems (SSS)*, pages 52–66, 2007. DOI: 10.1007/978-3-540-76627-8_7 Cited on page(s) 12, 117, 119, 128, 129, 130, 131, 132

[18] D. Canepa and M. Gradinariu Potop-Butucaru. Stabilizing flocking via leader election in robot networks. Technical Report 6268, INRIA, 2007. DOI: 10.1007/978-3-540-76627-8_7 Cited on page(s) 128, 129, 130, 131

[19] R. Carli and F. Bullo. Quantized coordination algorithms for rendezvous and deployment. *SIAM Journal on Control and Optimization*, 48(3):1251–1274, 2009. DOI: 10.1137/070709906 Cited on page(s) 105

[20] J. Chalopin, P. Flocchini, B. Mans, and N. Santoro. Network exploration by silent and oblivious robots. In *Proceedings of 36th International Workshop on Graph Theoretic Concepts in Computer Science (WG)*, pages 208–219, 2010. DOI: 10.1007/978-3-642-16926-7_20 Cited on page(s) 3, 148, 149, 151

[21] I. Chatzigiannakis, M. Markou, and S. Nikoletseas. Distributed circle formation for anonymous oblivious robots. In *Proceedings of 3rd International Workshop on Experimental and Efficient Algorithms (WEA)*, pages 159 –174, 2004. DOI: 10.1007/978-3-540-24838-5_12 Cited on page(s) 3, 12, 65, 84

[22] S. G. Chaudhuri and K. Mukhopadhyaya. Gathering asynchronous transparent fat robots. In *Proceedings of 6th International Conference on Distributed Computing and Internet Technology (ICDCIT)*, pages 170–175, 2010. DOI: 10.1007/978-3-642-11659-9_17 Cited on page(s) 11, 143

[23] Q. Chen and J. Y. S. Luh. Coordination and control of a group of small mobile robots. In *Proceedings of 1994 IEEE International Conference on Robotics and Automation*, pages 2315–2320, 1994. DOI: 10.1109/ROBOT.1994.350940 Cited on page(s) 117

[24] M. Cieliebak, P. Flocchini, G. Prencipe, and N. Santoro. Solving the gathering problem. In *Proceedings of 30th International Colloquium on Automata, Languages and Programming (ICALP)*, pages 1181–1196, 2003. Cited on page(s) 21, 25

[25] M. Cieliebak, P. Flocchini, G. Prencipe, and N. Santoro. Distributed computing by mobile robots: Gathering. *SIAM Journal on Computing*, 2012. Cited on page(s) 21, 28, 34, 35

[26] M. Cieliebak and G. Prencipe. Gathering autonomous mobile robots. In *Proceedings of 9th International Colloquium on Structural Information and Communication Complexity (SIROCCO)*, pages 57–72, 2002. Cited on page(s) 35, 55

[27] J. Clark and R. Fierro. Mobile robotic sensors for perimeter detection and tracking. *ISA Transactions*, 46(1):3–13, 2007. DOI: 10.1016/j.isatra.2006.08.001 Cited on page(s) 1

[28] R. Cohen and D. Peleg. Convergence properties of the gravitational algorithm in asynchronous robot systems. *SIAM Journal on Computing*, 34:1516–1528, 2005. DOI: 10.1137/S0097539704446475 Cited on page(s) 3, 12, 17, 22, 25, 26, 27, 48

[29] R. Cohen and D. Peleg. Convergence of autonomous mobile robots with inaccurate sensors and movements. In *Proceedings of 23rd International Symposium on Theoretical Aspects of Computer Science (STACS)*, pages 549—560, 2006. DOI: 10.1007/11672142_45 Cited on page(s) 51, 52, 53, 54

[30] R. Cohen and D. Peleg. Local spreading algorithms for autonomous robot systems. *Theoretical Computer Science*, 399·71–82, 2008. DOI: 10.1016/j.tcs.2008.02.007 Cited on page(s) 3, 12, 105, 106, 107

[31] A. Cord-Landwehr, B. Degener, M. Fischer, M. Hüllmann, B. Kempkes, A. Klaas, P. Kling, S. Kurras, M. Mrtens, F. Meyer auf der Heide, C. Raupach, K. Swierkot, D. Warner, C. Weddemann, and D. Wonisch. Collision-less gathering of robots with an extent. In *Proceedings of 37th International Conference on Current Trends in Theory and Practice of Computer Science (SOFSEM)*, pages 178–189, 2011. Cited on page(s) 11, 143

[32] A. Cord-Landwehr, B. Degener, M. Fischer, M. Hüllmann, B. Kempkes, A. Klaas, P. Kling, S. Kurras, M. Mrtens, F. Meyer auf der Heide, C. Raupach, K. Swierkot, D. Warner, C. Weddemann, and D. Wonisch. A new approach for analyzing convergence algorithms for mobile robots. In *Proceedings of 38th International Colloquium on Automata, Languages and Programming (ICALP)*, pages 650–661. Springer, 2011. DOI: 10.1007/978-3-642-22012-8_52 Cited on page(s) 27

[33] J. Czyzowicz, L. Gasieniec, and A. Pelc. Gathering few fat mobile robots in the plane. *Theoretical Computer Science*, 410(6–7):481–499, 2009. DOI: 10.1016/j.tcs.2008.10.005 Cited on page(s) 11, 13, 139, 140, 143

[34] G. D'Angelo, G. Di Stefano, R. Klasing, and A. Navarra. Gathering of robots on anonymous grids without multiplicity detection. In *Proceedings of 19th International Colloquium on Structural Information and Communication Complexity (SIROCCO)*, pages 327–338, 2012. DOI: 10.1007/978-3-642-31104-8_28 Cited on page(s) 148

[35] G. D'Angelo, G. Di Stefano, and A. Navarra. Gathering of six robots on anonymous symmetric rings. In *Proceedings of 18th International Colloquium on Structural Information and Communication Complexity (SIROCCO)*, pages 174–185, 2011. DOI: 10.1007/978-3-642-22212-2_16 Cited on page(s) 147

[36] G. D'Angelo, G. Di Stefano, and A. Navarra. How to gather asynchronous oblivious robots on anonymous rings. In *26th International Symposium on Distributed Computing*, to appear, 2012. Cited on page(s) 147

[37] S. Das, P. Flocchini, S. Kutten, A. Nayak, and N. Santoro. Map construction of unknown graphs by multiple agents. *Theoretical Computer Science*, 385(1-3):34–48, 2007. DOI: 10.1016/j.tcs.2007.05.011 Cited on page(s) 1

[38] S. Das, P. Flocchini, G. Prencipe, N. Santoro, and M. Yamashita. The power of lights: Synchronizing asynchronous robots using visible bits. In *Proceedings of 32nd International Conference on Distributed Computing Systems (ICDCS)*, 2012. (to appear). Cited on page(s) 9, 135, 136, 137, 138

[39] S. Das, P. Flocchini, N. Santoro, and M. Yamashita. On the computational power of oblivious robots: forming a series of geometric patterns. In *Proceedings of 29th Annual ACM Symposium on Principles of Distributed Computing (PODC)*, pages 267–276, 2010. DOI: 10.1145/1835698.1835761 Cited on page(s) 98, 99, 100, 101

[40] S. Das, E. Mesa-Barrameda, and N. Santoro. Deployment of asynchronous robotic sensors in unknown orthogonal environments. In *Proceedings of 4th International Workshop on Algorithmic Aspects of Wireless Sensor Networks (ALGOSENSOR)*, pages 25–140, 2008. DOI: 10.1007/978-3-540-92862-1_11 Cited on page(s) 3, 12, 113, 114, 115

[41] X. A. Debest. Remark about self-stabilizing systems. *Communication of the ACM*, 2(38):115–177, 1995. Cited on page(s) 84

[42] X. Défago, M. Gradinariu, S. Messika, and P. R. Parvédy. Fault-tolerant and self-stabilizing mobile robots gathering. In *Proceedings of 20th International Symposium on Distributed Computing (DISC)*, pages 46–60, 2006. DOI: 10.1007/11864219_4 Cited on page(s) 9, 21, 25, 55, 59

[43] X. Défago and A. Konagaya. Circle formation for oblivious anonymous mobile robots with no common sense of orientation. In *Proceedings of 2nd Workshop on Principles of Mobile Computing*, pages 97–104, 2002. DOI: 10.1145/584490.584509 Cited on page(s) 3, 12, 65, 84, 86

[44] X. Défago and S. Souissi. Non-uniform circle formation algorithm for oblivious mobile robots with convergence toward uniformity. *Theoretical Computer Science*, 396(1-3):97–112, 2008. DOI: 10.1016/j.tcs.2008.01.050 Cited on page(s) 65, 84, 86

[45] B. Degener, B. Kempkes, T. Langner, F. Meyer auf der Heide, P. Pietrzyk, and R. Wattenhofer. A tight runtime bound for synchronous gathering of autonomous robots with limited visibility. In *Proceedings of 23rd ACM Symposium on Parallelism in algorithms and architectures (SPAA)*, pages 139–148, 2011. DOI: 10.1145/1989493.1989515 Cited on page(s) 39

[46] S. Devismes. Optimal exploration of small rings. In *Proceedings of 3rd International Workshop on Reliability, Availability, and Security (WRAS)*, pages 1–9, 2010. DOI: 10.1145/1953563.1953571 Cited on page(s) 3, 150

[47] S. Devismes, A. Lamani, F. Petit, P. Raymond, and S. Tixeuil. Optimal grid exploration by asynchronous oblivious robots. In *Proceedings of 14th International Conference on Stabilization, Safety, and Security in Distributed Systems (SSS)*, 2012. (to appear). Cited on page(s) 151

[48] S. Devismes, F. Petit, and S. Tixeuil. Optimal probabilistic ring exploration by semi-synchronous oblivious robots. In *Proceedings of 16th International Colloquium on Structural Information and Communication Complexity (SIROCCO)*, pages 95–208, 2009. DOI: 10.1007/978-3-642-11476-2_16 Cited on page(s) 150

[49] Y. Dieudonné, O. Labbani-Igbida, and F. Petit. Circle formation of weak mobile robots. *ACM Transactions on Autonomous and Adaptive Systems*, 3(4):16:1–16:20, 2008. DOI: 10.1145/1452001.1452006 Cited on page(s) 84, 89, 90, 91, 93, 94

[50] Y. Dieudonné and F. Petit. Circle formation of weak robots and lyndon words. *Information Processing Letters*, 4(104):156—162, 2007. DOI: 10.1016/j.ipl.2006.09.008 Cited on page(s) 84

[51] Y. Dieudonné and F. Petit. Squaring the circle with weak mobile robots. In *Proceedings of 19th International Symposium on Algorithms and Computation (ISAAC)*, pages 354–365, 2008. DOI: 10.1007/978-3-540-92182-0_33 Cited on page(s) 94

[52] Y. Dieudonné and F. Petit. Scatter of weak mobile robots. *Parallel Processing Letters*, 19(1):175–184, 2009. Cited on page(s) 104

[53] Y. Dieudonné and F. Petit. Self-stabilizing gathering with strong multiplicity detection. *Theoretical Computer Science*, 428((13)), 2012. DOI: 10.1016/j.tcs.2011.12.010 Cited on page(s) 37, 38

[54] Y. Dieudonné, F. Petit, and V. Villain. Leader election problem versus pattern formation problem. In *Proceedings of 24th International Symposium on Distributed Computing (DISC)*, pages 267–281, 2010. DOI: 10.1007/978-3-642-15763-9_26 Cited on page(s) 70, 71

[55] E. W. Dijkstra. *Selected Writings on Computing: A Personal Perspective*. Springer-Verlag, 1982. DOI: 10.1007/978-1-4612-5695-3 Cited on page(s) 3

[56] E.W. Dijkstra. Self stabilizing systems in spite of distributed control. *Communications of the Association of the Computing Machinery*, 17:643–644, 1974. DOI: 10.1145/361179.361202 Cited on page(s) 11

[57] S. Dolev. *Self-Stabilization*. The MIT Press, 2000. Cited on page(s) 3, 11

[58] S. Dubois and S. Tixeuil. A taxonomy of daemons in self-stabilization. Technical Report 1110.0334, ArXiv eprint, October 2011. Cited on page(s) 9

[59] S. Durocher and D. Kirkpatrick. The projection median of a set of points. *Computational Geometry: Theory and Applications*, 42(5):364–375, 2009. DOI: 10.1016/j.comgeo.2008.06.006 Cited on page(s) 28

[60] Y. Elor and A. M. Bruckstein. Uniform multi-agent deployment on a ring. *Theoretical Computer Science*, 412:783–795, 2011. DOI: 10.1016/j.tcs.2010.11.023 Cited on page(s) 152

[61] N. Fatès. Solving the decentralized gathering problem with a reaction-diffusion-chemotaxis scheme. *Swarm Intelligence*, 4, 2010. DOI: 10.1007/s11721-010-0038-4 Cited on page(s) 1

[62] P. Flocchini, D. Ilcinkas, A. Pelc, and N. Santoro. How many oblivious robots can explore a line. *Information Processing Letters*, 111(20):1027–1031, 2011. DOI: 10.1016/j.ipl.2011.07.018 Cited on page(s) 149

[63] P. Flocchini, D. Ilcinkas, A. Pelc, and N. Santoro. Remembering without memory: Tree exploration by asynchronous oblivious robots. *Theoretical Computer Science*, 411((14-15)), 2012. DOI: 10.1016/j.tcs.2010.01.007 Cited on page(s) 149, 150

[64] P. Flocchini, D. Ilcinkas, A. Pelc, and N. Santoro. Ring exploration by asynchronous oblivious robots. *Algorithmica*, 2012. DOI: 10.1007/s00453-011-9611-5 Cited on page(s) 3, 150

[65] P. Flocchini, G. Prencipe, and N. Santoro. Self-deployment algorithms for mobile sensors on a ring. *Theoretical Computer Science*, 402(1):67–80, 2008. DOI: 10.1016/j.tcs.2008.03.006 Cited on page(s) 12, 86, 94, 95, 96, 108, 111, 112

[66] P. Flocchini, G. Prencipe, and N. Santoro. Computing by mobile robotic sensors. In S. Nikoletseas and J. Rolim, editors, *Theoretical Aspects of Distributed Computing in Sensor Networks*, chapter 21, pages 655–693. Springer, 2011. DOI: 10.1007/978-3-642-14849-1 Cited on page(s) 10

[67] P. Flocchini, G. Prencipe, N. Santoro, and P. Widmayer. Hard tasks for weak robots: The role of common knowledge in pattern formation by autonomous mobile robots. In *Proceedings of 10th International Symposium on Algorithms and Computation (ISAAC)*, pages 93–102, 1999. DOI: 10.1007/3-540-46632-0_10 Cited on page(s) 8

[68] P. Flocchini, G. Prencipe, N. Santoro, and P. Widmayer. Gathering of asynchronous mobile robots with limited visibility. *Theoretical Computer Science*, 337:147–168, 2005. DOI: 10.1016/j.tcs.2005.01.001 Cited on page(s) 3, 12, 25, 38, 42, 45

[69] P. Flocchini, G. Prencipe, N. Santoro, and P. Widmayer. Arbitrary pattern formation by asynchronous oblivious robots. *Theoretical Computer Science*, 407(1-3):412–447, 2008. DOI: 10.1016/j.tcs.2008.07.026 Cited on page(s) 3, 12, 65, 68, 69, 71, 72, 75, 76, 78

[70] N. Foukia, J. G. Hulaas, and J. Harms. Intrusion Detection with Mobile Agents. In *Proceedings of 11th Annual Conference of the Internet Society (INET 2001)*, 2001. http://www.isoc.org. Cited on page(s) 1

[71] J. Fredslund and M. J. Matarić. A general algorithm for robot formations using local sensing and minimal communication. *IEEE Transactions on Robotics and Automation*, 18(5):837–846, 2002. DOI: 10.1109/TRA.2002.803458 Cited on page(s) 1

[72] N. Fujinaga, Y. Yamauchi, S. Kijima, and M. Yamashita. Asynchronous pattern formation by anonymous oblivious mobile robots. In *26th International Symposium on Distributed Computing*, to appear, 2012. Cited on page(s) 84

[73] N. Fujinaga, H. Ono, S. Kijima, and M. Yamashita. Pattern formation through optimum matching by oblivious CORDA robots. In *Proceedings of 14th International Conference on Principles of Distributed Systems (OPODIS)*, pages 1–15, 2010. DOI: 10.1007/978-3-642-17653-1_1 Cited on page(s) 78, 80

[74] A. Ganguli, J. Cortés, and F. Bullo. Multirobot rendezvous with visibility sensors in nonconvex environments. *IEEE Transactions on Robotics*, 25(2):340–352, 2009. DOI: 10.1109/TRO.2009.2013493 Cited on page(s) 40, 41

[75] V. Gervasi and G. Prencipe. Coordination without communication: The case of the flocking problem. *Discrete Applied Mathemathics*, 144(3):324–344, 2003. DOI: 10.1016/j.dam.2003.11.010 Cited on page(s) 119, 120, 122, 123

[76] V. Gervasi and G. Prencipe. Robotic cops: The intruder problem. In *Proceedings of the 2003 IEEE International Conference on Systems, Man, and Cybernetics*, pages 2284–2289, 2003. DOI: 10.1109/ICSMC.2003.1244224 Cited on page(s) 84, 125, 126, 127

[77] V. Gervasi and G. Prencipe. On the efficient capture of dangerous criminals. In *Proceedings of 3rd International Conference on Fun With Algorithms*, pages 184–196, 2004. Cited on page(s) 126, 127

[78] N. Gordon, Y. Elor, and A. M. Bruckstein. Gathering multiple robotic agents with crude distance sensing capabilities. In *Proceedings of 6th International Conference on Ant Colony Optimizatin and Swarm Intelligence*, pages 72–83, 2008. DOI: 10.1007/978-3-540-87527-7_7 Cited on page(s) 51

[79] N. Gordon, I. A. Wagner, and A. M. Bruckstein. Gathering multiple robotic a(ge)nts with limited sensing capabilities. In *Proceedings of 2nd International Conference on Ant Colony Optimization and Swarm Intelligence*, pages 142–153, 2004. DOI: 10.1007/978-3-540-28646-2_13 Cited on page(s) 1, 51

[80] S. Guilbault and A. Pelc. Gathering asynchronous oblivious agents with local vision in regular bipartite graphs. In *Proceedings of 18th International Colloquium on Structural Information and Communication Complexity (SIROCCO)*, pages 162–173, 2011. DOI: 10.1007/978-3-642-22212-2_15 Cited on page(s) 148

[81] N. Heo and P. K. Varshney. Energy-efficient deployment of intelligent mobile sensor networks. *IEEE Transactions on Systems, Man, and CyberNetics - Part A: Systems and Humans*, 35(1):78–92, 2005. DOI: 10.1109/TSMCA.2004.838486 Cited on page(s) 2

[82] A. Howard, M. J. Mataric, and G. S. Sukhatme. An incremental self-deployment algorithm for mobile sensor networks. *Autonomous Robots*, 13(2):113–126, 2002. DOI: 10.1023/A:1019625207705 Cited on page(s) 2

[83] T.-R. Hsiang, E. Arkin, M. A. Bender, S. Fekete, and J. Mitchell. Algorithms for rapidly dispersing robot swarms in unknown environments. In *Proceedings of 5th Workshop on Algorithmic Foundations of Robotics (WAFR)*, pages 77–94, 2002. Cited on page(s) 3, 12

[84] T. Izumi, Z. Bouzid, S. Tixeuil, and K. Wada. Brief Announcement: The BG-simulation for Byzantine mobile robots. In *Proceedings of 25th International Symposium on Distributed Computing (DISC)*, pages 330–331, 2011. DOI: 10.1007/978-3-642-24100-0_32 Cited on page(s) 59

[85] T. Izumi, T. Izumi, S. Kamei, and F. Ooshita. Mobile robots gathering algorithm with local weak multiplicity in rings. In *Proceedings of 17th International Colloquium on Structural Information and Communication Complexity (SIROCCO)*, pages 101–113, 2010. DOI: 10.1007/978-3-642-13284-1_9 Cited on page(s) 147

[86] T. Izumi, Y. Katayama, N. Inuzuka, and K. Wada. Gathering autonomous mobile robots with dynamic compasses: An optimal results. In *Proceedings of 21st International Symposium on Distributed Computing (DISC)*. Springer, 2007. DOI: 10.1007/978-3-540-75142-7_24 Cited on page(s) 35, 36, 37

[87] T. Izumi, M. Gradinariu Potop-Butucaru, and S. Tixeuil. Connectivity-preserving scattering of mobile robots with limited visibility. In *Proceedings of 12th International Symposium on Stabilization, Safety, and Security of Distributed Systems (SSS)*, pages 319—331, 2010. DOI: 10.1007/978-3-642-16023-3_27 Cited on page(s) 105

[88] T. Izumi, S. Souissi, Y. Katayama, N. Inuzuka, X. Defago, K. Wada, and M. Yamashita. The gathering problem for two oblivious robots with unreliable compasses. *Siam Journal on Computing*, 41(1):26–46, 2012. DOI: 10.1137/100797916 Cited on page(s) 18, 21, 23, 24, 25

[89] D. Jung, G. Cheng, and A. Zelinsky. Experiments in realising cooperation between autonomous mobile robots. In *Proceedings of 5th International Symposium on Experimental Robotics (ISER)*, pages 513–524, 1997. Cited on page(s) 25

[90] S. Kamei, A. Lamani, F. Ooshita, and S. Tixeuil. Asynchronous mobile robot gathering from symmetric configurations without global multiplicity detection. In *Proceedings of 18th Int. Colloquium on Structural Information and Communication Complexity (SIROCCO)*, pages 150–161, 2011. DOI: 10.1007/978-3-642-22212-2_14 Cited on page(s) 147

[91] A. Kansal, W. Kaiser, G. Pottie, M. Srivastava, and G. S. Sukhatme. Reconfiguration methods for mobile sensor networks. *ACM Transactions on Sensor Networks*, 3(4):22–23, 2007. DOI: 10.1145/1281492.1281497 Cited on page(s) 1, 2

[92] M. Kasuya, N. Ito, N. Inuzuka, and K. Wada. A pattern formation algorithm for a set of autonomous distributed robots with agreement on orientation along one axis. *Systems and Computers in Japan*, 37(10):89–100, 2006. DOI: 10.1002/scj.20331 Cited on page(s) 65

[93] Y. Katayama, Y. Tomida, H. Imazu, N. Inuzuka, and K. Wada. Dynamic compass models and gathering algorithms for autonomous mobile robots. In *Proceedings of 14th Colloquium*

on Structural Information and Communication Complexity (SIROCCO), pages 274–288, 2007. DOI: 10.1007/978-3-540-72951-8_22 Cited on page(s) 13

[94] B. Katreniak. Biangular circle formation by asynchronous mobile robots. In *Proceedings of 12th International Colloquium on Structural and Communication Complexity (SIROCCO)*, pages 185–199, 2005. DOI: 10.1007/11429647_16 Cited on page(s) 3, 12, 65, 84, 87, 88, 89

[95] B. Katreniak. Convergence with limited visibility by asynchronous mobile robots. In *Proceedings of 18th Int. Colloquium on Structural Information and Communication Complexity (SIROCCO)*, pages 125–137, 2011. DOI: 10.1007/978-3-642-22212-2_12 Cited on page(s) 41, 42

[96] R. Klasing, A. Kosowski, and A. Navarra. Taking advantage of symmetries: Gathering of many asynchronous oblivious robots on a ring. *Theoretical Computer Science*, 411:3235–3246, 2010. DOI: 10.1016/j.tcs.2010.05.020 Cited on page(s) 146

[97] R. Klasing, E. Markou, and A. Pelc. Gathering asynchronous oblivious mobile robots in a ring. *Theoretical Computer Science*, 390:27–39, 2008. DOI: 10.1016/j.tcs.2007.09.032 Cited on page(s) 3, 146, 147

[98] Y. Kupitz and H. Martini. Geometric aspects of the generalized Fermat-Torricelli problem. *Intuitive Geometry*, 6:55–127, 1997. Cited on page(s) 28

[99] A. Lamani, S. Kamei, F. Ooshita, and S. Tixeuil. Gathering an even number of robots in a symmetric ring without global multiplicity detection. In *Proceedings of 37th International Conference on Mathematical Foundations of Computer Science (MFCS)*, 2012. (to appear). Cited on page(s) 147

[100] A. Lamani, M. Gradinariu Potop-Butucaru, and S. Tixeuil. Optimal deterministic ring exploration with oblivious asynchronous robots. In *Proceedings of 17th Int. Colloquium on Structural Information and Communication Complexity (SIROCCO)*, pages 183–196, 2010. DOI: 10.1007/978-3-642-13284-1_15 Cited on page(s) 3, 151

[101] X. Li, M. F. Ercan, and Y. F. Fung. Decentralized control for swarm flocking in 3d space. In *Proceedings of 2nd International Conference on Intelligent Robotics and Applications (ICIRA)*, pages 744–754, 2009. DOI: 10.1007/978-3-642-10817-4_74 Cited on page(s) 1, 2, 133

[102] J. Lin, A.S. Morse, and B.D.O. Anderson. The multi-agent rendezvous problem. part 1: The synchronous case. *SIAM Journal on Control and Optimization*, 46(6):2096–2119, 2007. DOI: 10.1137/040620564 Cited on page(s) 1, 38, 40

[103] J. Lin, A.S. Morse, and B.D.O. Anderson. The multi-agent rendezvous problem. part 2: The asynchronous case. *SIAM Journal on Control and Optimization*, 46(6):2120–2147, 2007. DOI: 10.1137/040620564 Cited on page(s) 9, 38, 41

[104] L. Loo, E. Lin, M. Kam, and P. Varshney. Cooperative multi-agent constellation formation under sensing and communication constraints. *Cooperative Control and Optimization*, pages 143–170, 2002. DOI: 10.1007/0-306-47536-7_8 Cited on page(s) 1

[105] S. Martínez. Practical multiagent rendezvous through modified circumcenter algorithms. *Automatica*, 45(9):2010–2017, 2009. DOI: 10.1016/j.automatica.2009.05.013 Cited on page(s) 51, 54

[106] S. Martinez, F. Bullo, J. Cortes, and E. Frazzoli. On synchronous robotic networks - part ii: Time complexity of rendezvous and deployment algorithms. *IEEE Transactions on Automatic Control*, 52(12):2214–2226, 2007. DOI: 10.1109/TAC.2007.908304 Cited on page(s) 105

[107] S. Martínez, F. Bullo, J. Cortes, and E. Frazzoli. On synchronous robotic networks -part ii: Time complexity of rendezvous and deployment algorithms. *IEEE Transactions on Automatic Control*, 52(12):2214–2226, 2007. DOI: 10.1109/TAC.2007.908304 Cited on page(s) 1

[108] M. J Matarić. *Interaction and Intelligent Behavior*. PhD thesis, MIT, 1994. Cited on page(s) 117

[109] T. Miyamae, S. Ichikawa, and F. Hara. Emergent approach to circle formation by multiple autonomous modular robots. *Journal of Robotics and Mechatronics*, 21(1):3–11, 2009. Cited on page(s) 144, 145

[110] I. Navarro, Á. Gutiérrez, F. Matía, , and F. Monasterio-Huelin. An approach to flocking of robots using minimal local sensing and common orientation. In *Proceedings of 3rd International Workshop on Hybrid Artificial Intelligence Systems (HAIS)*, pages 616–624, 2008. DOI: 10.1007/978-3-540-87656-4_76 Cited on page(s) 117

[111] F. Ooshita and S. Tixeuil. On the self-stabilization of mobile oblivious robots in uniform rings. In *Proceedings of 14th International Conference on Stabilization, Safety, and Security in Distributed Systems (SSS)*, 2012. (to appear). Cited on page(s) 147

[112] L. Pagli, G. Prencipe, and G. Viglietta. Getting close without touching. In *Proceedings of 19th Int. Colloquium on Structural Information and Communication Complexity (SIROCCO)*, pages 315–326, 2012. DOI: 10.1007/978-3-642-31104-8_27 Cited on page(s) 48, 50, 51

[113] G. Prencipe. The effect of synchronicity on the behavior of autonomous mobile robots. *Theory Of Computing Systems*, 38:539–558, 2005. DOI: 10.1007/s00224-005-1101-1 Cited on page(s) 138

[114] G. Prencipe. Impossibility of gathering by a set of autonomous mobile robots. *Theoretical Computer Science*, 384(2-3):222–231, 2007. DOI: 10.1016/j.tcs.2007.04.023 Cited on page(s) 18, 21

[115] C.W. Reynolds. Flocks, herds, and schools: A distributed behavioral model. *Computer Graphics*, 21(4):25–34, 1987. DOI: 10.1145/37402.37406 Cited on page(s) 117, 132

[116] S. Souissi. *Fault-resilient cooperation of autonomous mobile robots with unreliable compass sensors.* PhD thesis, Japan Advanced Institute of Science and Technology, 2007. Cited on page(s) 47

[117] S. Souissi, X. Défago, and T. Katayama. Convergence of a uniform circle formation algorithm for distributed autonomous mobile robots. In *Proceedings of Journés Scientifiques Francophones (JSF)*, 2004. Cited on page(s) 84, 86

[118] S. Souissi, X. Défago, and M. Yamashita. Using eventually consistent compasses to gather memory-less mobile robots with limited visibility. *ACM Transactions on Autonomous and Adaptive Systemse*, 4(1):1–27, 2009. DOI: 10.1145/1462187.1462196 Cited on page(s) 21, 38, 45, 47

[119] S. Souissi, Y. Yang, and X. Défago. Fault-tolerant flocking in a k -bounded asynchronous system. In *Proceedings of 12th International Conference on Principles of Distributed Systems (OPODIS)*, pages 145–163, 2008. DOI: 10.1007/978-3-540-92221-6_11 Cited on page(s) 117, 119

[120] S. Souissi, Y. Yang, X. Défago, and M. Takizawa. Fault-tolerant flocking for a group of autonomous mobile robots. *The Journal of Systems and Software*, 84:29–36, 2011. Cited on page(s) 117, 119

[121] K. Sugihara and I. Suzuki. Distributed algorithms for formation of geometric patterns with many mobile robots. *Journal of Robotics Systems*, 13:127–139, 1996. DOI: 10.1002/(SICI)1097-4563(199603)13:3%3C127::AID-ROB1%3E3.0.CO;2-U Cited on page(s) 12, 25, 65, 84, 143

[122] I. Suzuki and M. Yamashita. Distributed anonymous mobile robots. In *Proceedings of 3rd International Colloquium on Structural Information and Communication Complexity (SIROCCO)*, pages 313–330, 1996. Cited on page(s) 9

[123] I. Suzuki and M. Yamashita. Distributed anonymous mobile robots: Formation of geometric patterns. *SIAM Journal on Computing*, 28(4):1347–1363, 1999. DOI: 10.1137/S009753979628292X Cited on page(s) 12, 13, 18, 22, 25, 28, 65, 66, 81

[124] O. Tanaka. Forming a circle by distributed anonymous mobile robots. Master's thesis, Department of Electrical Engineering, 1992. Cited on page(s) 65, 84, 144

[125] R. Vaughan, N. Sumpter, J. Henderson, A. Frost, and S. Cameron. Experiments in automatic flock control. *Robotics and Autonomous Systems*, 31(1–2):109–117, 2000. DOI: 10.1016/S0921-8890(99)00084-6 Cited on page(s) 1, 132

[126] G. Wang, G. Cao, and T. La Porta. Movement-assisted sensor deployment. *IEEE Transactions on Mobile Computing*, 5(6):640–652, 2006. DOI: 10.1109/TMC.2006.80 Cited on page(s) 2

[127] P. K. C. Wang. Navigation Strategies for Multiple Autonomous Mobile Robots Moving in Formation. *Journal of Robotic Systems*, 8(2):177–195, 1991. DOI: 10.1002/rob.4620080204 Cited on page(s) 65, 117

[128] E. Weiszfeld. Sur le point pour lequel la somme des distances de n points donnés est minimum. *Tohoku Mathematical*, 43:355–386, 1936. Cited on page(s) 28

[129] E. Welzl. Smallest enclosing disks (balls and ellipsoids). *New Results and New Trends in Computer Science*, 555:359–370, 1991. DOI: 10.1007/BFb0038202 Cited on page(s) 15

[130] N. Xiong, J. He, Y. Yang, Y. He, T. Kim, and C. Lin. A survey on decentralized flocking schemes for a set of autonomous mobile robots. *Journal of Communications*, 5(1):31–38, 2010. DOI: 10.4304/jcm.5.1.31-38 Cited on page(s) 117

[131] M. Yamashita and I. Suzuki. Characterizing geometric patterns formable by oblivious anonymous mobile robots. *Theoretical Computer Science*, 411(26-28):2433–2453, 2010. DOI: 10.1016/j.tcs.2010.01.037 Cited on page(s) 81

[132] Y. Yang, N. Xiong, N. Y. Chong, and X. Défago. A decentralized and adaptive flocking algorithm for autonomous mobile robots. In *Proceedings of 3rd International Conference on Grid and Pervasive Computing Workshops*, pages 262–268, 2008. DOI: 10.1109/GPC.WORKSHOPS.2008.18 Cited on page(s) 132, 133

[133] D. Yoshida, T. Masuzawa, and H. Fujiwara. Fault-tolerant distributed algorithms for autonomous mobile robots with crash faults. *Systems and Computers in Japanl*, 28, 1997. DOI: 10.1002/(SICI)1520-684X(199702)28:2%3C33::AID-SCJ4%3E3.3.CO;2-1 Cited on page(s) 14

Authors' Biographies

PAOLA FLOCCHINI

Paola Flocchini received her Ph.D. in Computer Science from the University of Milan, Italy, in 1995. She held positions at the Université de Montreal and Université du Quebec en Outaouais before joining the University of Ottawa in 1999. She is Professor and University Research Chair in Distributed Computing at the School of Electrical Engineering and Computer Science (University of Ottawa). Her main research interests are in distributed algorithms, distributed computing, algorithms for mobile agents and autonomous robots, and cellular automata.

GIUSEPPE PRENCIPE

Giuseppe Prencipe has received his Ph.D. in Computer Science in 2002 from the University of Pisa, Italy, with a thesis on distributed mobile robots. After his Ph.D. studies, he has continued his investigations on distributed mobile computing as a Visiting Researcher in Ottawa, at Carleton University and at the University of Ottawa, and in Zurich at ETH. He has been involved in the PC of several distributed computing conferences, and has been PC co-Chair of SIROCCO in 2007. He is currently Assistant Professor at the Department of Computer Science of the University of Pisa. His main research interests are distributed algorithms, distributed computing, mobile agents computing, and design of algorithms for autonomous mobile robots.

NICOLA SANTORO

Nicola Santoro is Distinguished Research Professor of Computer Science at Carleton University. Initially interested in philosophy, he is one of the first computer science graduates in Italy (Pisa'74), discovering the beauty of algorithms and data structures. During his Ph.D. on information structure (Waterloo '79), he discovers the net (then called ARPANET) and email, and starts thinking in distributed terms. He contributes seminal papers focusing on the algorithmic aspects and starts some of the main theoretical conferences in the field (PODC, DISC, SIROCCO). He is the author of the book *Design and Analysis of Distributed Algorithms* (Wiley 2007). In 2010 he has been awarded the SIROCCO *Prize for Innovation in Distributed Computing*. His current research interests include distributed computations by mobile entities (agents, robots, sensors) and in time-varying networks (dynamic, delay-tolerant, vehicular).

Index